THE ART OF JESUS

Sandro Sehic

Printed in the United States of America

ISBN: 978-1-949362-07-7 (Paperback)

ISBN: 978-1-949362-06-0 (eBook)

Library of Congress Control Number: 2018949739

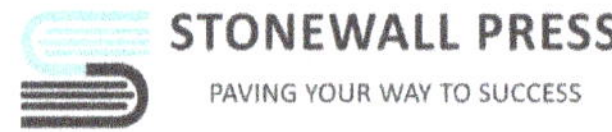

Stonewall Press
363 Paladium Court
Owings Mills, MD 21117
www.stonewallpress.com
1-888-334-0980

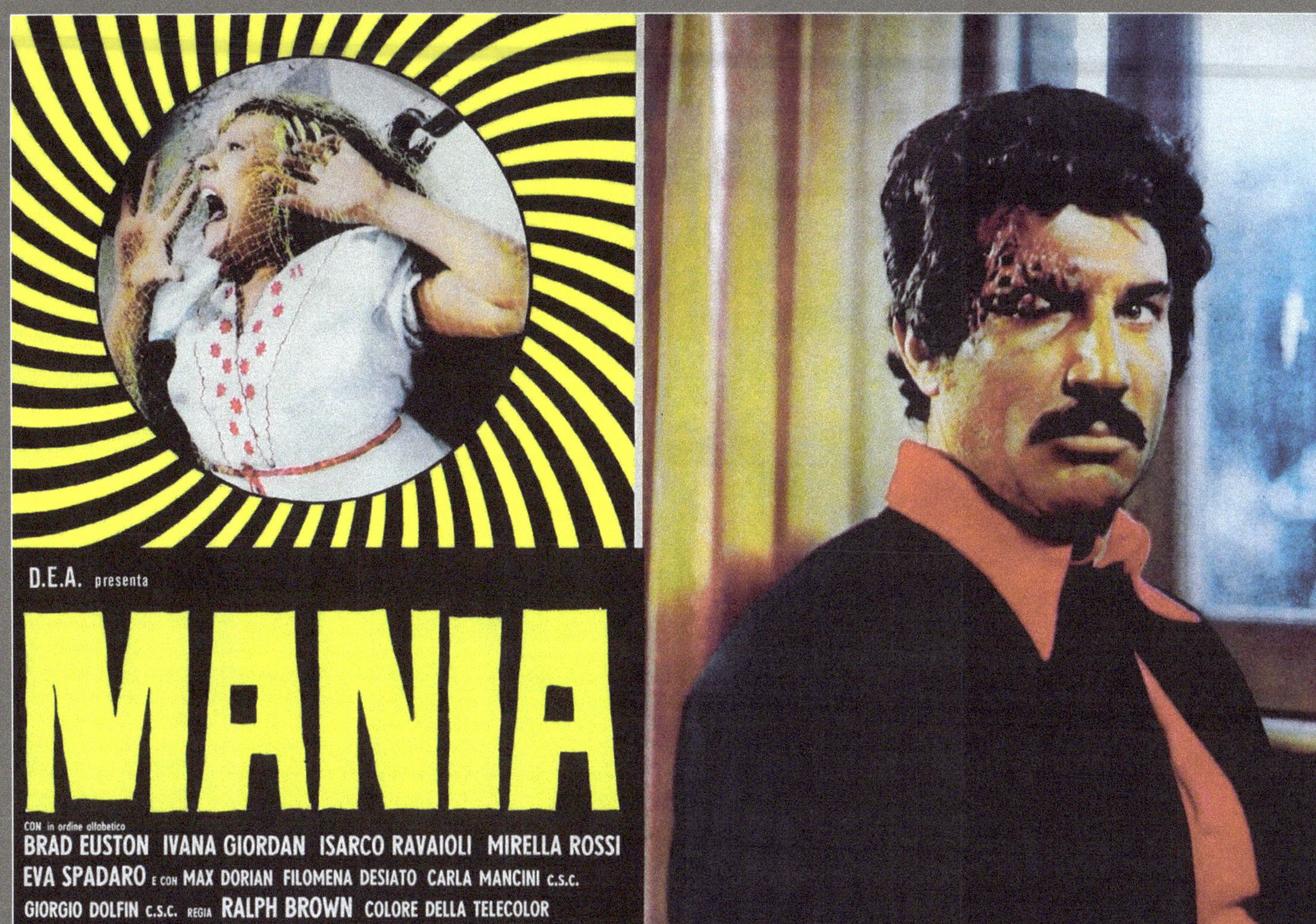

MANIA
("Mania")
Original Title: **Mania** (Italy, 1974)

OPPOSITE PAGE:

NUDA PER SATANA
("Nude For Satan")
Original Title: **Nuda Per Satana** (Italy, 1974)

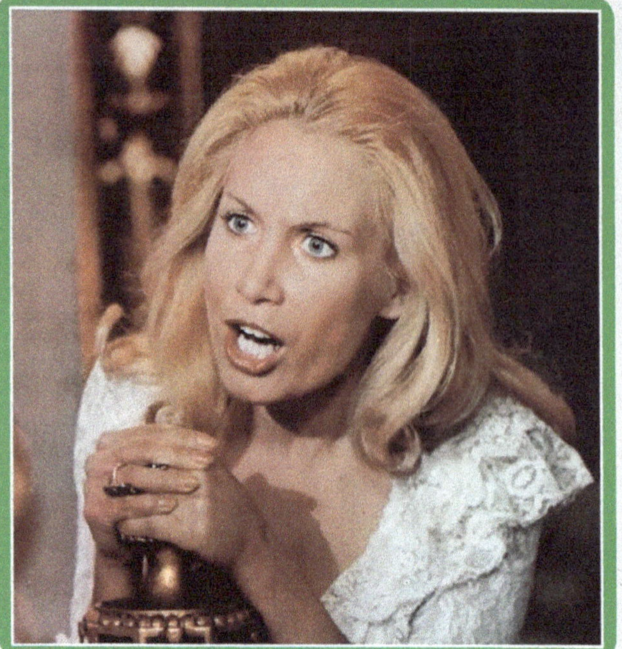

FEMI BENUSSI · GIACOMO ROSSI STUART · KRISTA NELL

LA SANGUISUGA
CONDUCE LA DANZA

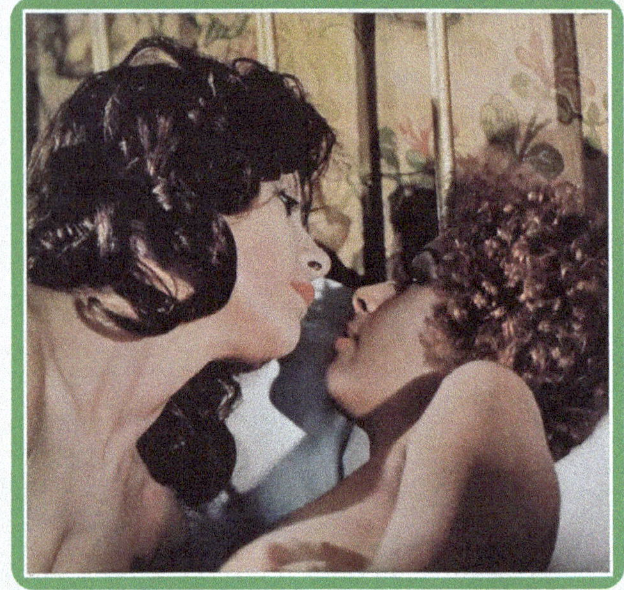

PATRIZIA DE ROSSI
ALAN COLLINS · MARIO DE ROSA · BARBARA MARZANO
MARZIA DAMONY · HALINA KIM · e con LEO VALERIANO
un film di ALFREDO RIZZO
musica di MARCELLO GIOMBINI · edizioni musicali NAZIONAL MUSIC
una produzione TO.RO. Cinematografica - Roma · TECHNICOLOR
pab

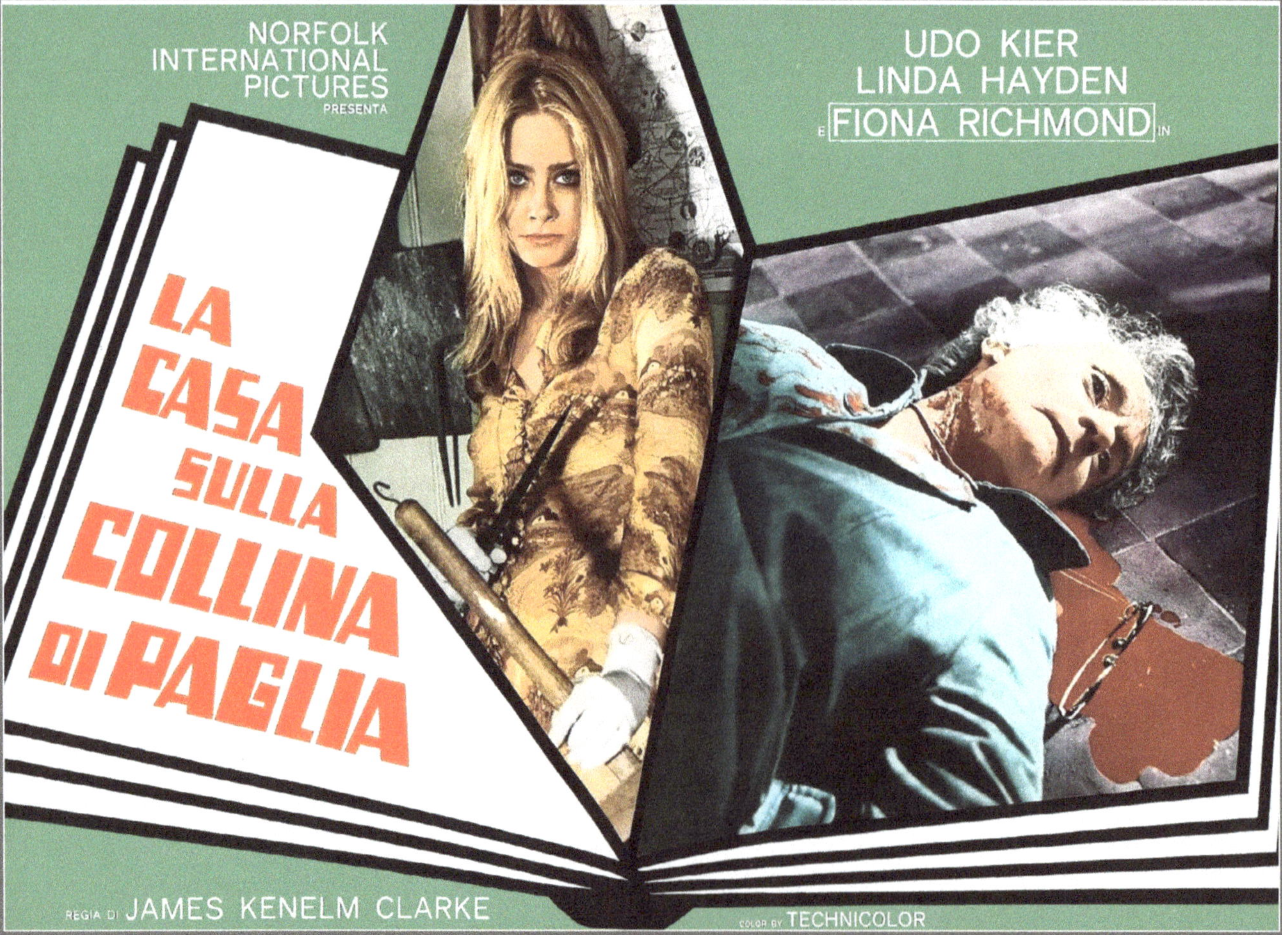

NORFOLK
INTERNATIONAL
PICTURES
presenta

UDO KIER
LINDA HAYDEN
e FIONA RICHMOND in

LA CASA
SULLA
COLLINA
DI PAGLIA

REGIA DI JAMES KENELM CLARKE
COLOR BY TECHNICOLOR

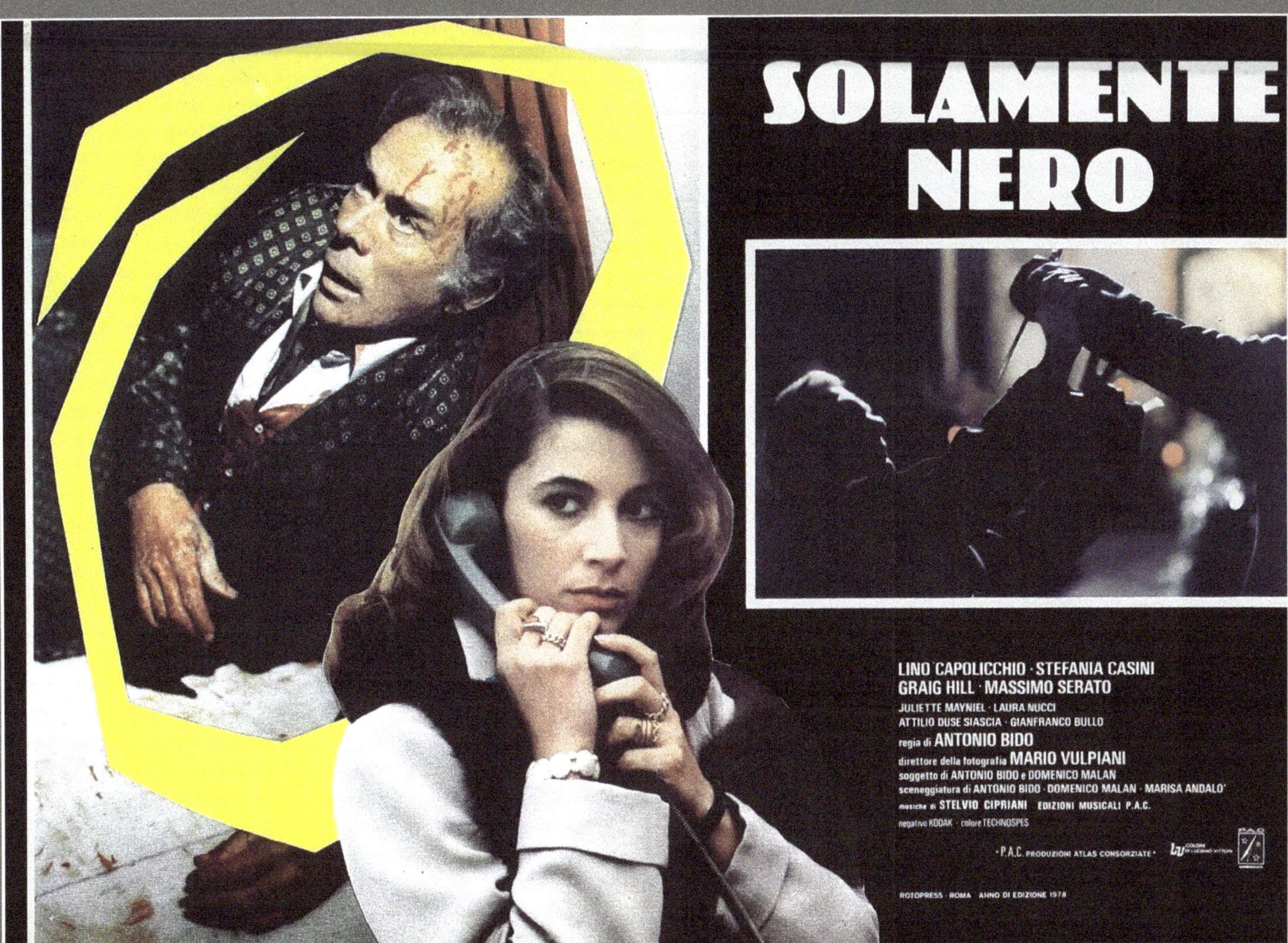

SOLAMENTE NERO
(''Nothing But Black'')
Original Title: **Solamente Nero** (Italy, 1978)

LA SANGUISUGA CONDUCE LA DANZA
(''The Bloodsucker Leads The Dance'')
Original Title: **La Sanguisuga Conduce La Danza** (Italy, 1975)

LA CASA SULLA COLLINA DI PAGLIA
(''The House On Straw Hill'')
Original Title: **Exposé** (UK, 1976)

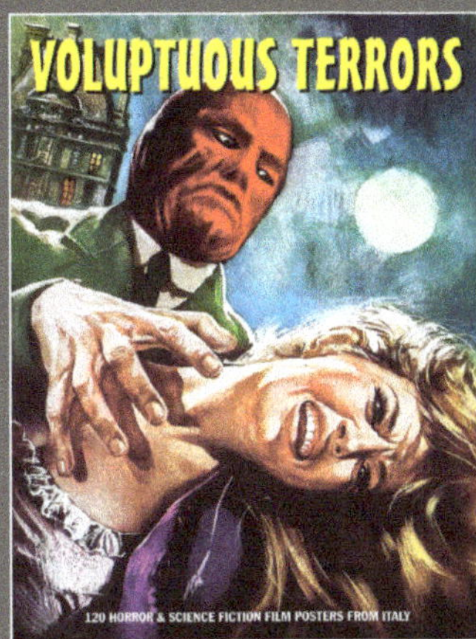
VOLUPTUOUS TERRORS
120 HORROR & SCIENCE FICTION FILM POSTERS FROM ITALY

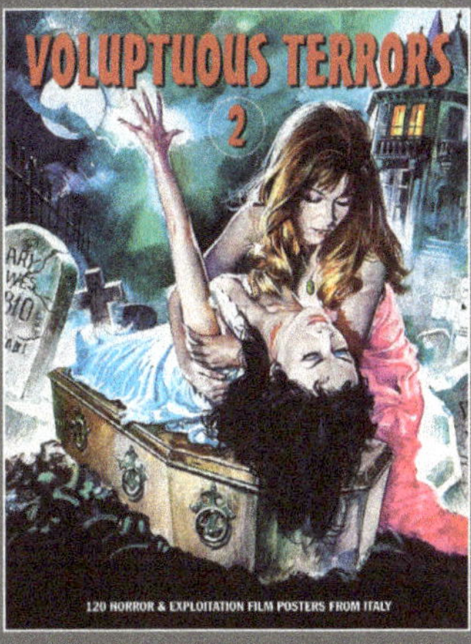
VOLUPTUOUS TERRORS
2
120 HORROR & EXPLOITATION FILM POSTERS FROM ITALY

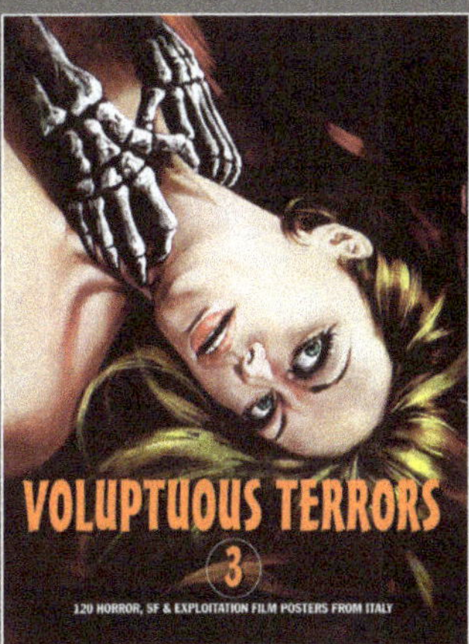
VOLUPTUOUS TERRORS
3
120 HORROR, SF & EXPLOITATION FILM POSTERS FROM ITALY

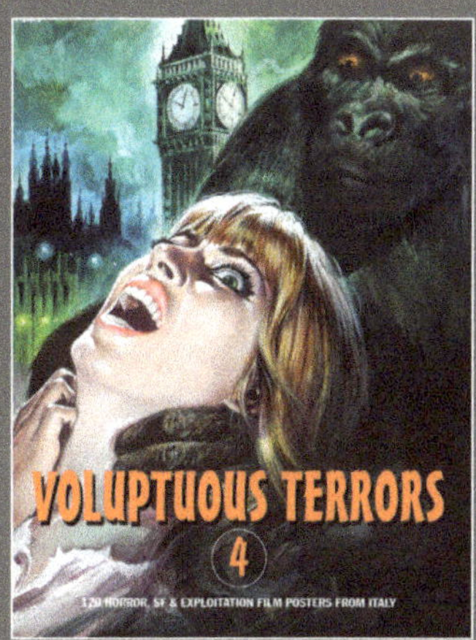
VOLUPTUOUS TERRORS
4
120 HORROR, SF & EXPLOITATION FILM POSTERS FROM ITALY

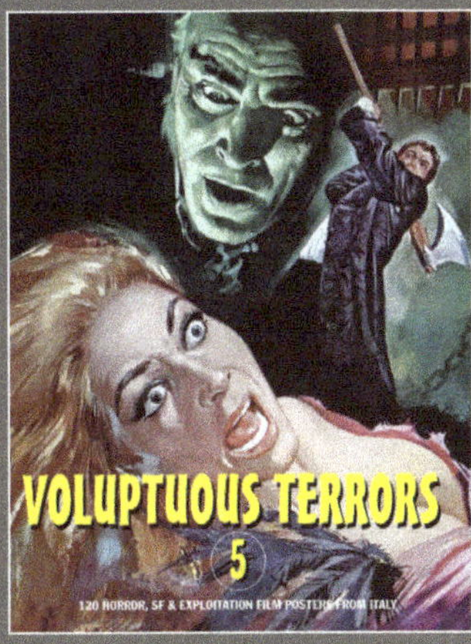
VOLUPTUOUS TERRORS
5
120 HORROR, SF & EXPLOITATION FILM POSTERS FROM ITALY

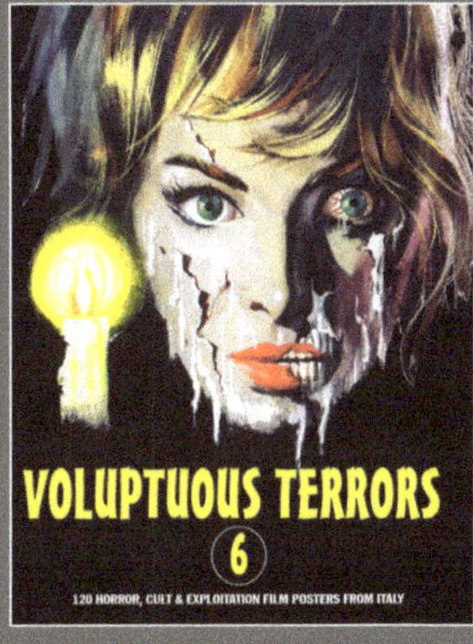
VOLUPTUOUS TERRORS
6
120 HORROR, CULT & EXPLOITATION FILM POSTERS FROM ITALY

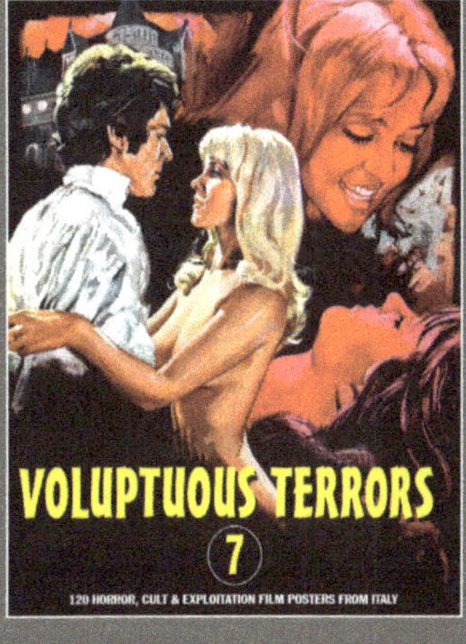
VOLUPTUOUS TERRORS
7
120 HORROR, CULT & EXPLOITATION FILM POSTERS FROM ITALY

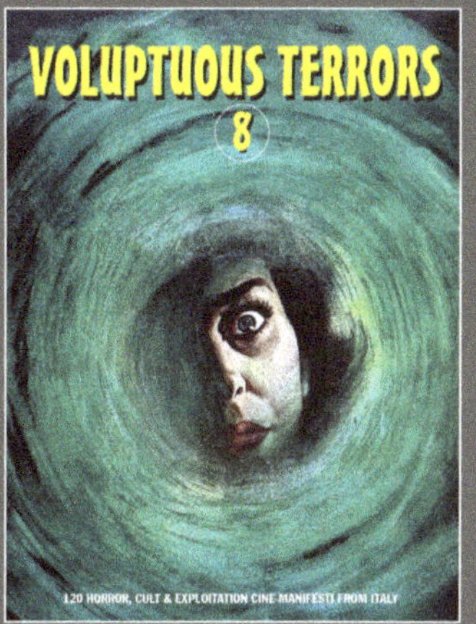
VOLUPTUOUS TERRORS
8
120 HORROR, CULT & EXPLOITATION CINE MANIFESTI FROM ITALY

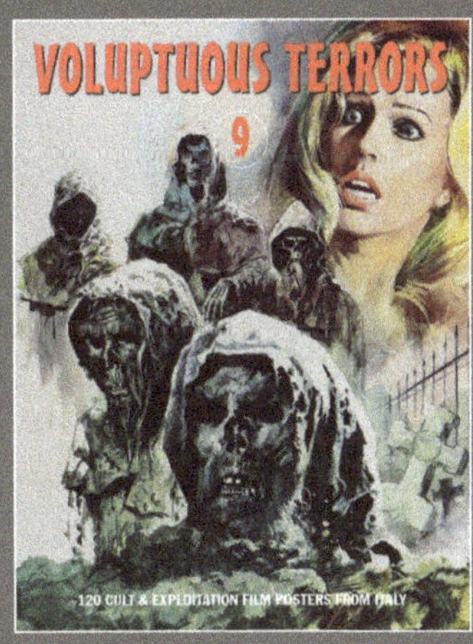
VOLUPTUOUS TERRORS
9
120 CULT & EXPLOITATION FILM POSTERS FROM ITALY

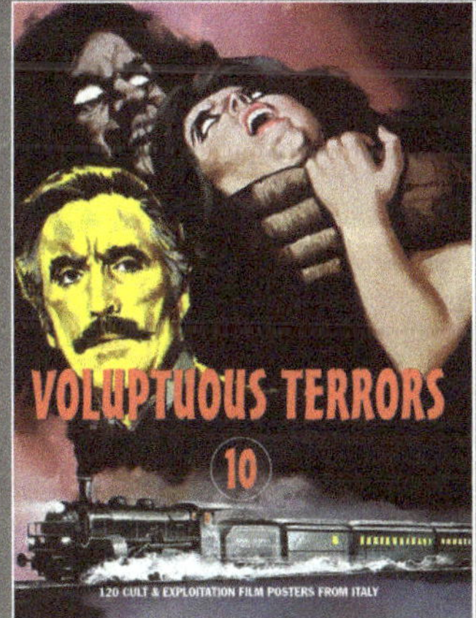
VOLUPTUOUS TERRORS
10
120 CULT & EXPLOITATION FILM POSTERS FROM ITALY

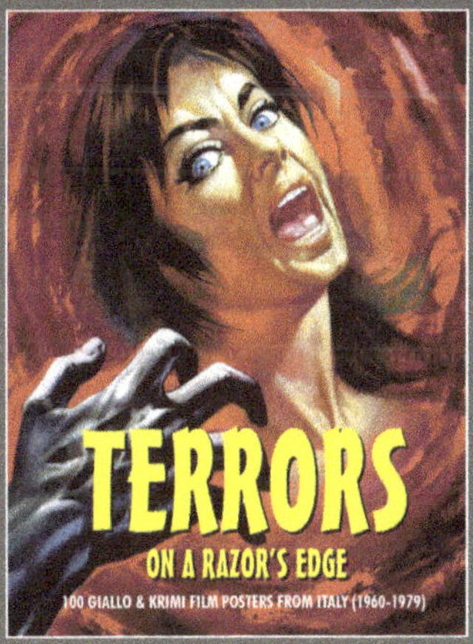
TERRORS
ON A RAZOR'S EDGE
100 GIALLO & KRIMI FILM POSTERS FROM ITALY (1960-1979)

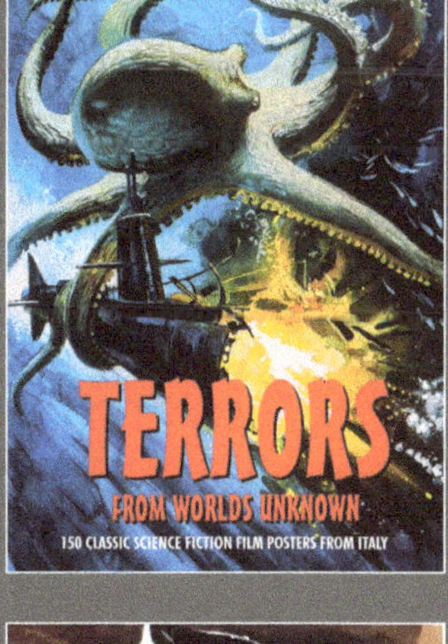
TERRORS
FROM WORLDS UNKNOWN
150 CLASSIC SCIENCE FICTION FILM POSTERS FROM ITALY

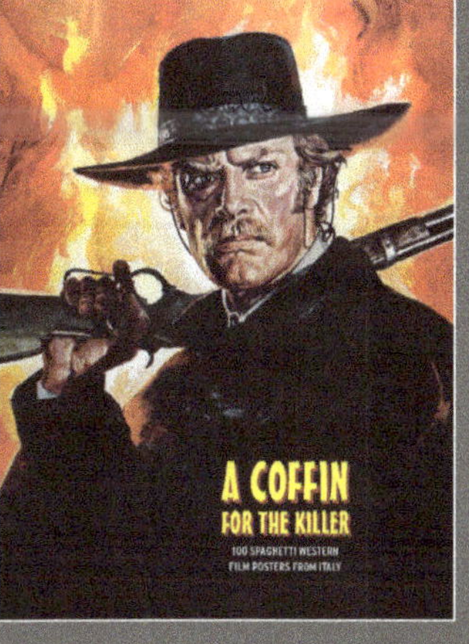
A COFFIN
FOR THE KILLER
100 SPAGHETTI WESTERN
FILM POSTERS FROM ITALY

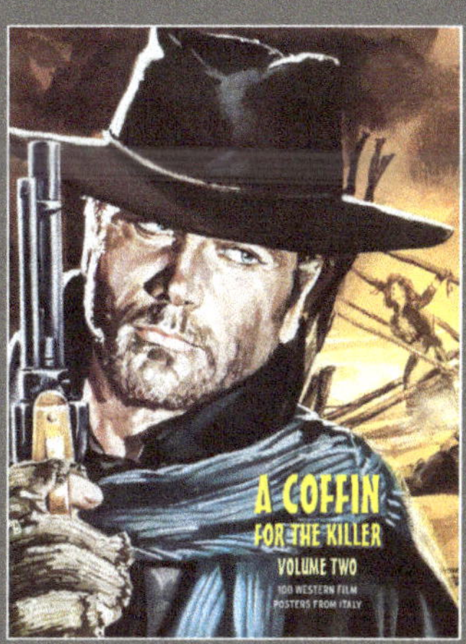
A COFFIN
FOR THE KILLER
VOLUME TWO
100 WESTERN FILM
POSTERS FROM ITALY

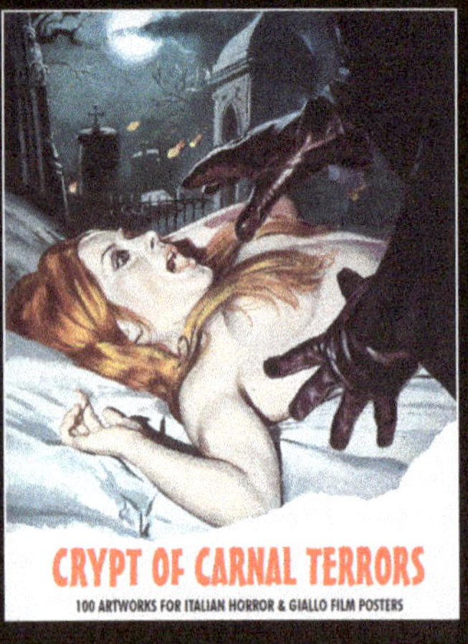
CRYPT OF CARNAL TERRORS
100 ARTWORKS FOR ITALIAN HORROR & GIALLO FILM POSTERS

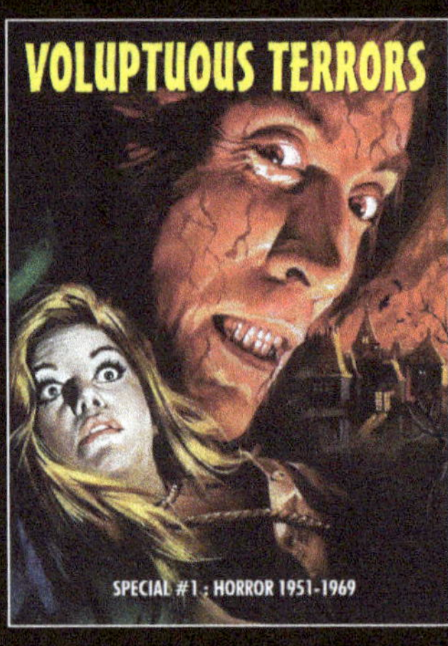
VOLUPTUOUS TERRORS
SPECIAL #1 : HORROR 1951-1969

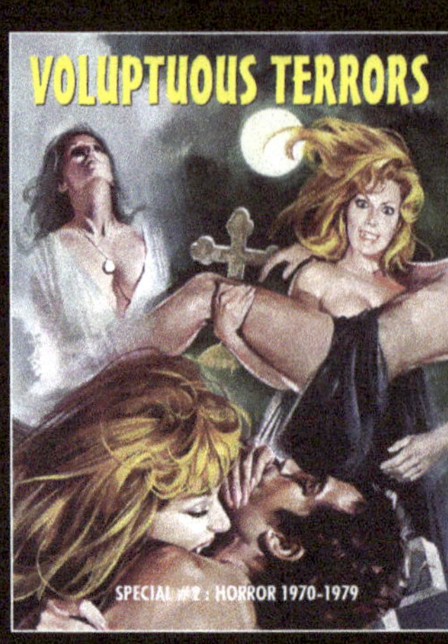
VOLUPTUOUS TERRORS
SPECIAL #2 : HORROR 1970-1979

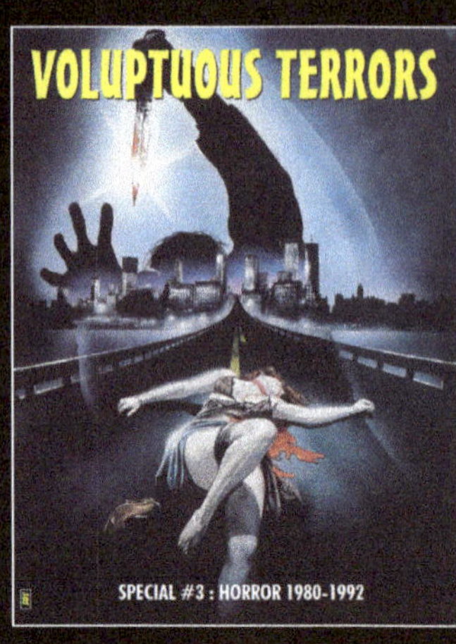
VOLUPTUOUS TERRORS
SPECIAL #3 : HORROR 1980-1992

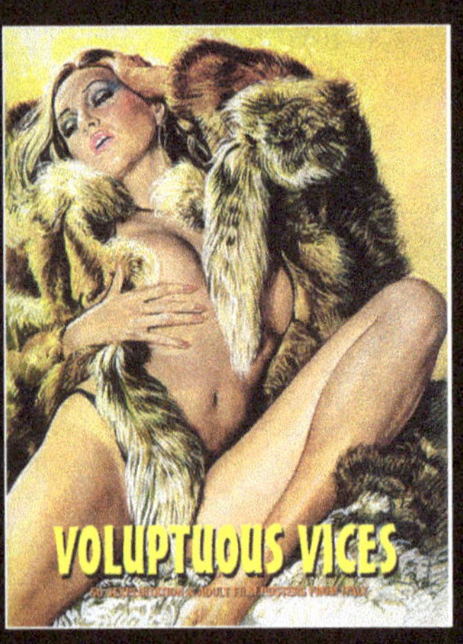
VOLUPTUOUS VICES

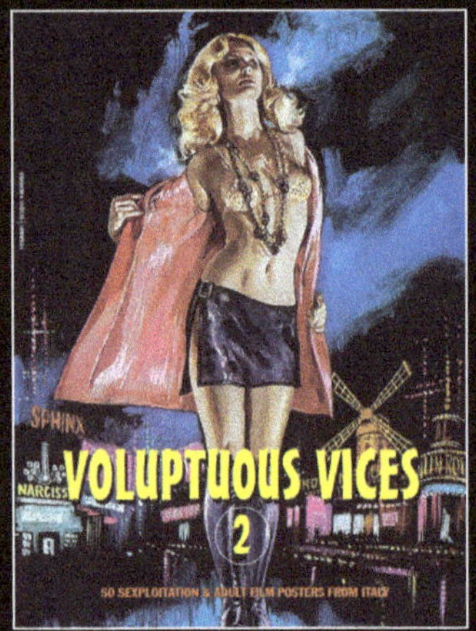
VOLUPTUOUS VICES
2
50 SEXPLOITATION & ADULT FILM POSTERS FROM ITALY

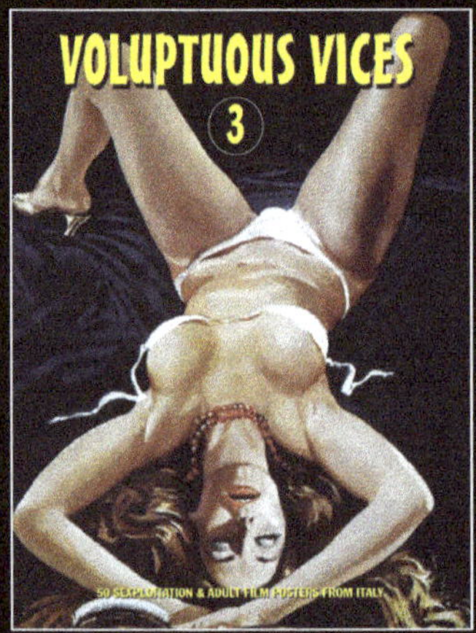
VOLUPTUOUS VICES
3
50 SEXPLOITATION & ADULT FILM POSTERS FROM ITALY

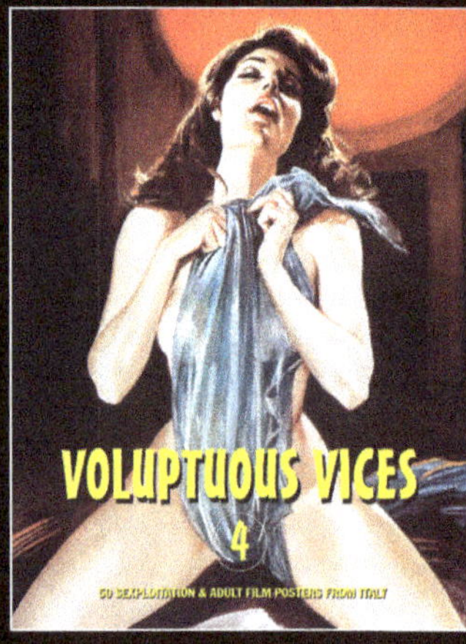
VOLUPTUOUS VICES
4
50 SEXPLOITATION & ADULT FILM POSTERS FROM ITALY

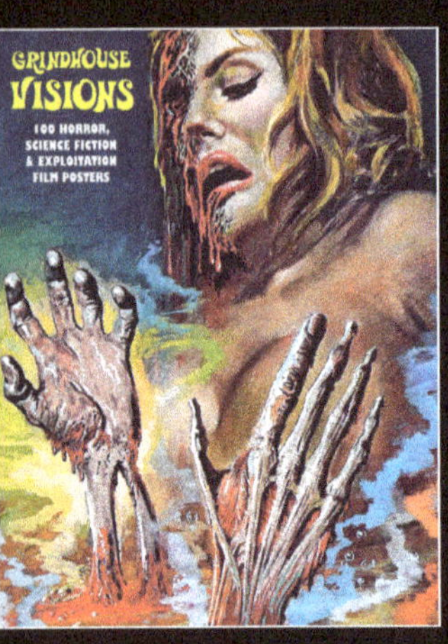
GRINDHOUSE
VISIONS
100 HORROR,
SCIENCE FICTION
& EXPLOITATION
FILM POSTERS

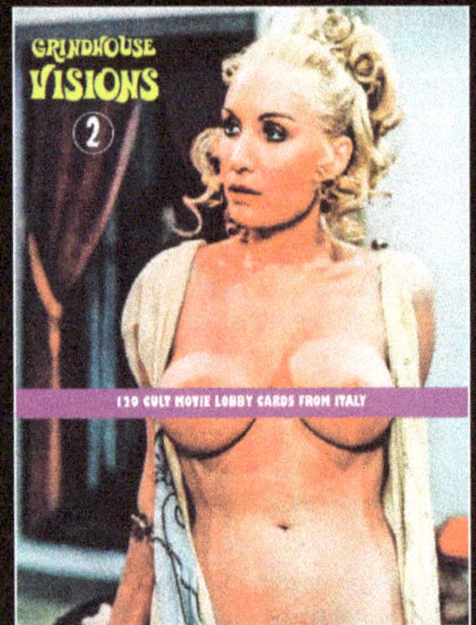
GRINDHOUSE
VISIONS
2
120 CULT MOVIE LOBBY CARDS FROM ITALY

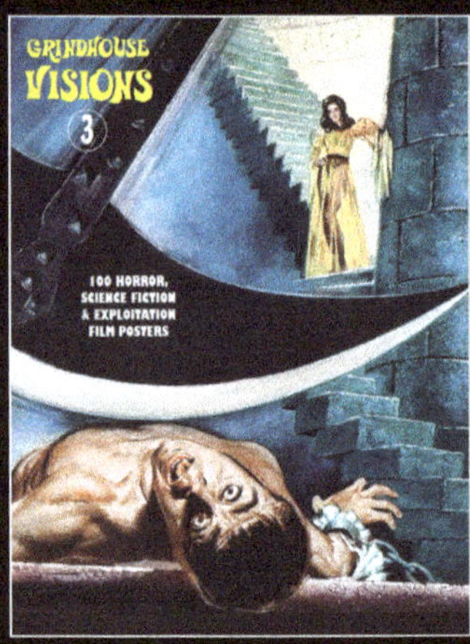
GRINDHOUSE
VISIONS
3
100 HORROR,
SCIENCE FICTION
& EXPLOITATION
FILM POSTERS

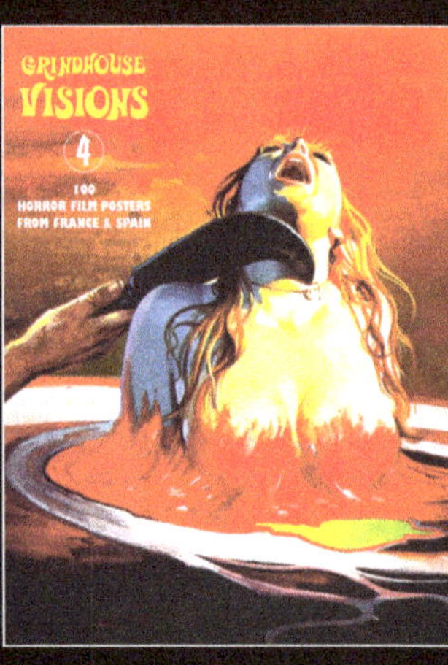
GRINDHOUSE
VISIONS
4
100 HORROR FILM POSTERS
FROM FRANCE & SPAIN

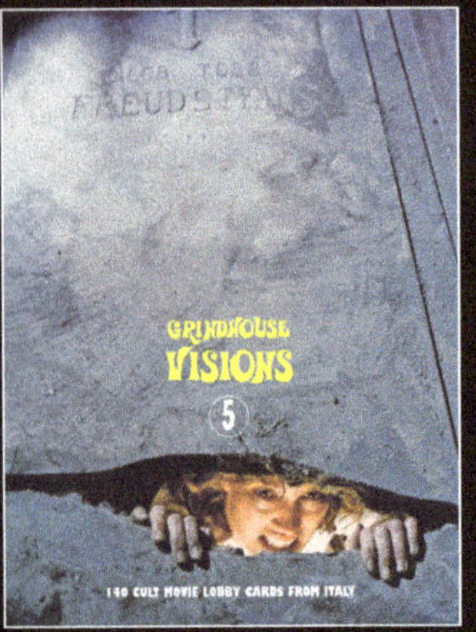
GRINDHOUSE
VISIONS
5
120 CULT MOVIE LOBBY CARDS FROM ITALY

Table of Contents

Page 1 .... Nativity of Jesus by Sandro Botticelli

Page 2 .... Jesus Walking On Water by Ivan Aivazovsky

Page 3 .... Jesus Walking On Water by Ivan Aivazovsky

Page 4 & 5 .... Appearance of Jesus to Maria Magdalena by Alexander Ivanov

Page 6 & 7 .... Ecce Homo by Antonio Ciseri

Page 8 & 9 .... Taking of Christ by Caravaggio

Page 10 .... Burial of Christ by Carl Bloch

Page 11 .... Christ at the Cross by Carl Bloch

Page 12 .... Gethsemane by Carl Bloch

Page 13 .... Raising of Lazarus by Carl Bloch

Page 14 .... Resurrection of Christ by Carl Bloch

Page 15 .... Suffer the Children by Carl Bloch

Page 16 & 17 .... Christ Healing the Sick by Carl Bloch

Page 18 .... The Last Supper by Carl Bloch

Page 19 .... Healing of the Blind Man by Carl Bloch

Page 20 .... The Sermon on the Mount by Carl Bloch

Page 21 .... The Shepherds and the Angel by Carl Bloch

Page 22 .... Transfiguration of Jesus by Carl Bloch

Page 23 .... Woman at the Well by Carl Bloch

Page 24 & 25 .... Flevit Super Illam by Enrique Simonet

Page 26 & 27 .... Farewell Discourse

Page 28 & 29 .... The Calling of the Apostles by Ghirlandaio

Page 30 .... Casting Out the Money Changers by Giotto

Page 31 .... Jesus Cleansing a Leper

Page 32 & 33 .... Jesus Enters Jerusalem by Giotto

Page 34 & 35 .... Christ and the Young Rich Ruler by Hofmann Heinrich

Page 36 & 37 .... 12-year Old Jesus in the Temple by Hofmann Heinrich

Page 38 & 39 .... Adoration by Shepherds by Gerard van Honthorst

Page 40 & 41 .... Jesus Talking to His Disciples by James Tissot

Page 42 & 43 .... Final Entry Into Jerusalem by Jean-Leon Gerome

Page 44 & 45 .... Last Supper by Juan de Juanes

Page 46 .... Last Supper

Page 47 .... Salvator Mundi by Leonardo Vinci

Page 48 & 49 .... Last Supper by Leonardo da Vinci

Page 50 .... The Baptism of Christ by Leonardo da Vinci

Page 51 .... Pieta from Krakow

Page 52 .... Crucifixion by Pietro Perguino

Page 53 .... Raising of Lazarus

Page 54 & 55 .... Giving Keys to St. Peter by Pietro Perguino

Page 56 .... Raising of Lazarus by Carl Bloch

Page 57 .... Pieta

Page 58 & 59 .... Woes of the Pharisees by James Tissot

Page 60 & 61 .... Pienta from Gorno Nerezi

Page 62 & 63 .... Avignon Pienta by Enguerrand Charonton

Page 64 .... Pieta by Rogier van der Weyden

Page 65 .... Deposition of Christ by Agnolo Bronzino

Page 66 .... Pieta by El Greco

Page 67 .... Jesus Alpha and Omega

Page 68 .... Veronica Holding Her Veil by Hans Memling

Page 69 .... Christ Giving His Blessing by Hans Memling

Page 70 & 71 .... Christ Surrounded by Musician Angels by Hans Memling

Page 72 .... Mater Dolorosa by Hans Memling

Page 73 .... Transfiguration by Raphael

Page 74 & 75 .... Advent and Triumph of Christ by Hans Memling

Page 76 & 77 .... Last Judgment by Hans Memling

Page 78 & 79 .... Virgin with Child by Hans Memling

Page 80 & 81 .... Transfiguration by Alexander Ivanov

Page 82 .... Transfiguration by Pietro Perugino

Page 83 .... Transfiguration by Cristofano Gherardi

Page 84............................ Transfiguration from Novgorod School

Page 85............................ Transfiguration from Yaroslav, Russia

Page 86 & 87..................... Walking on Water, Veneziano

Page 88 & 89.................... Christ Walking on the Sea by Amedee Varint

Page 90............................ Walking on Water by Francois Boucher

Page 91............................ Christ Crucified by Diego Velazquez

Page 92 & 93.................... Crucifixion of Jesus, Medieval Illustration

Page 94............................ Descendent from the Cross by Rubens

Page 95............................ Crucifixion by Agnolo Bronzino

Page 96............................ Way to Calvary by Andrea di Bartolo

Page 97............................ Crucifixion of Jesus from the Saint Bible

Page 98............................ What Our Lord Saw from the Cross by James Tissot

Page 99............................ Ecce Homo by Mateo Cerezo

Page 100.......................... Carrying the Cross Fresco from Decani Monastery, Serbia

Page 101.......................... Crucifixion of Christ by Michelangelo

Page 102.......................... Calvary by Paolo Veronese

Page 103.......................... Assisi Basilica by Pietro Lorenzetti

Page 104 & 105................ Lamentation of Christ by Sandro Botticelli

Page 106.......................... Lamentation Over the Dead Christ by Sandro Botticelli

Page 107.......................... Pala delle Convertite by Sandro Botticelli

Page 108 & 109................ Christ and the Apostles in the Garden by Caravaggio

Page 110.......................... Ecce Homo by Caravaggio

Page 111 .... La Flagellazione di Cristo by Caravaggio

Page 112.......................... Raising of Lazarus by Caravaggio

Page 113.......................... 12th Century Icon of Transfiguration

Page 114 & 115 .... Last Judgment by Stefan Lochner

Page 116 & 117 .... Last Judgment by Michelangelo

Page 118.......................... Last Judgment, 17th Century Icon, from Lipie

Page 119.......................... Last Judgment

Page 120.......................... Last Judgment, Russia, 18th Century

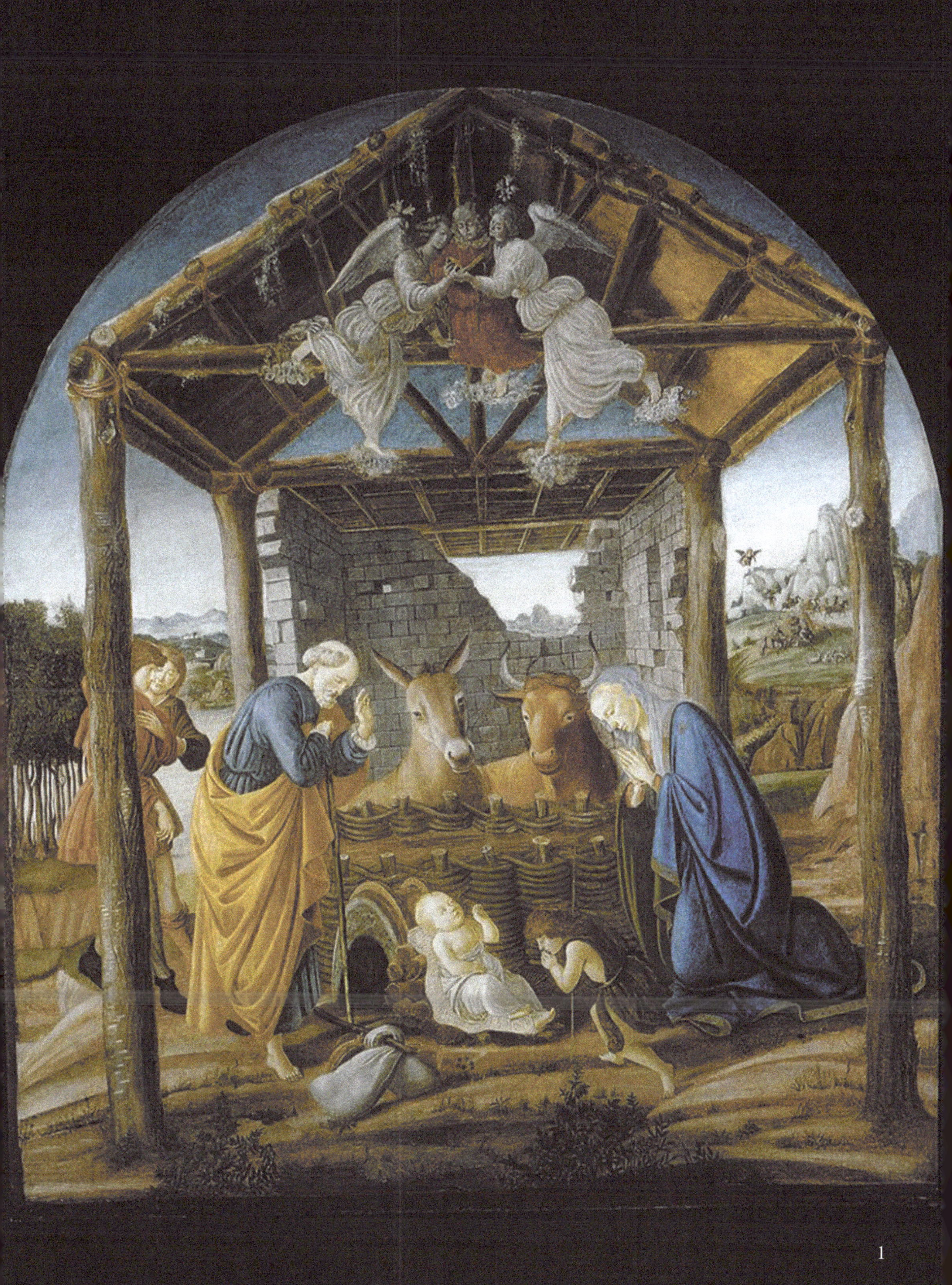

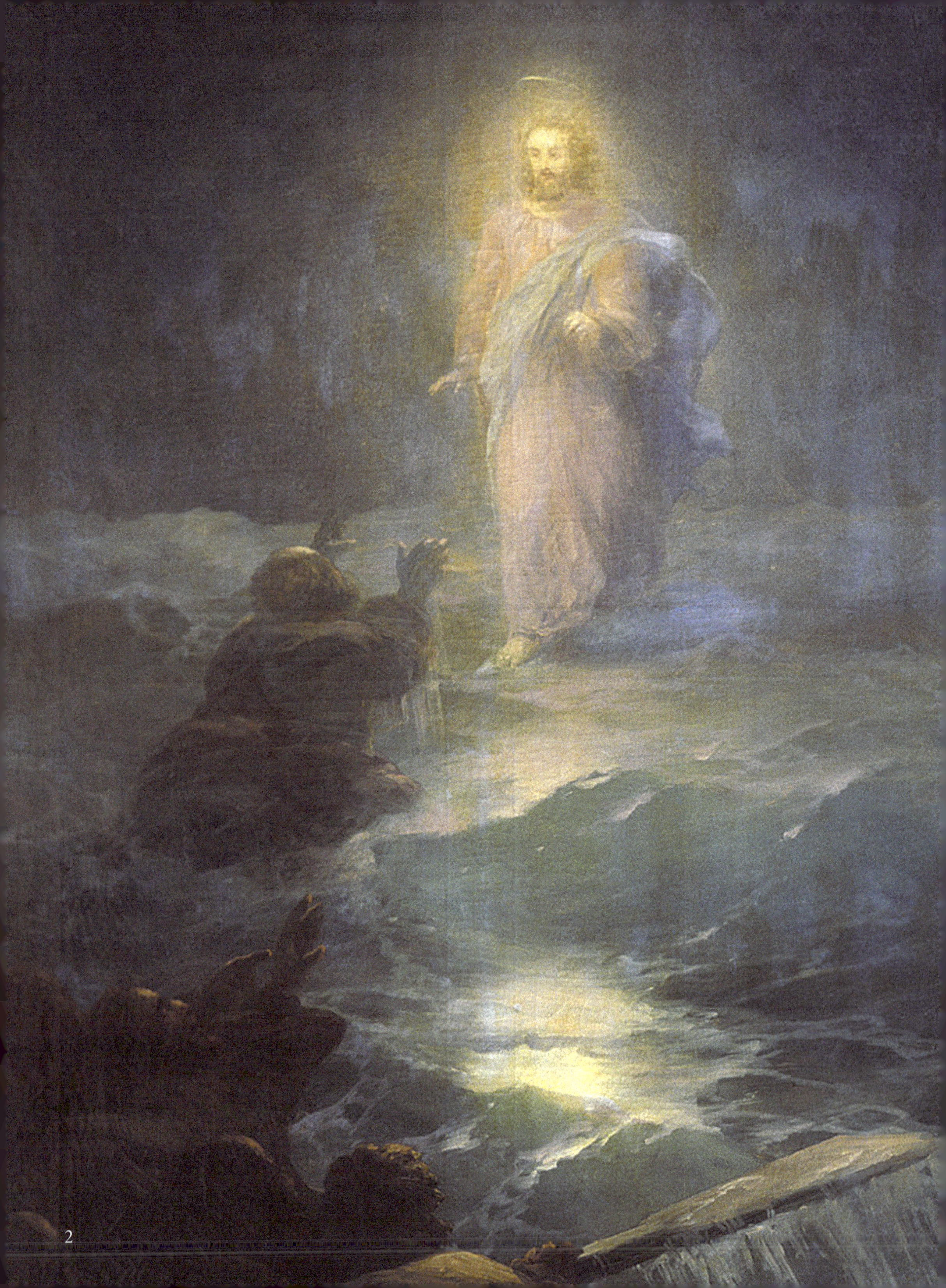

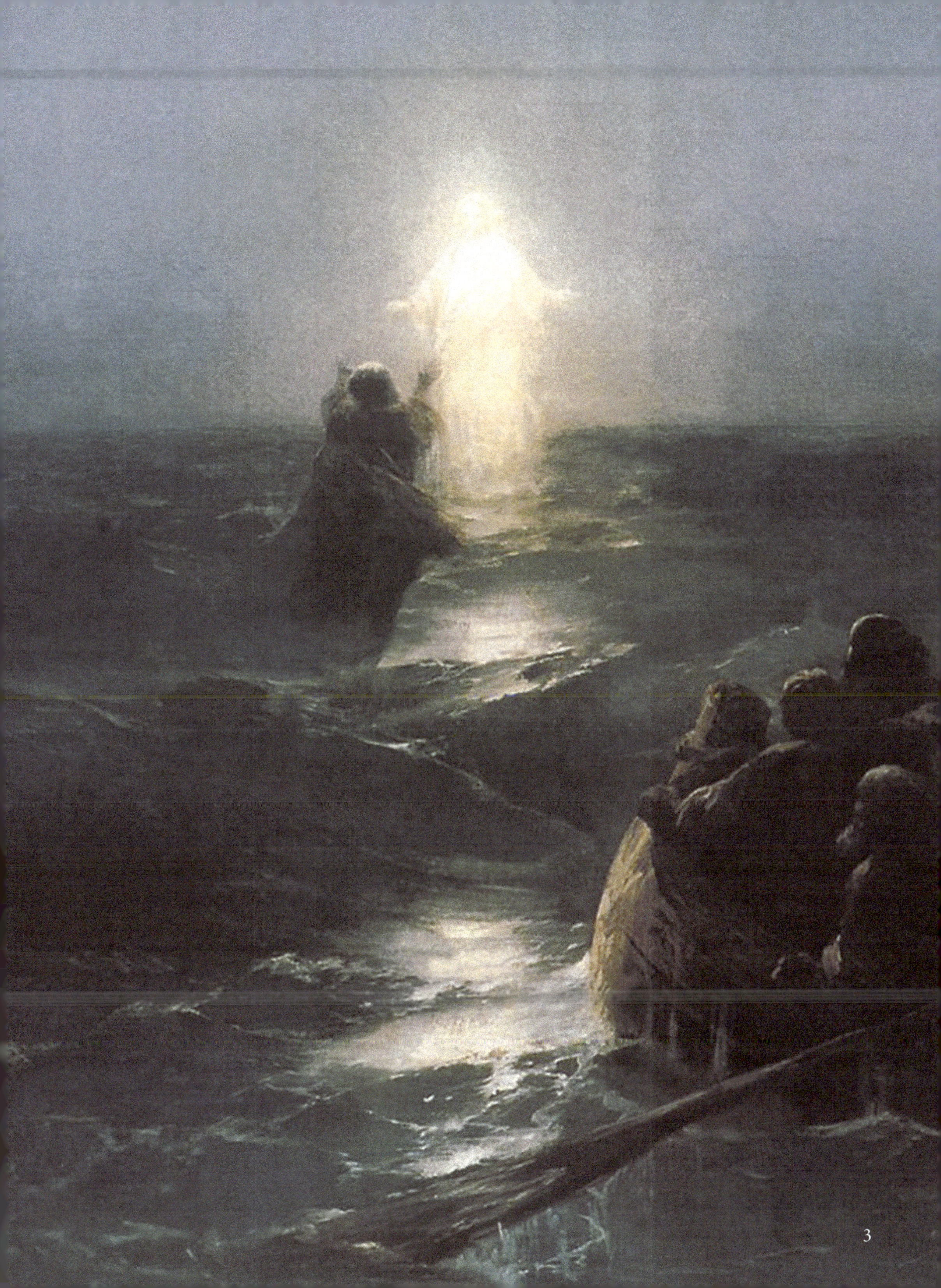

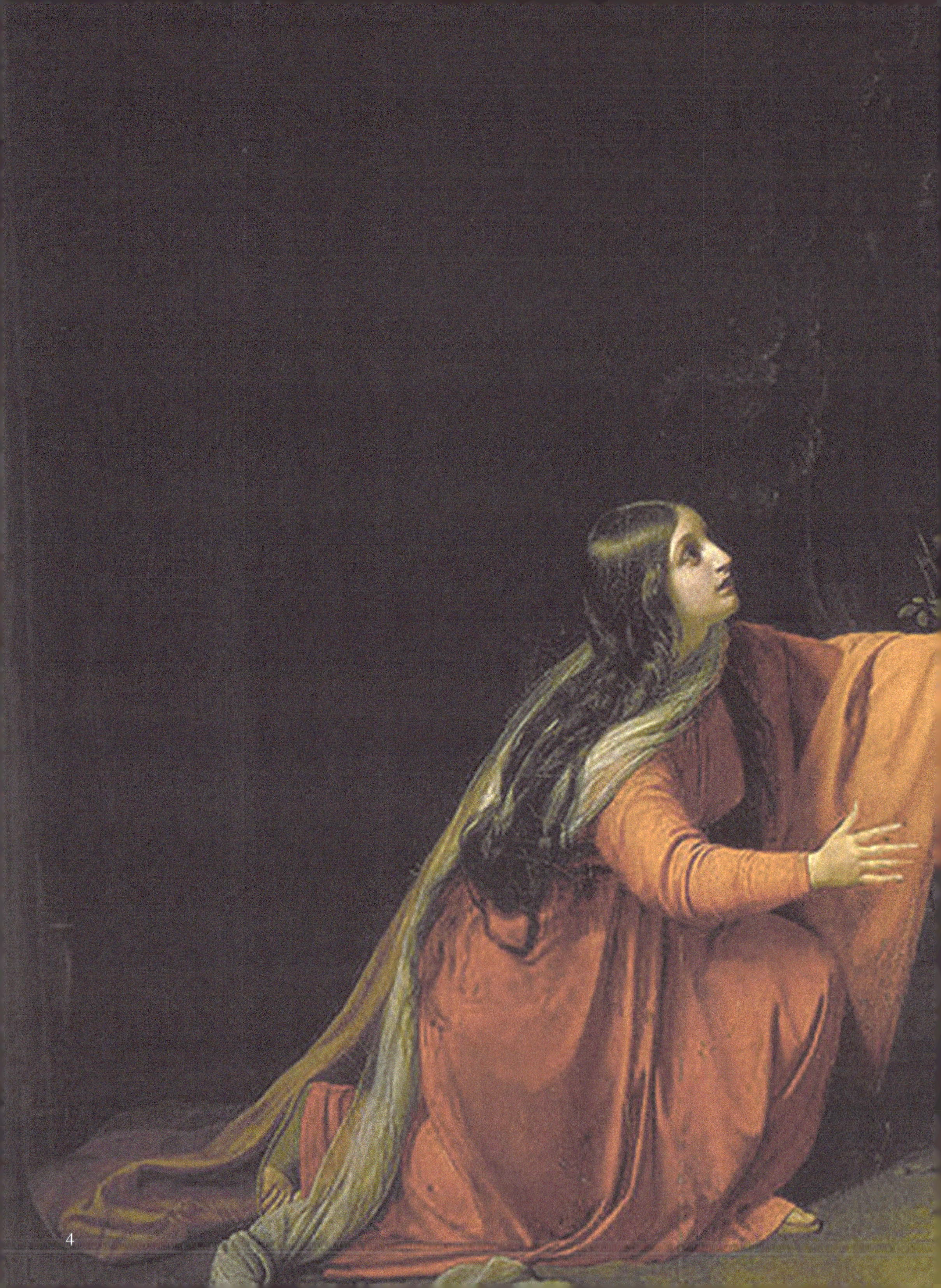

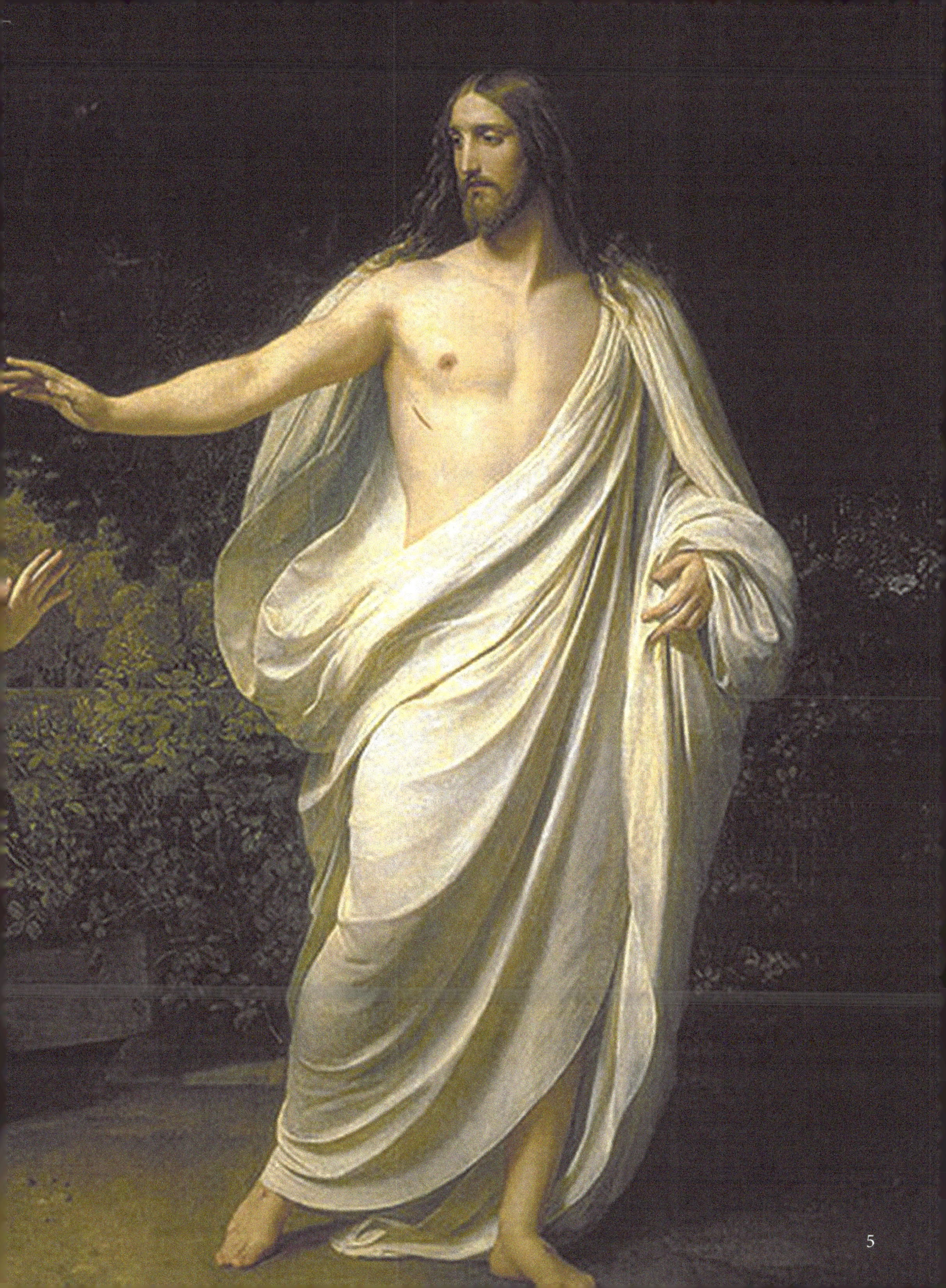

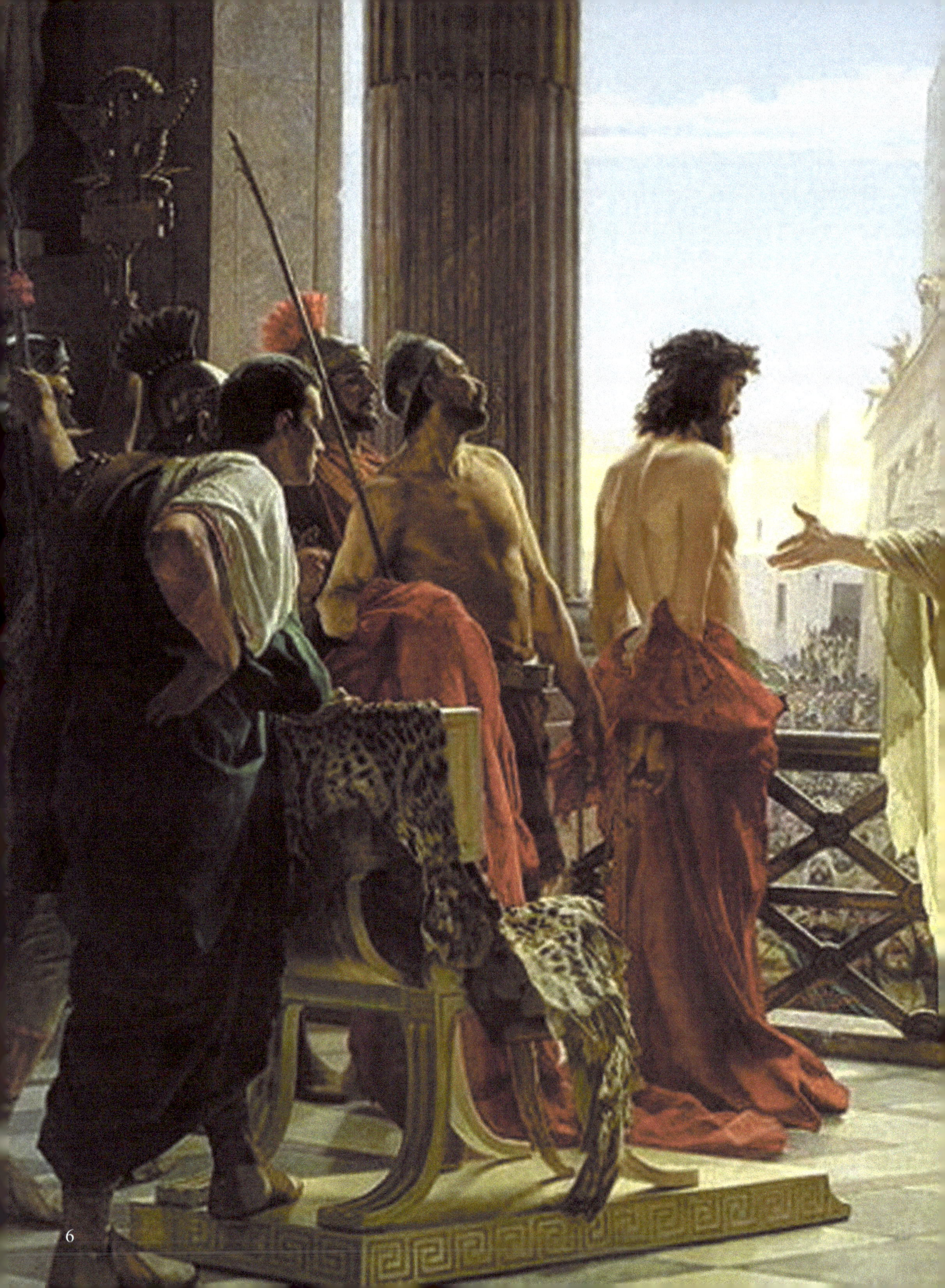

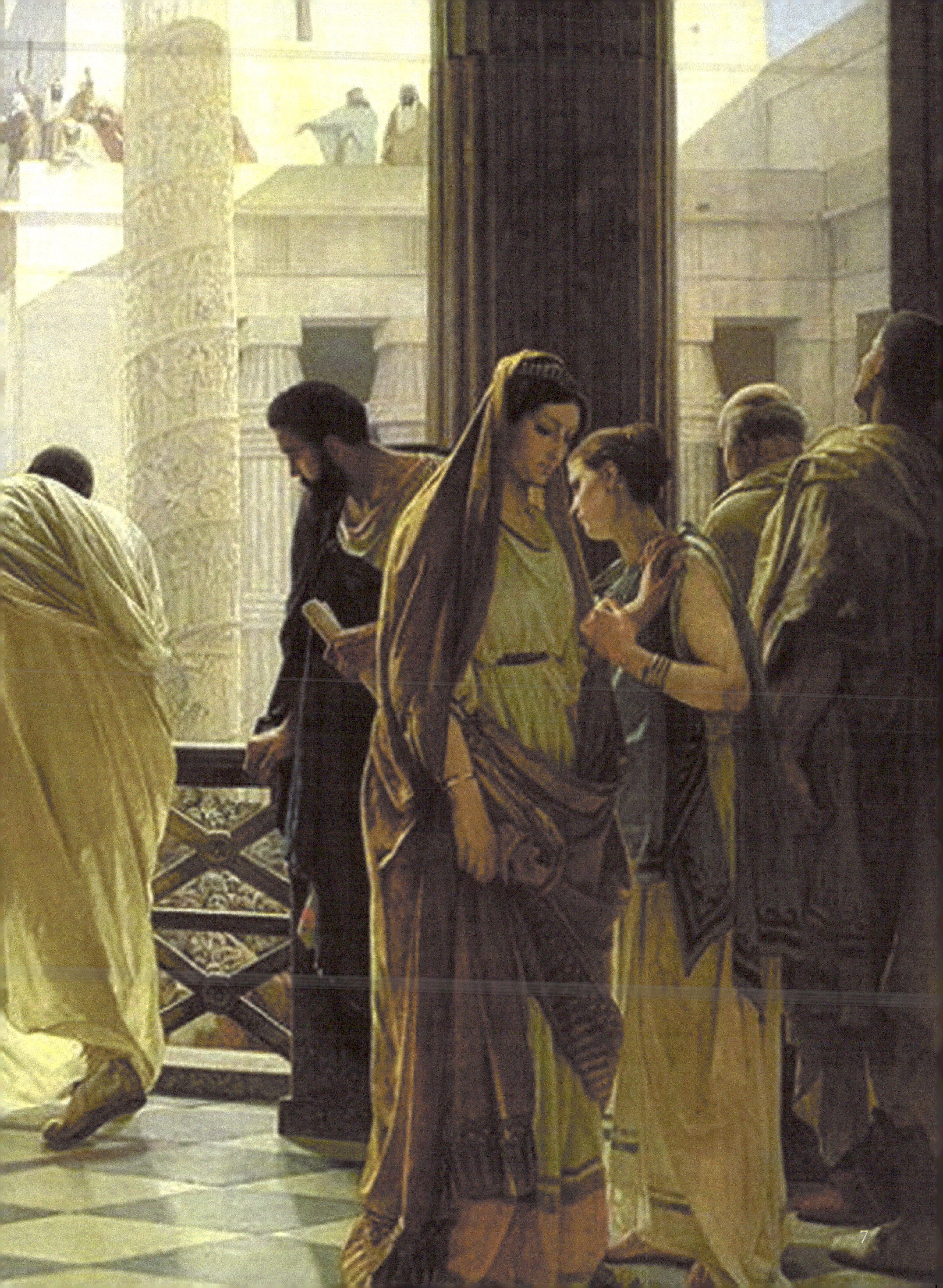

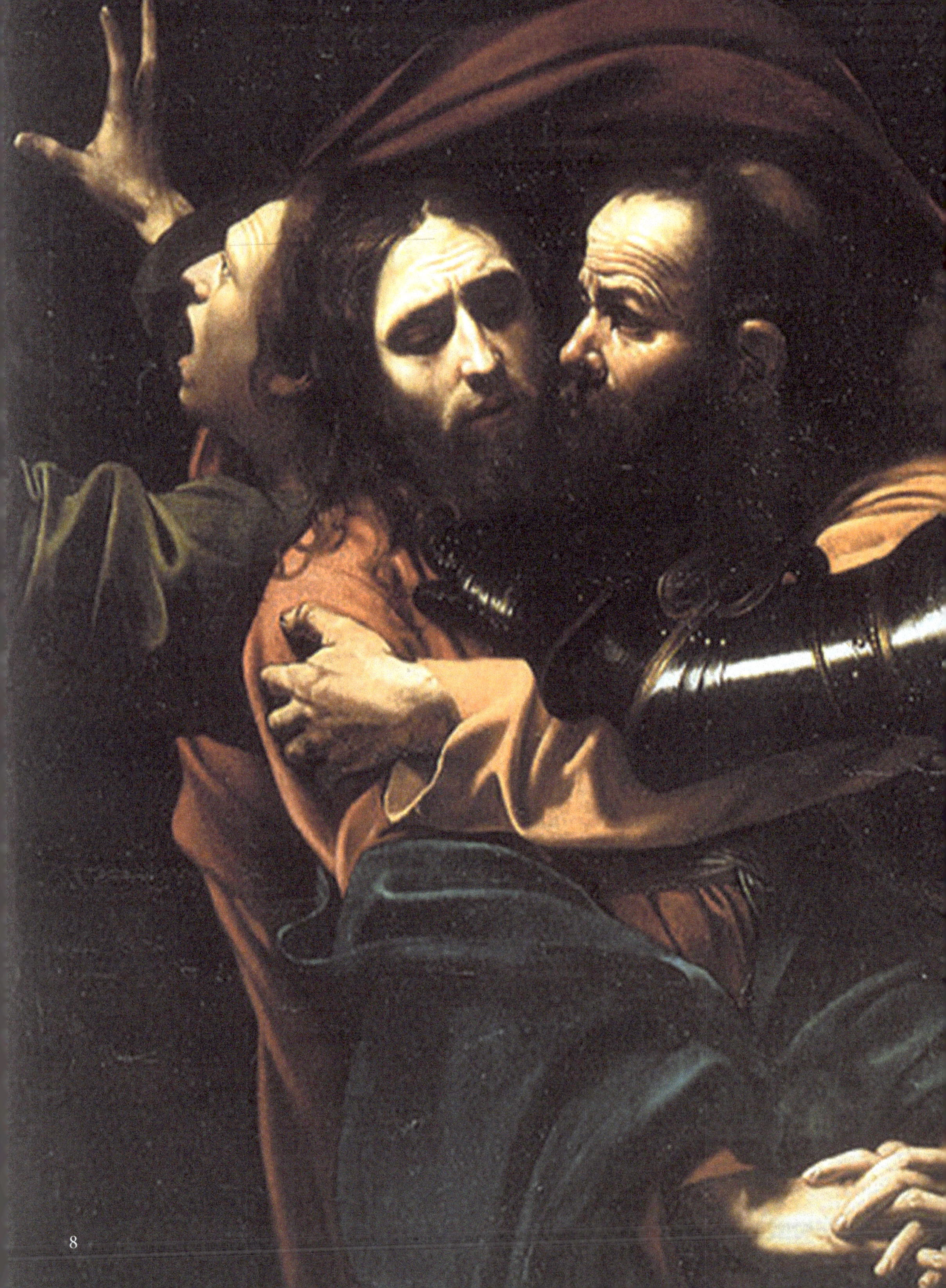

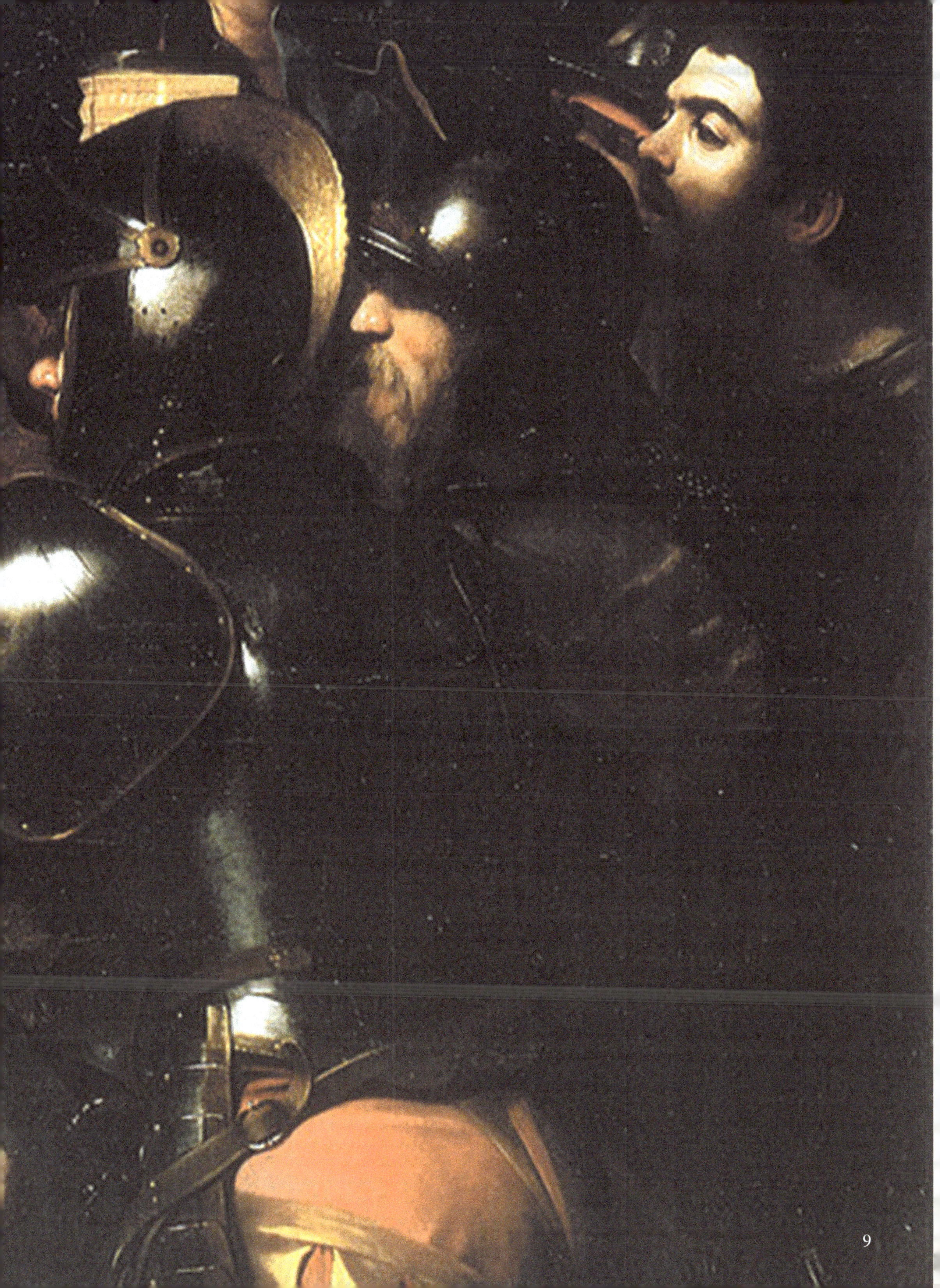

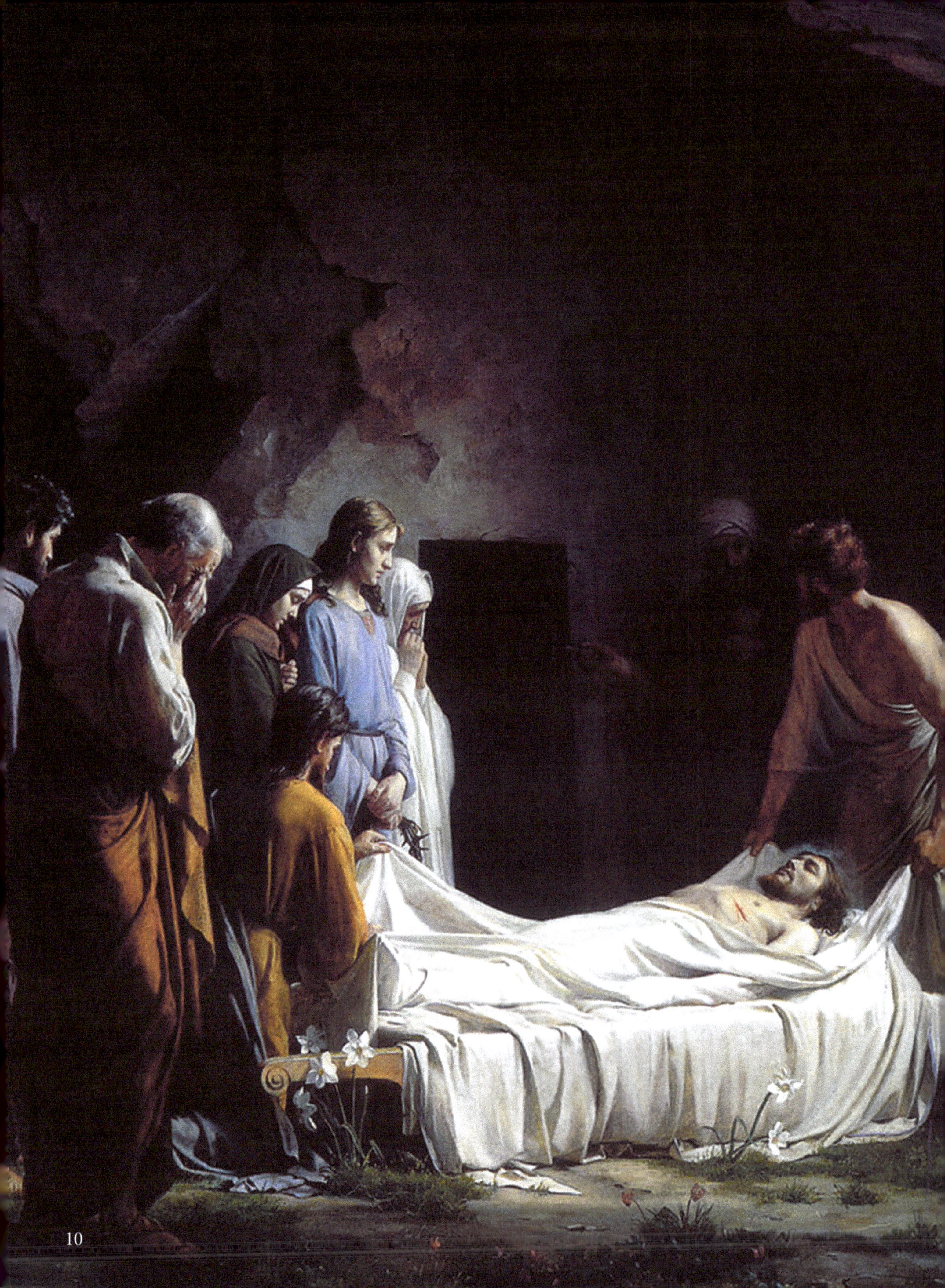

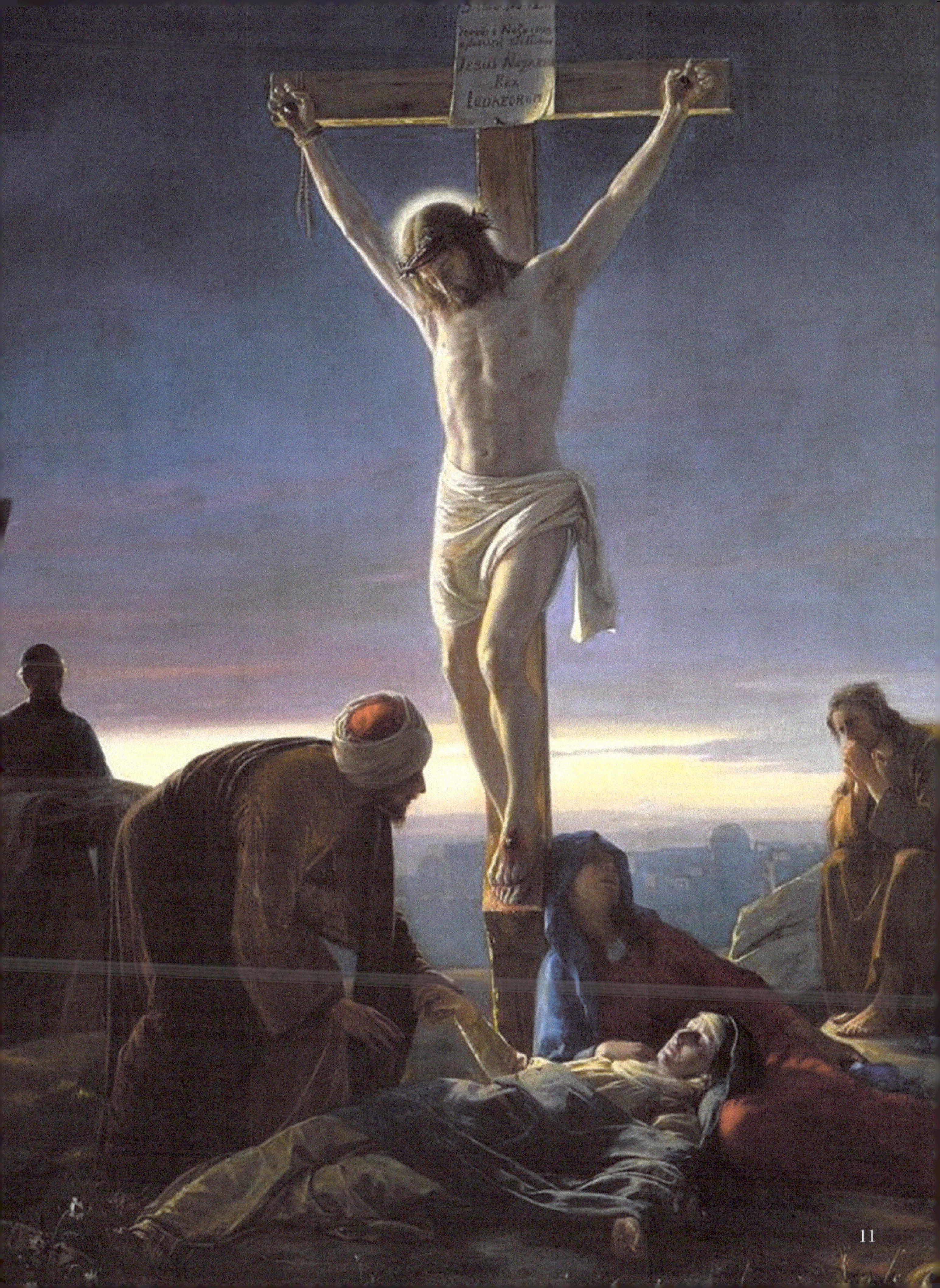

11

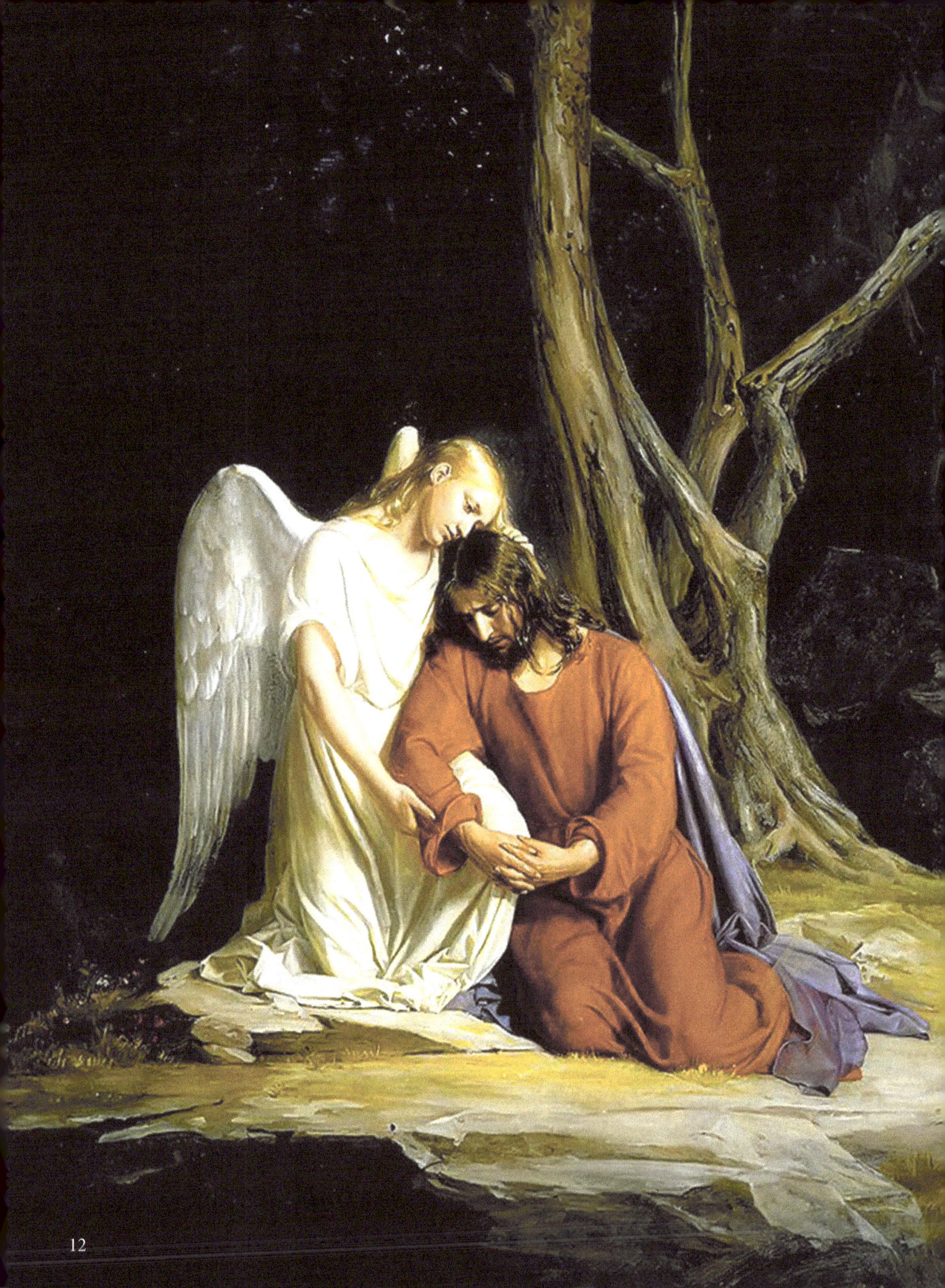

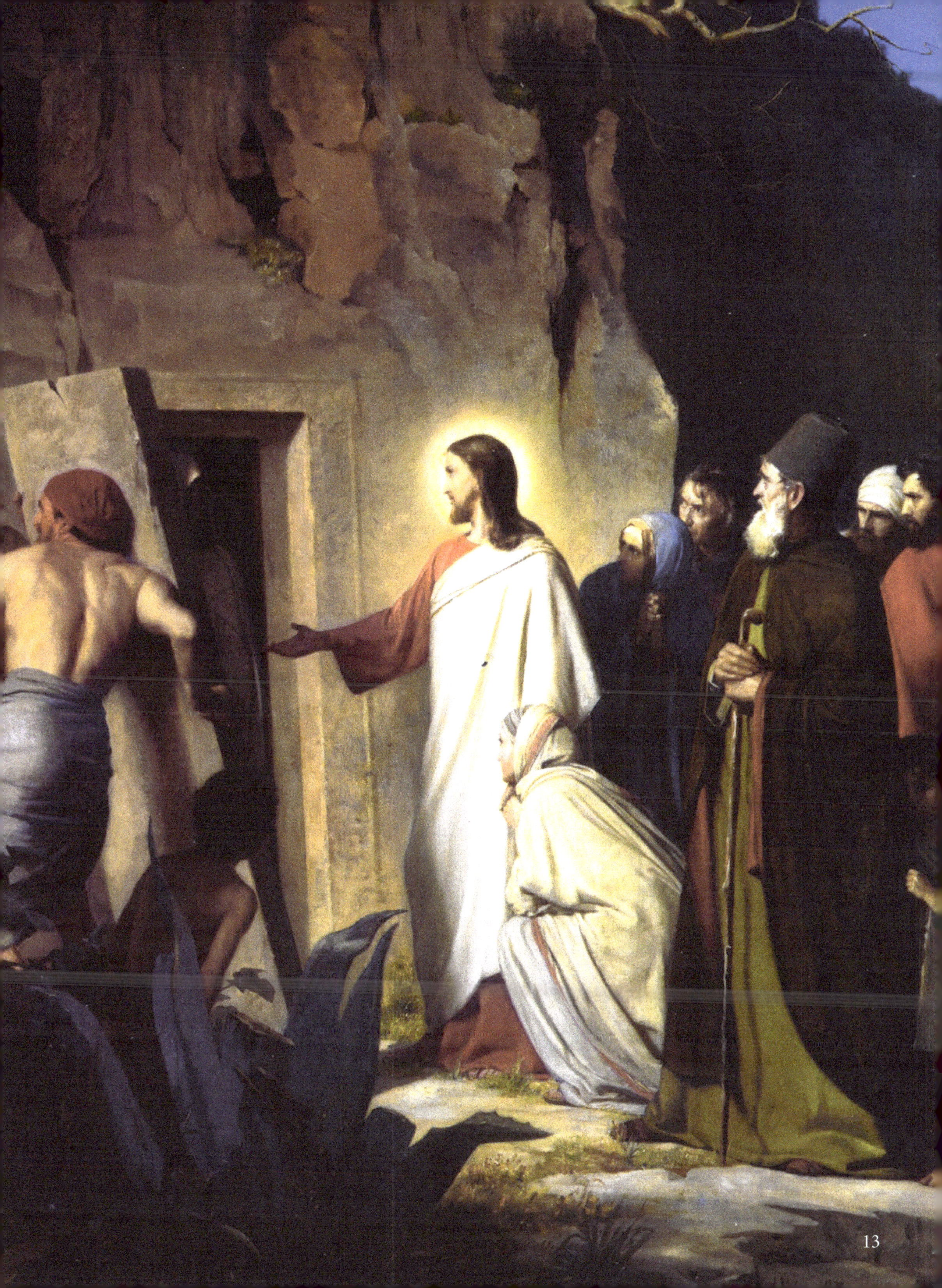

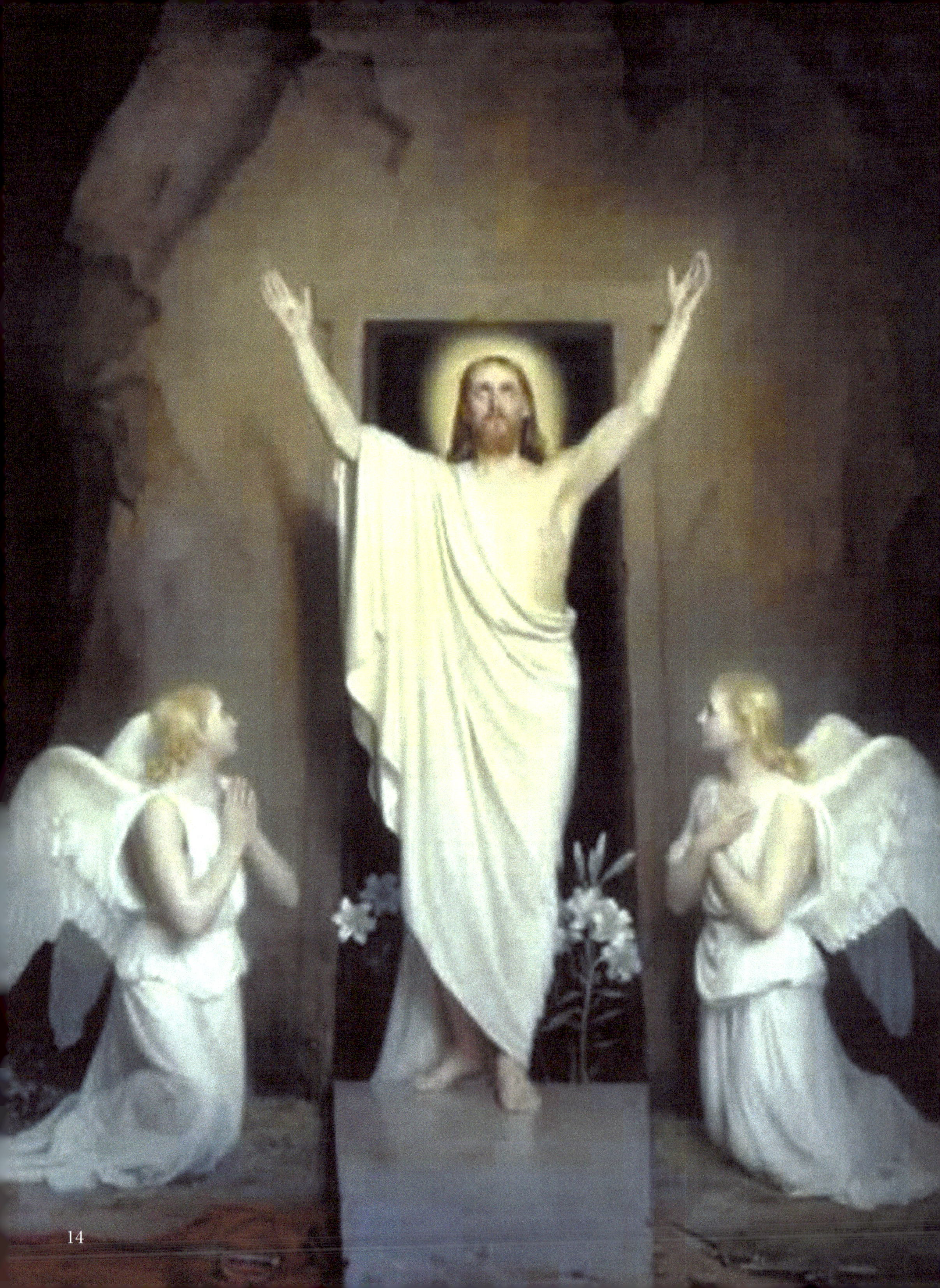

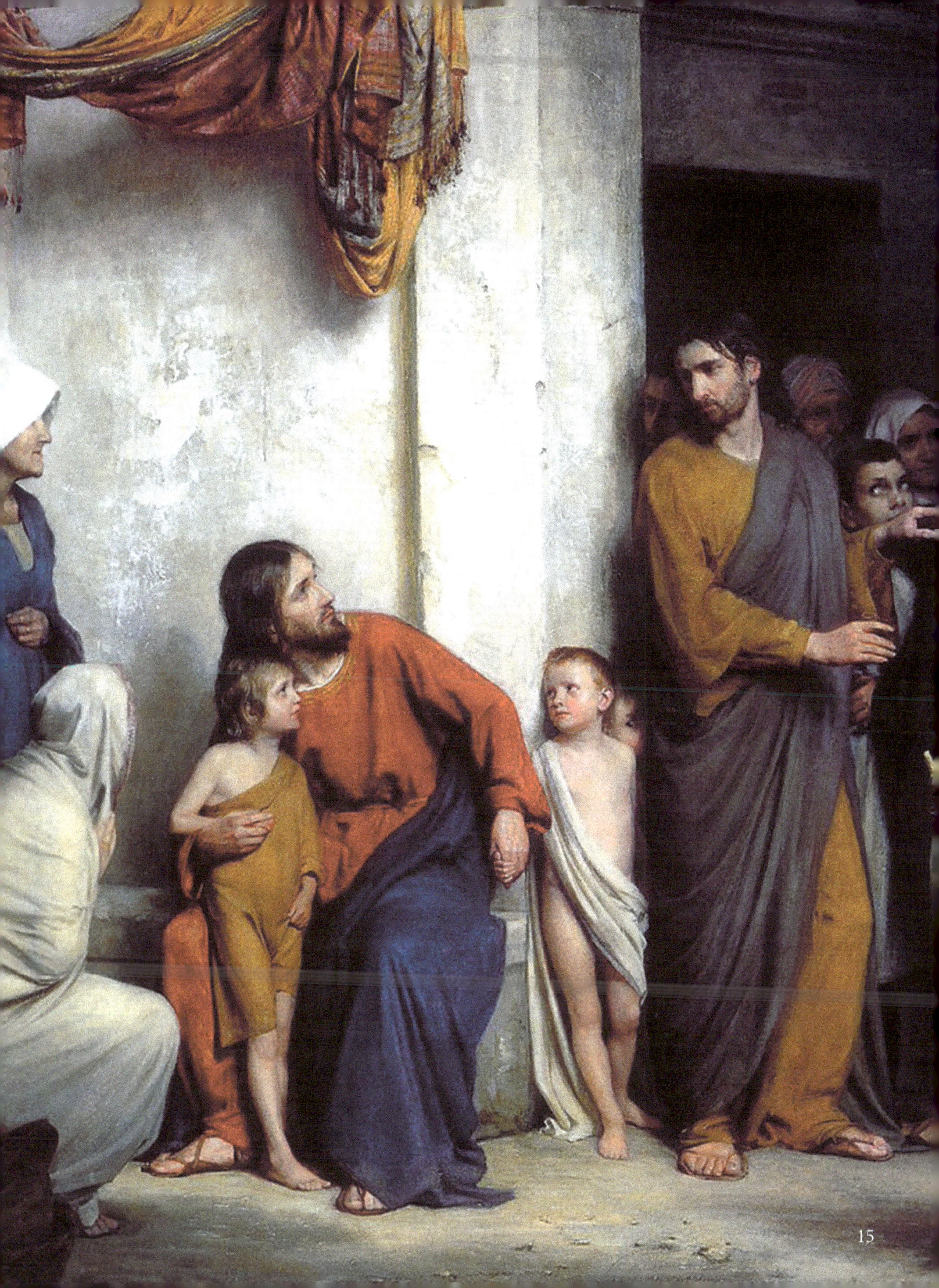

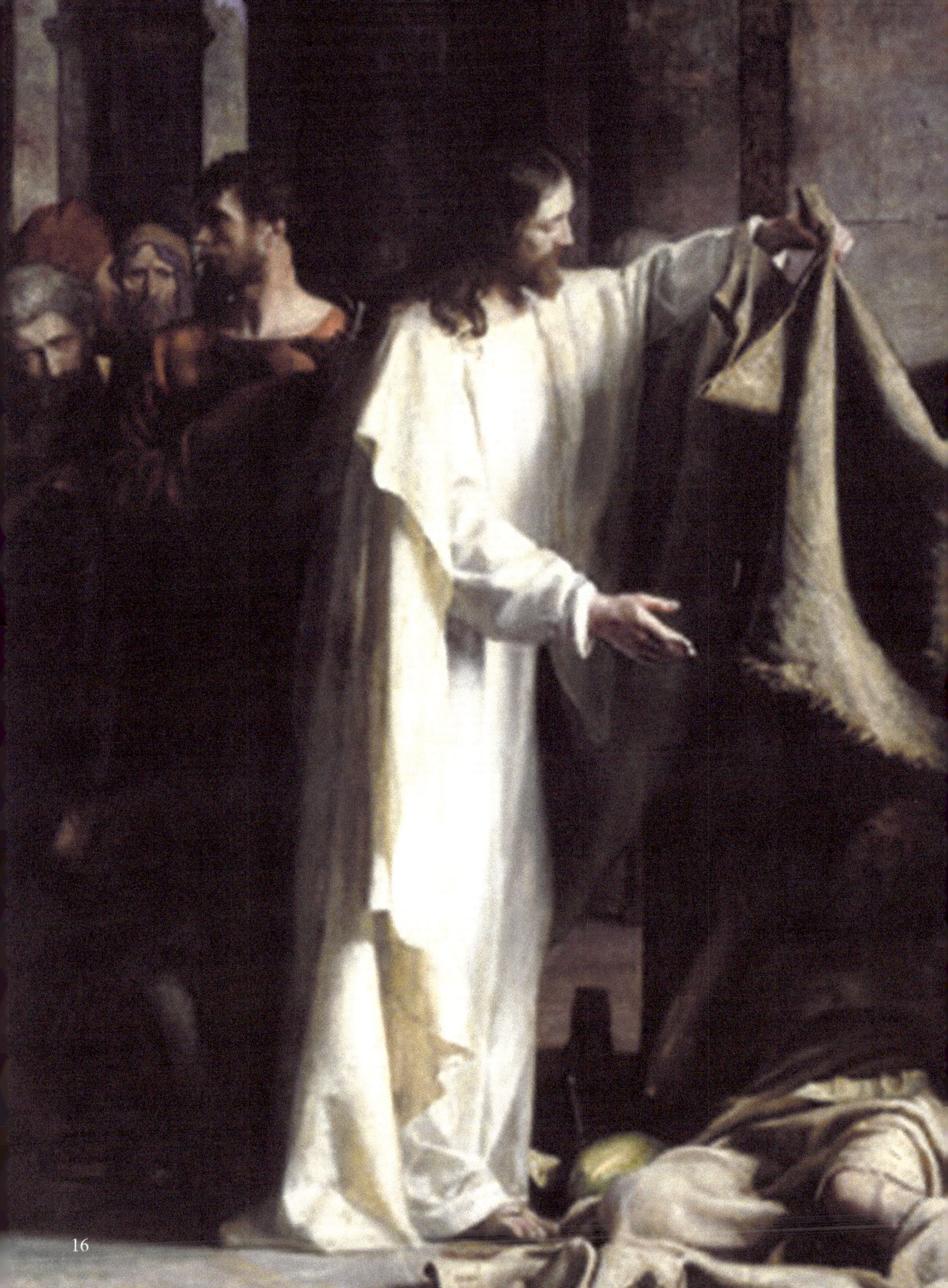

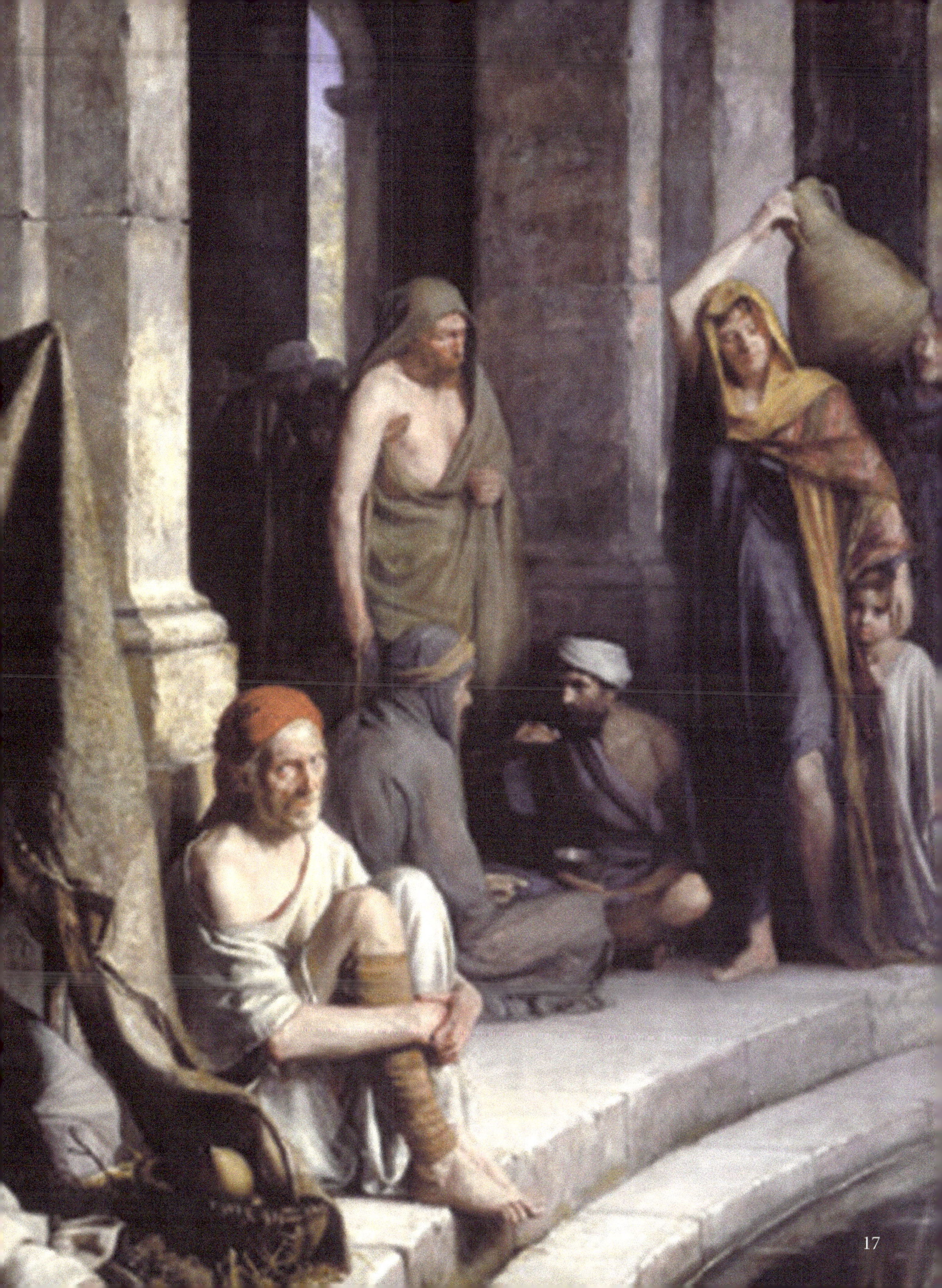

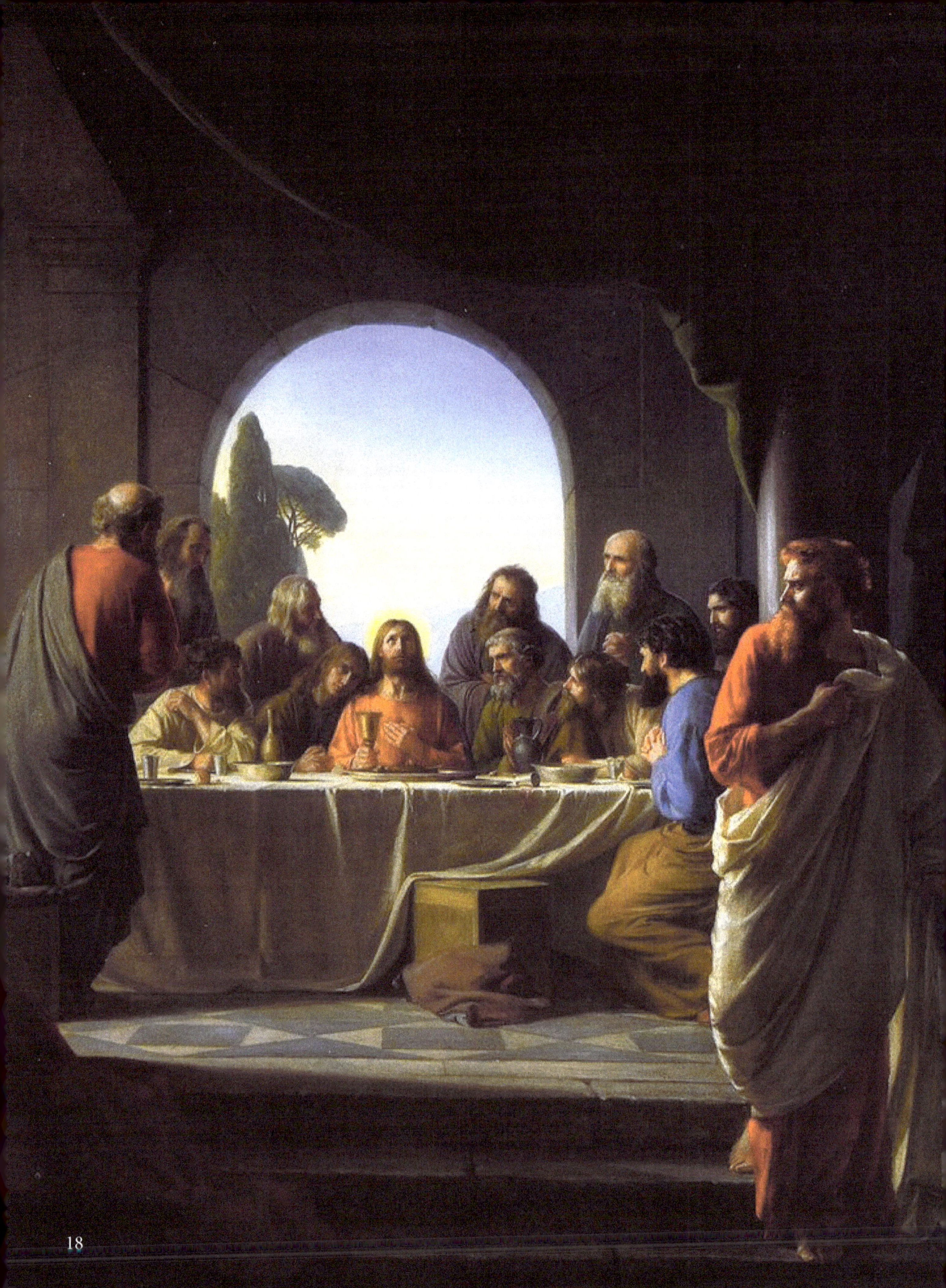

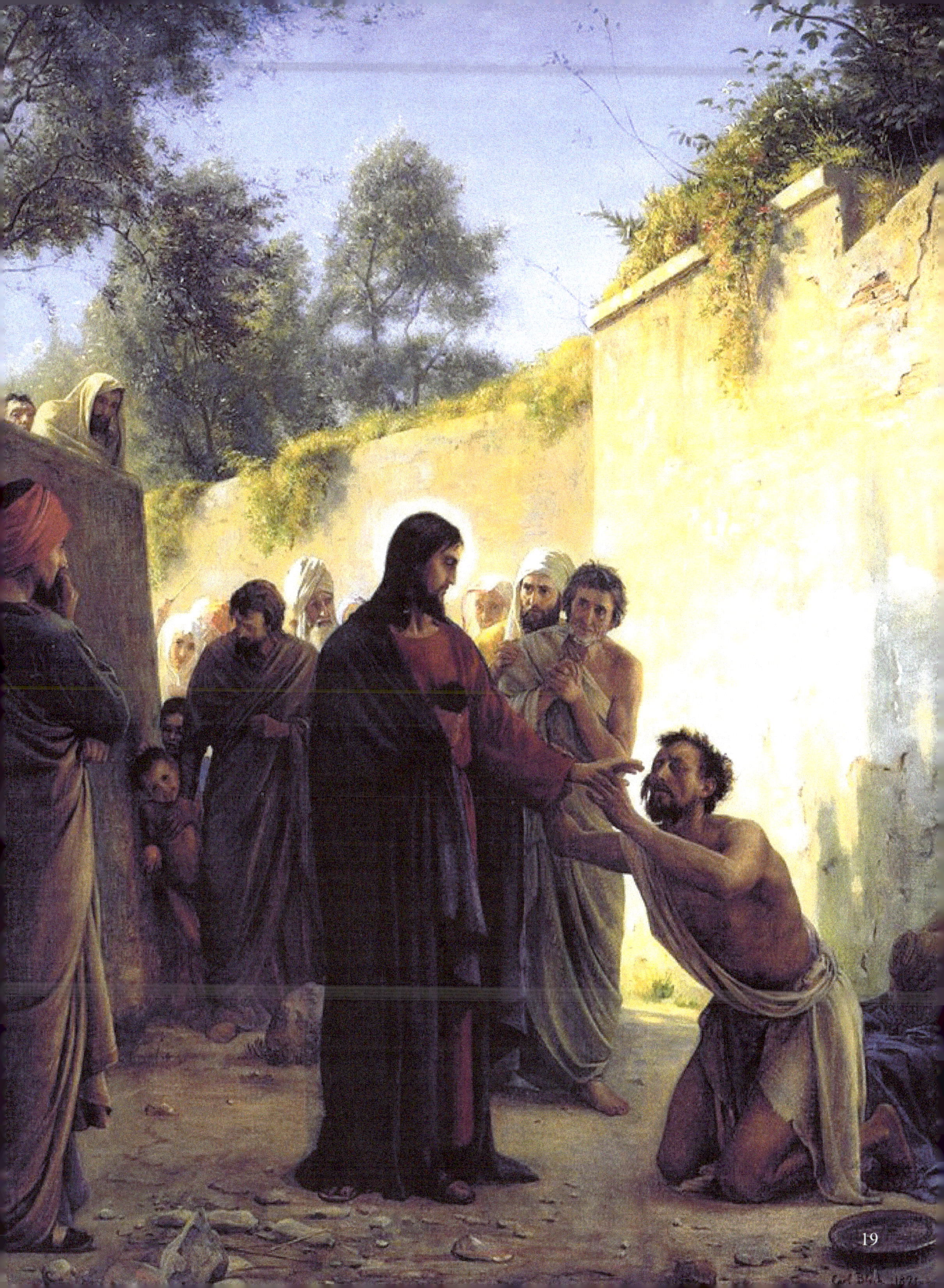

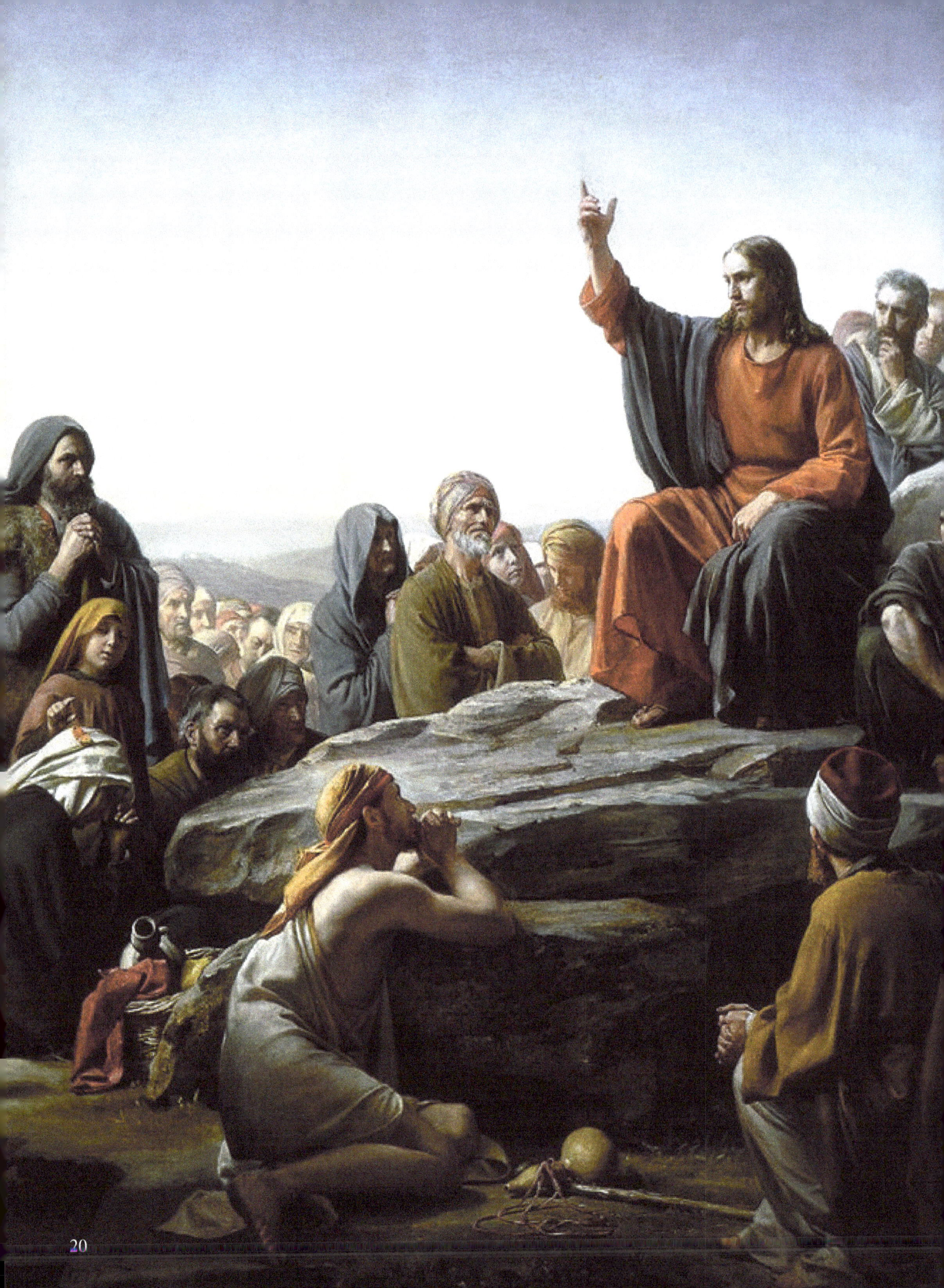

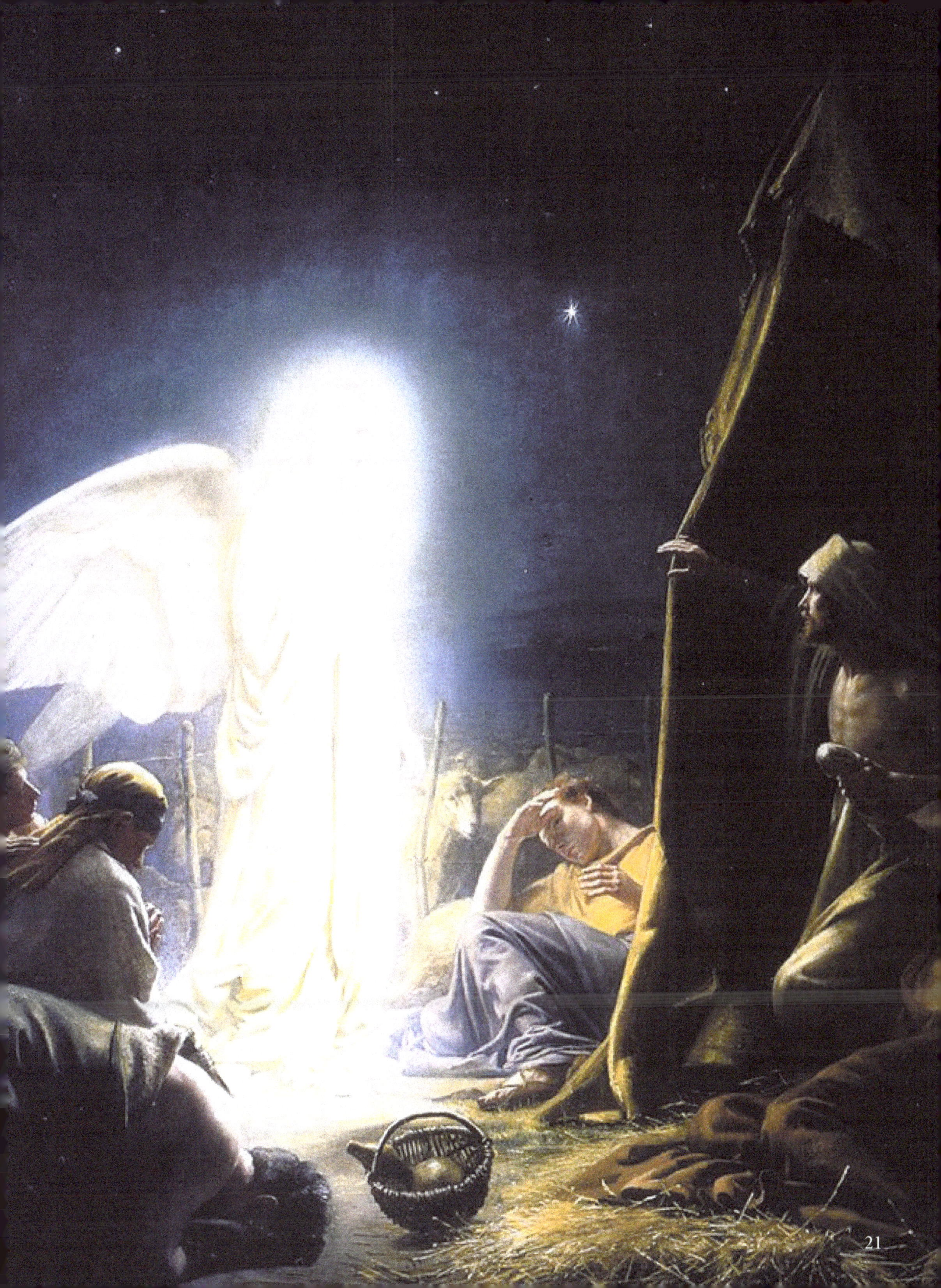

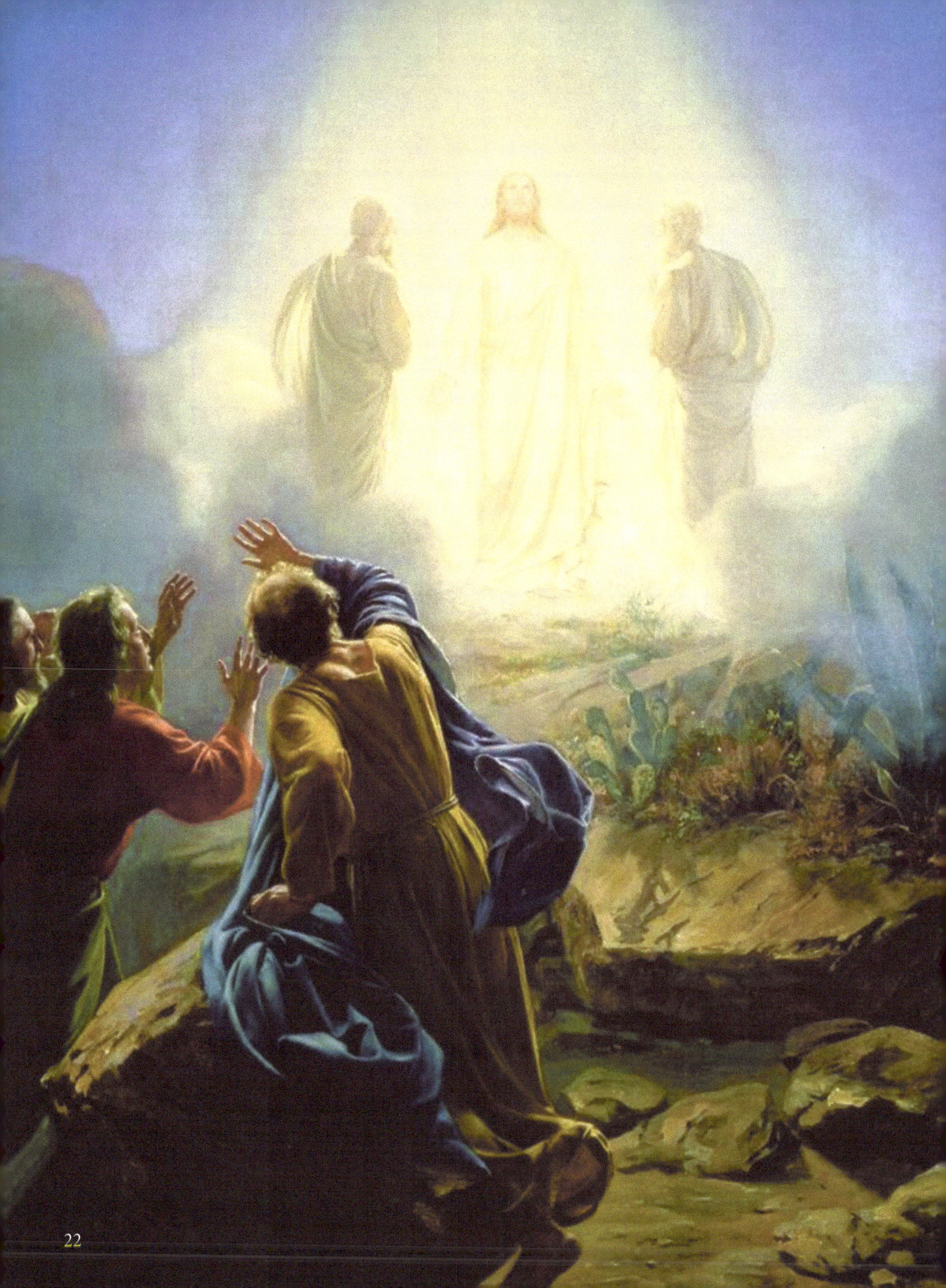

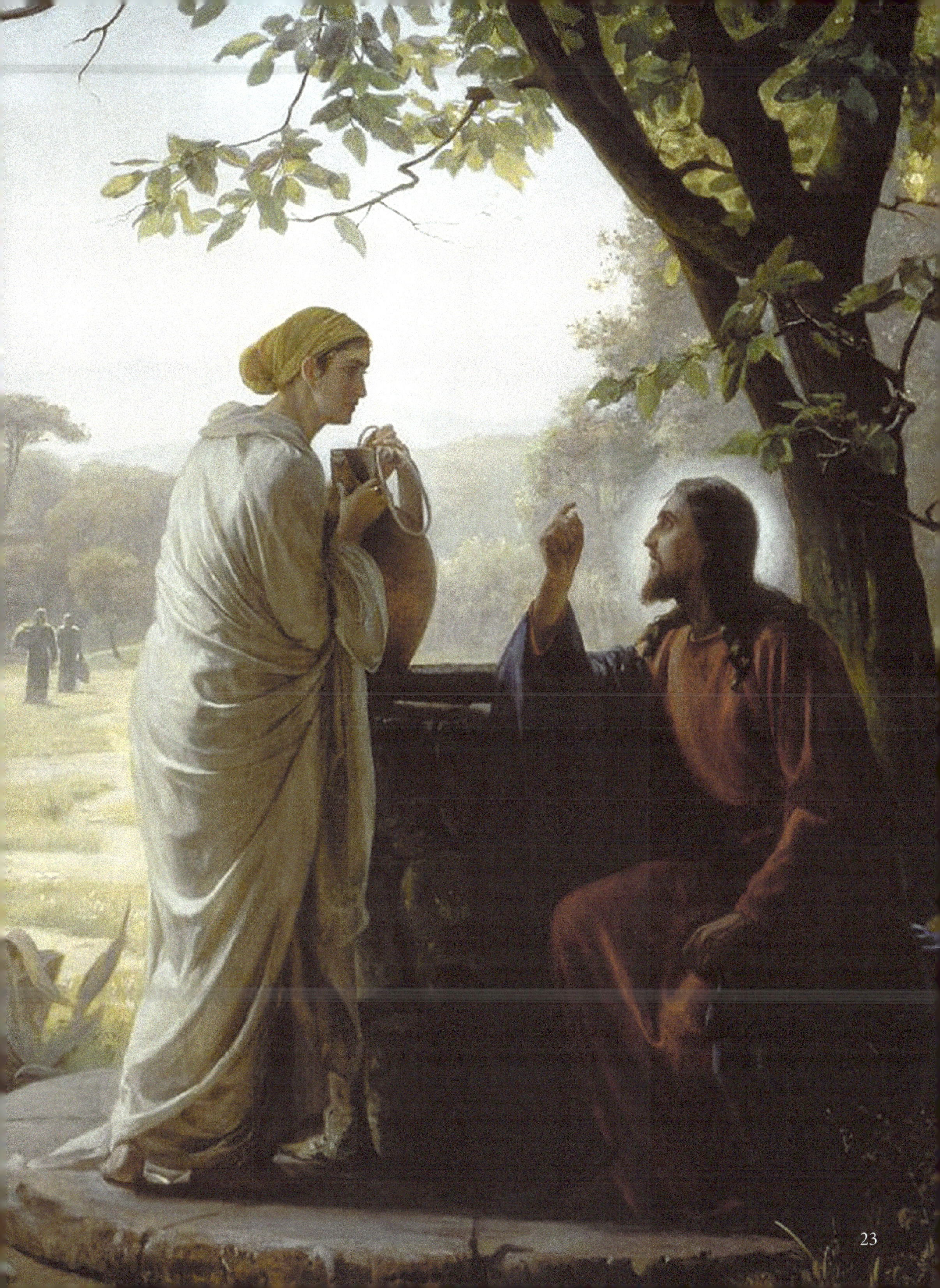

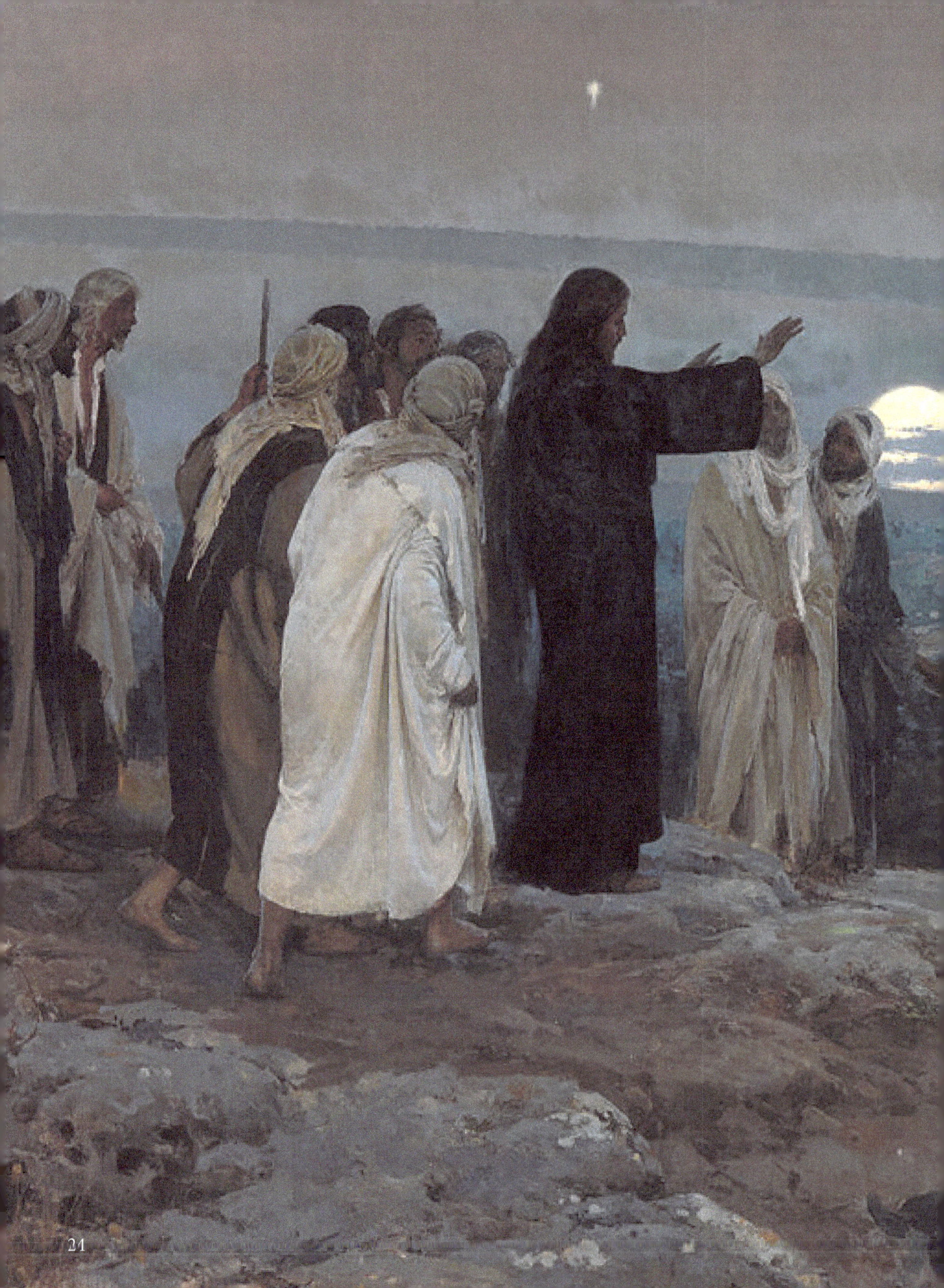

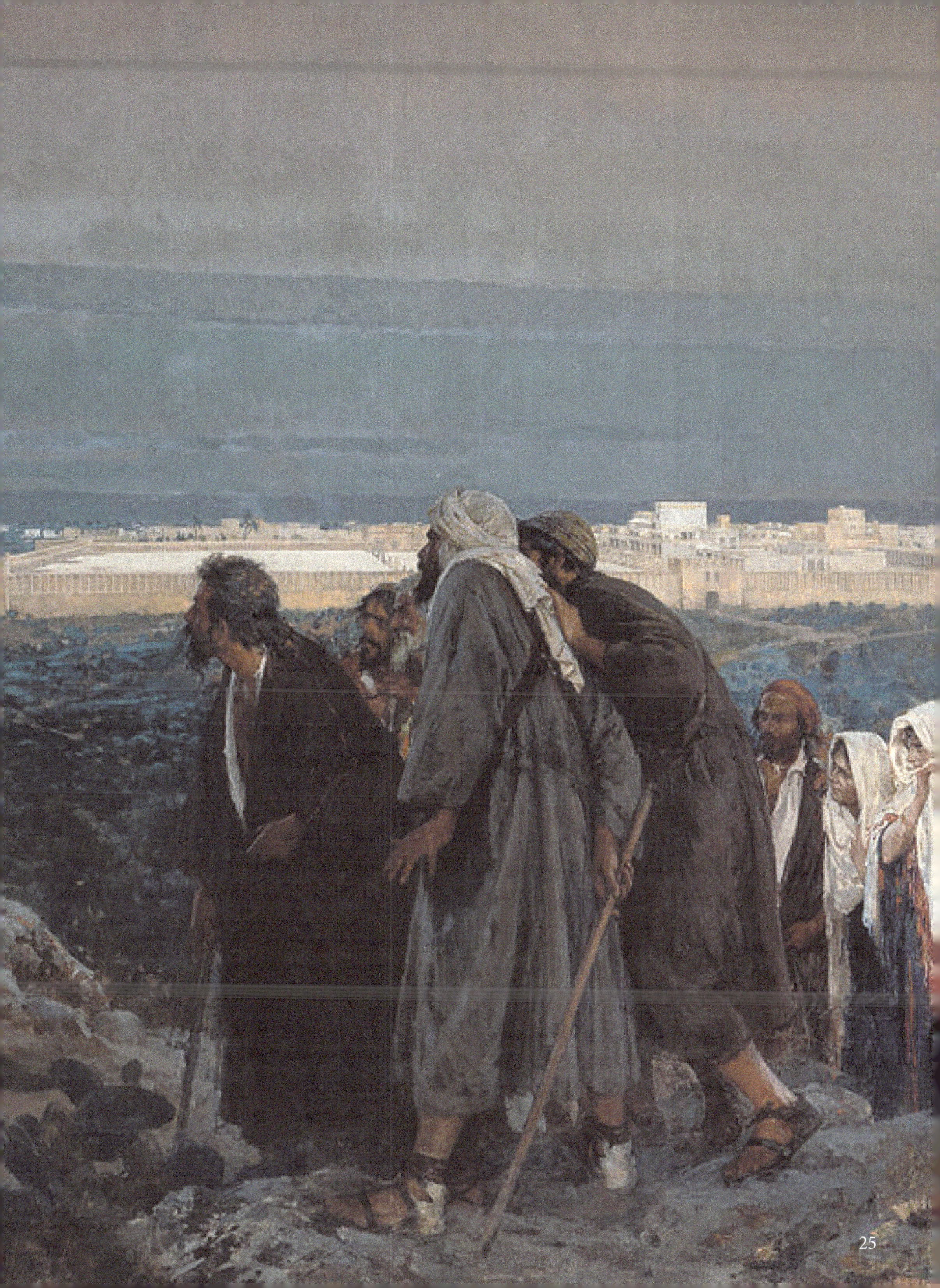

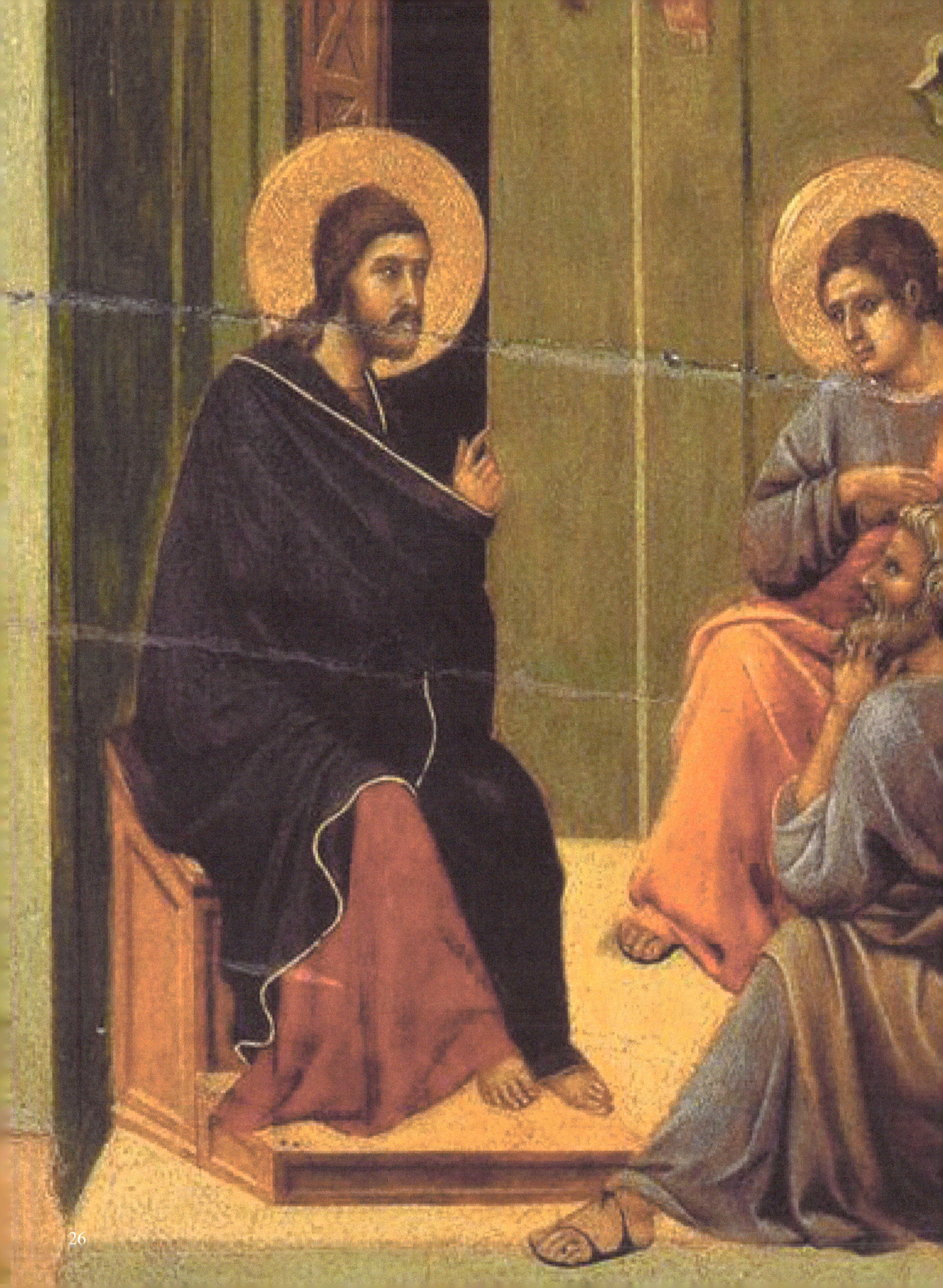

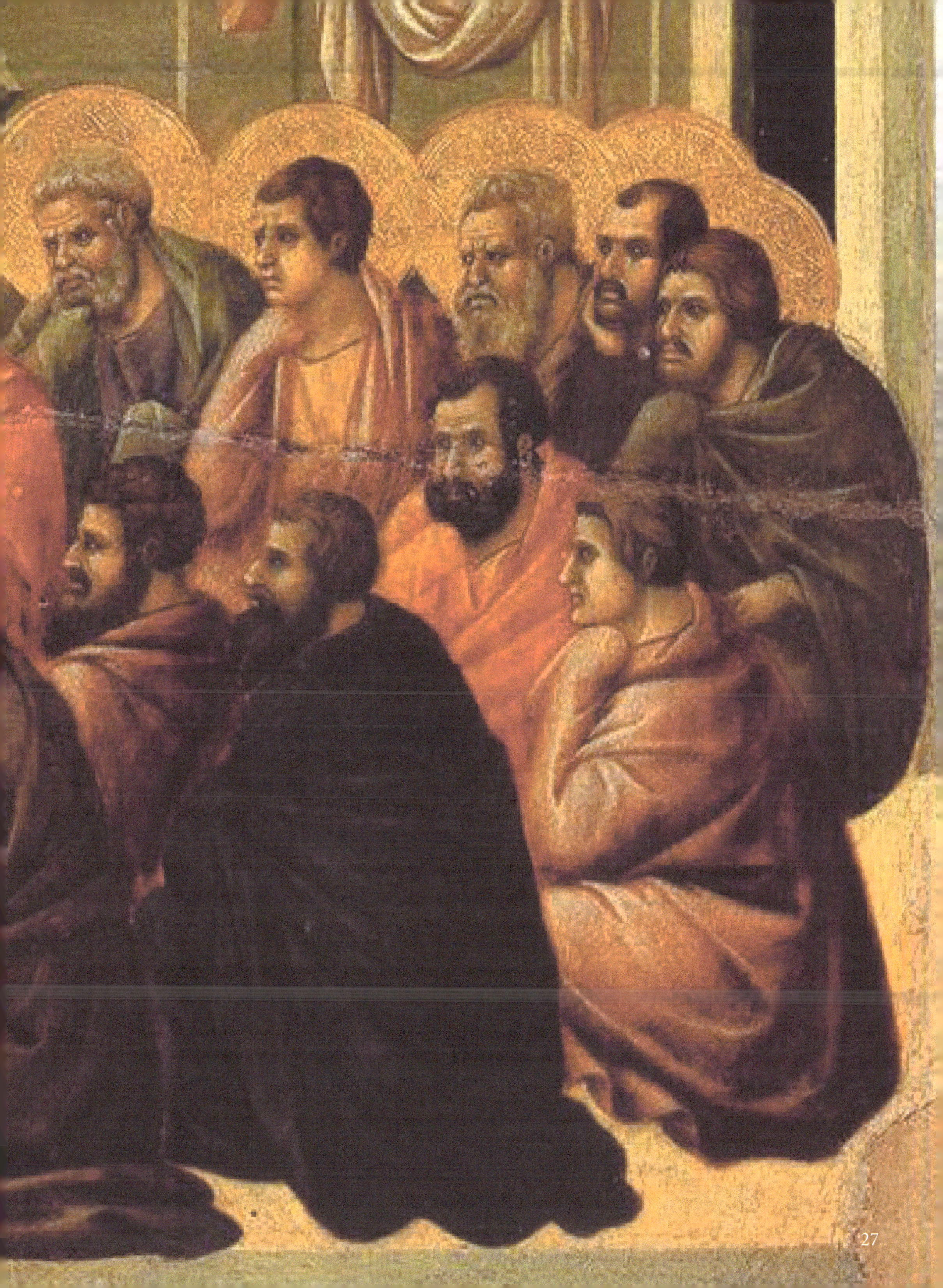

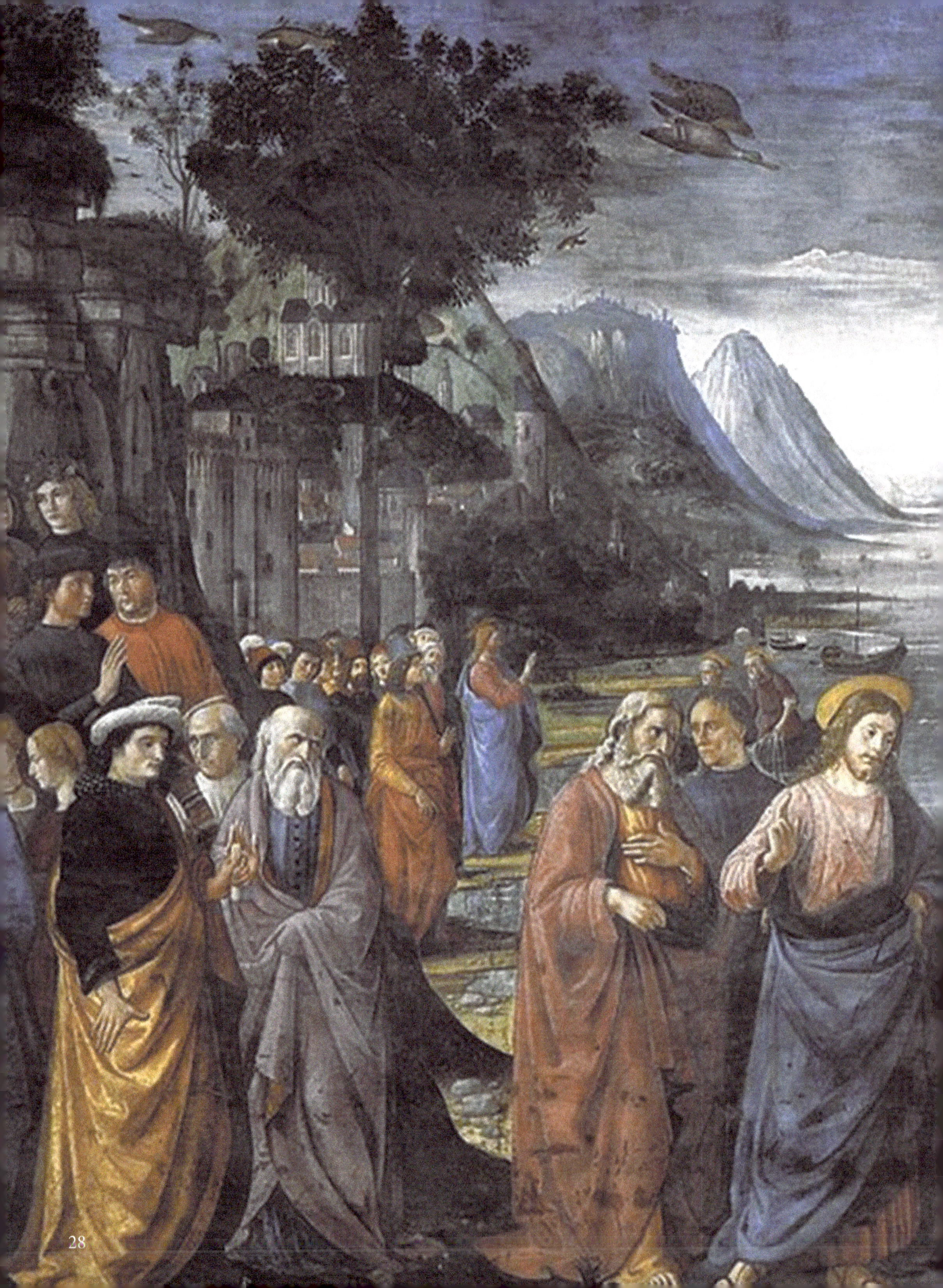

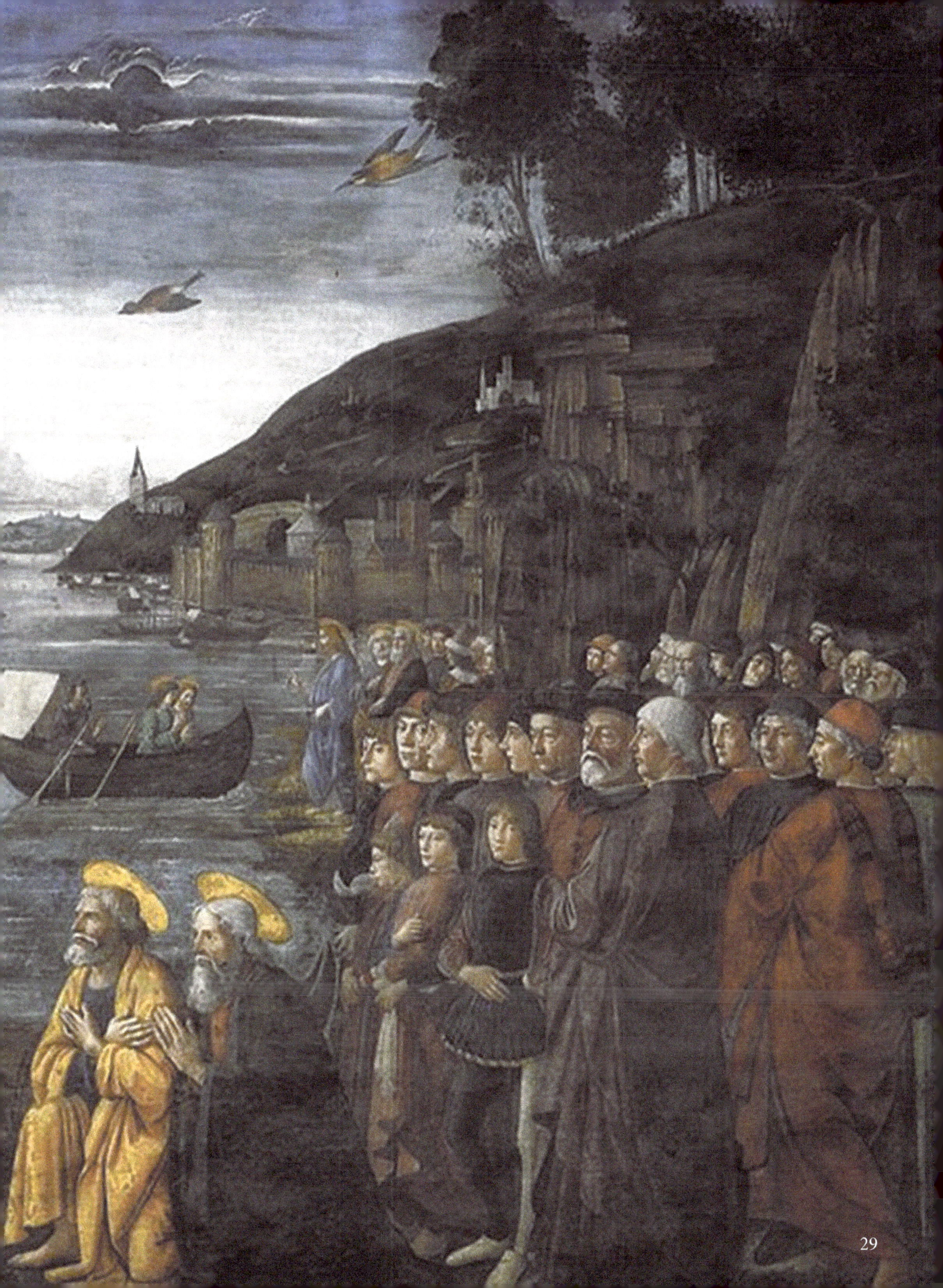

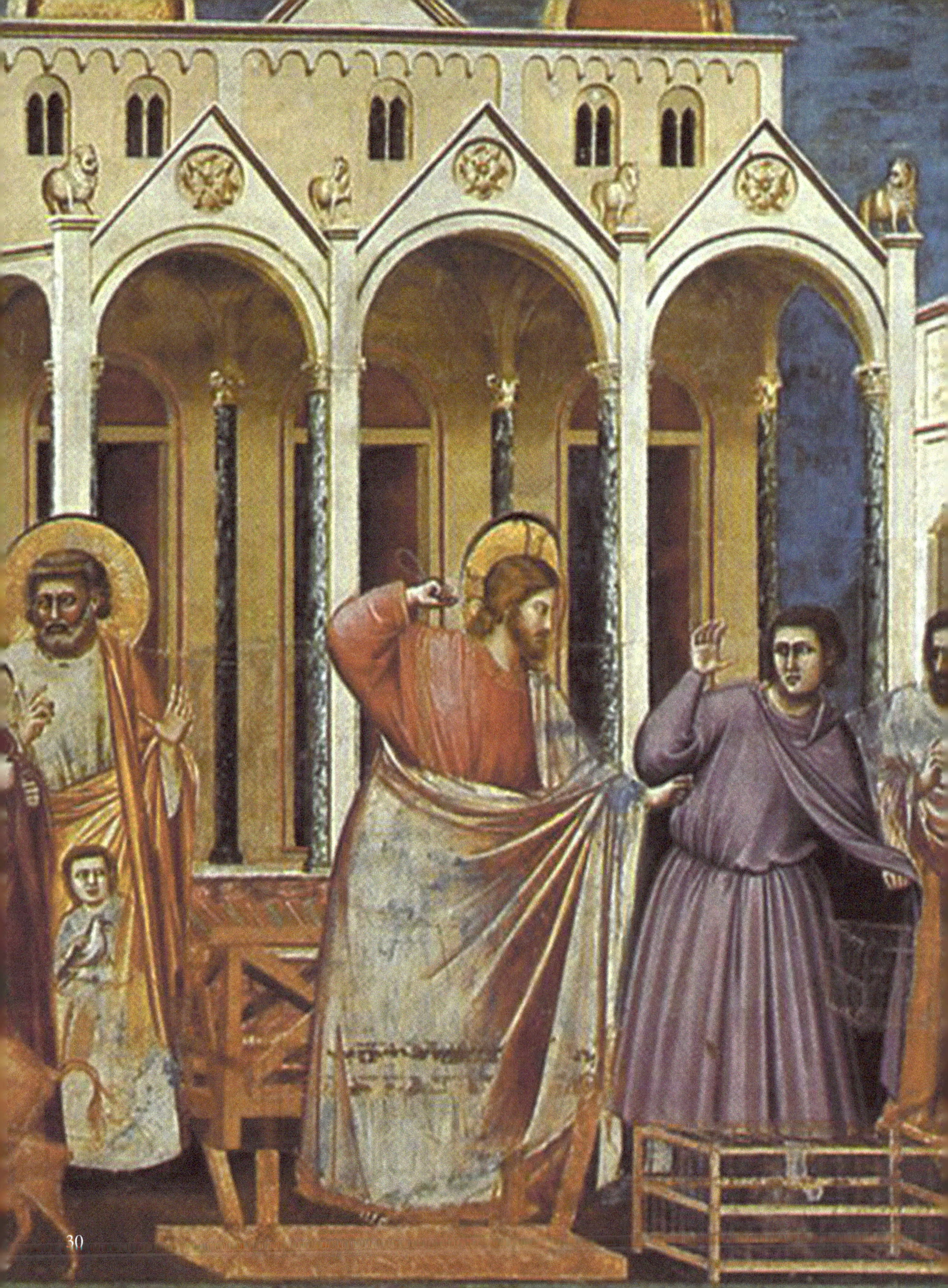

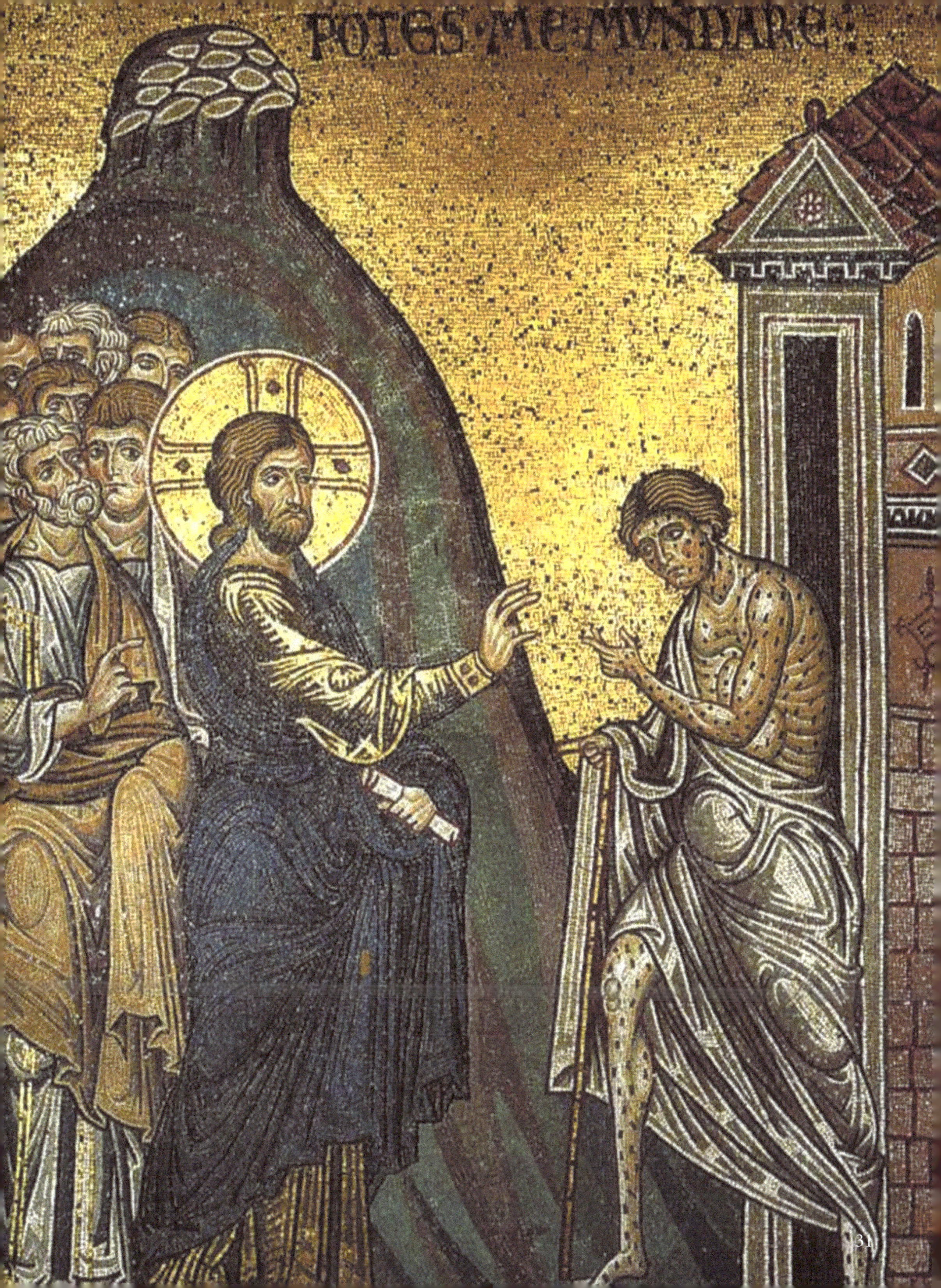

POTES ME MVNDARE

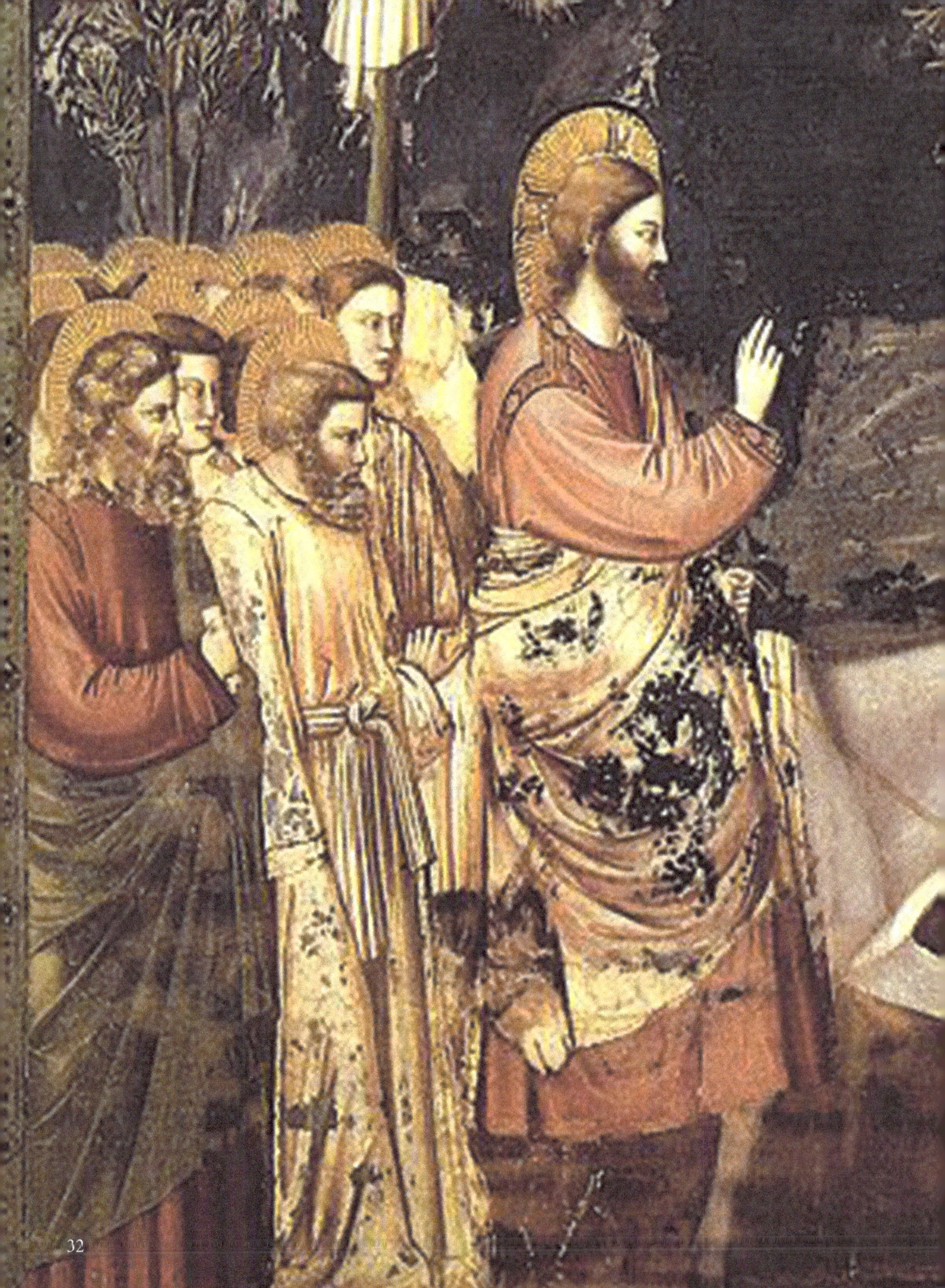

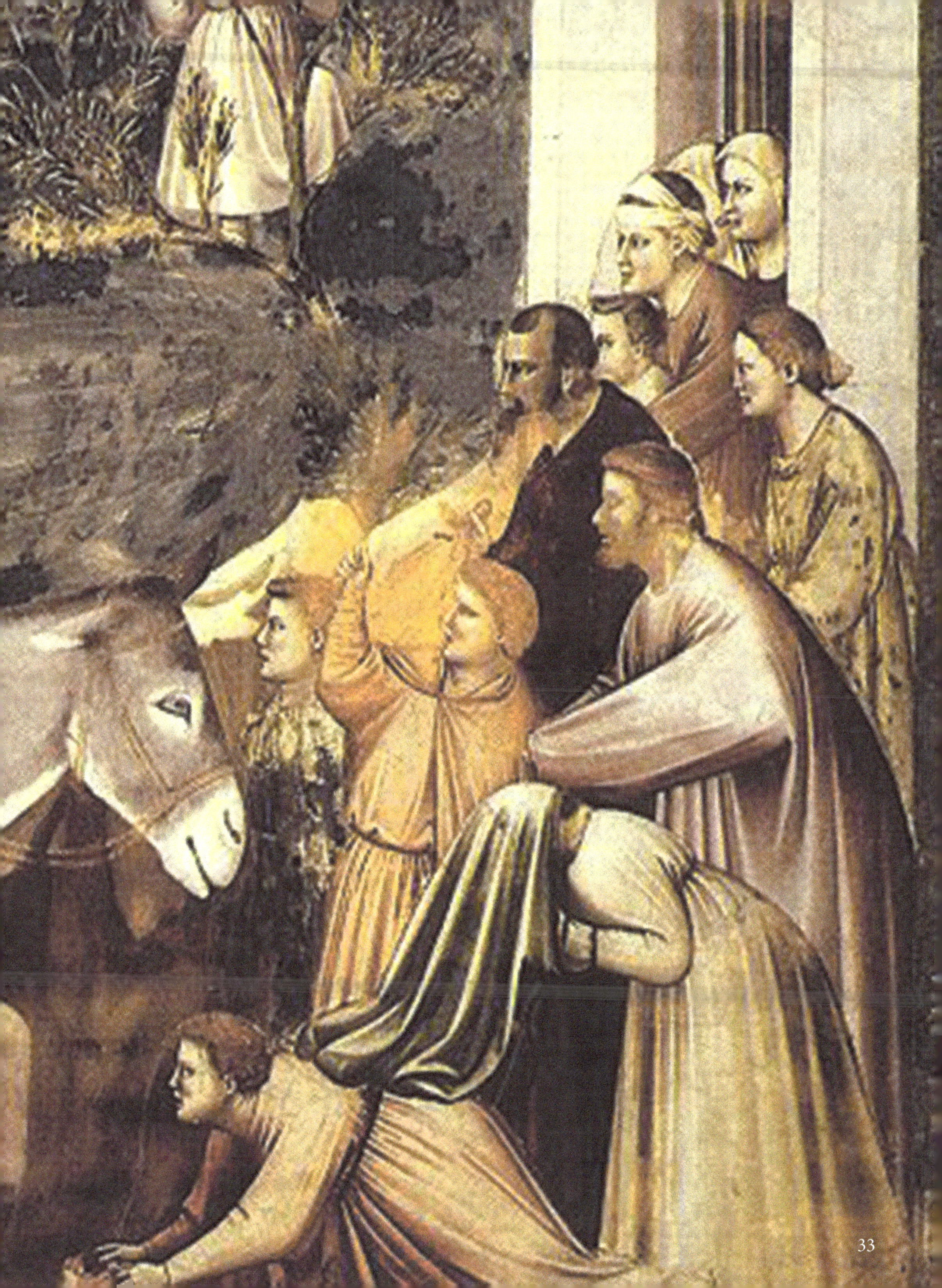

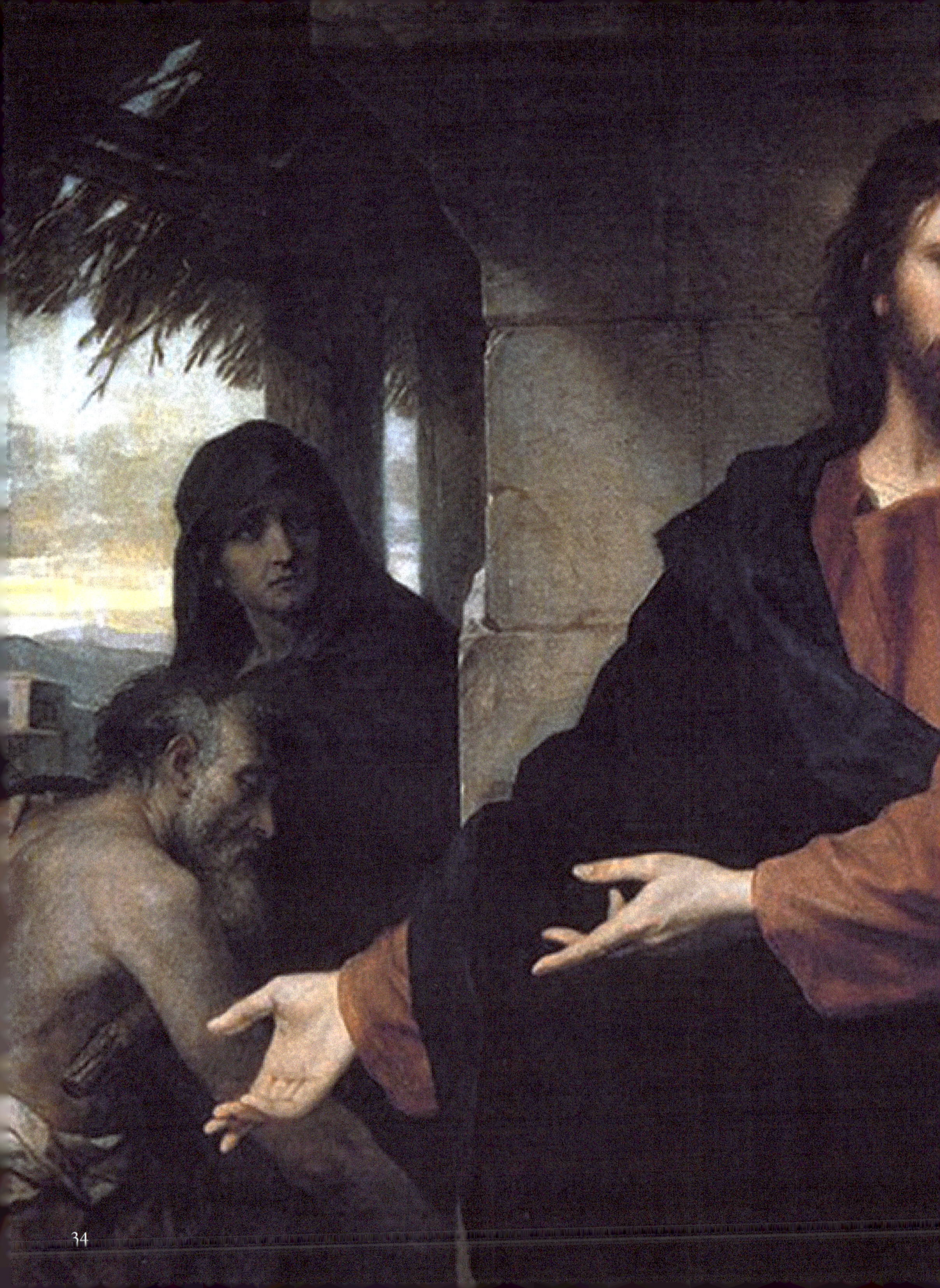

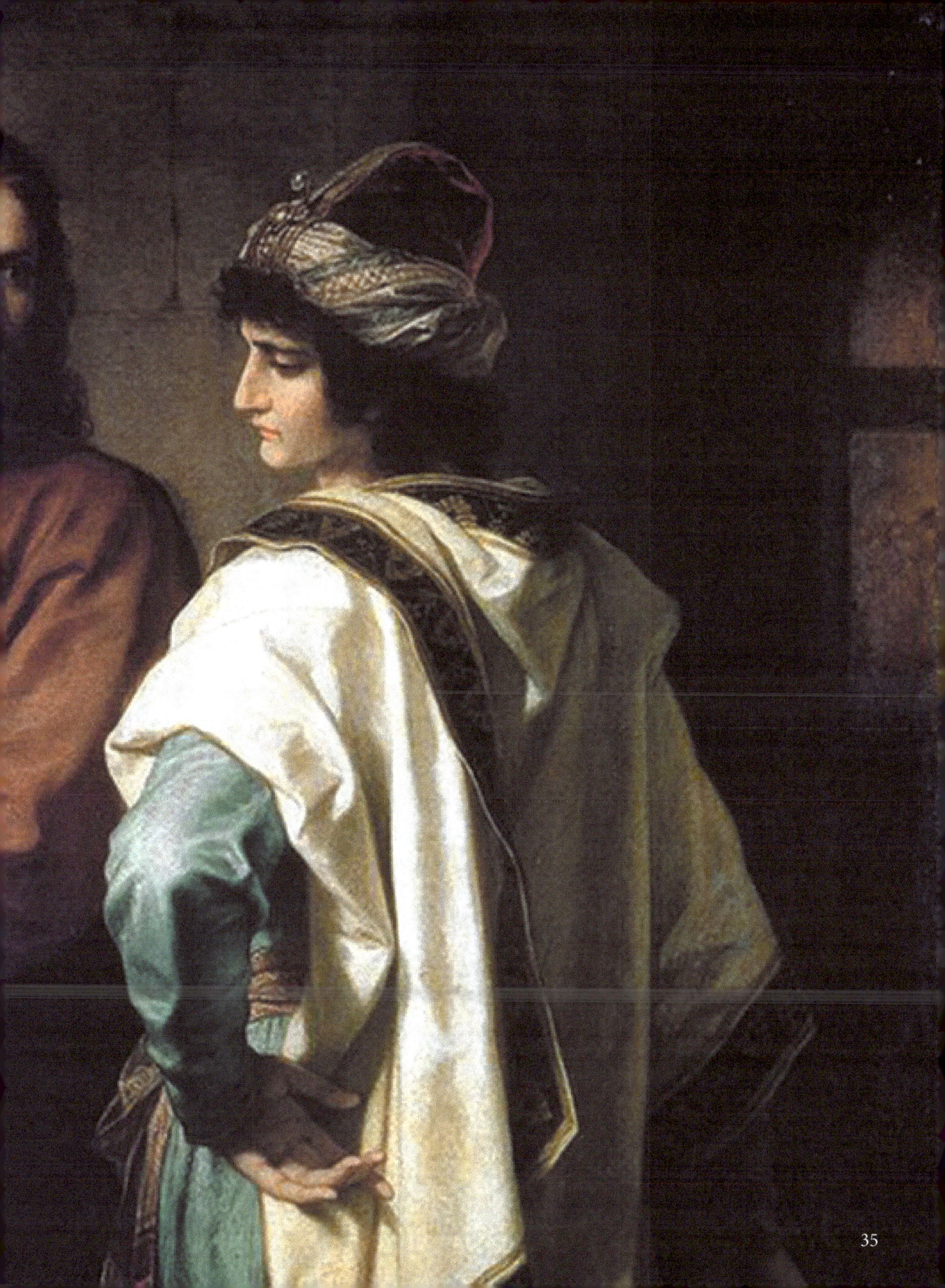

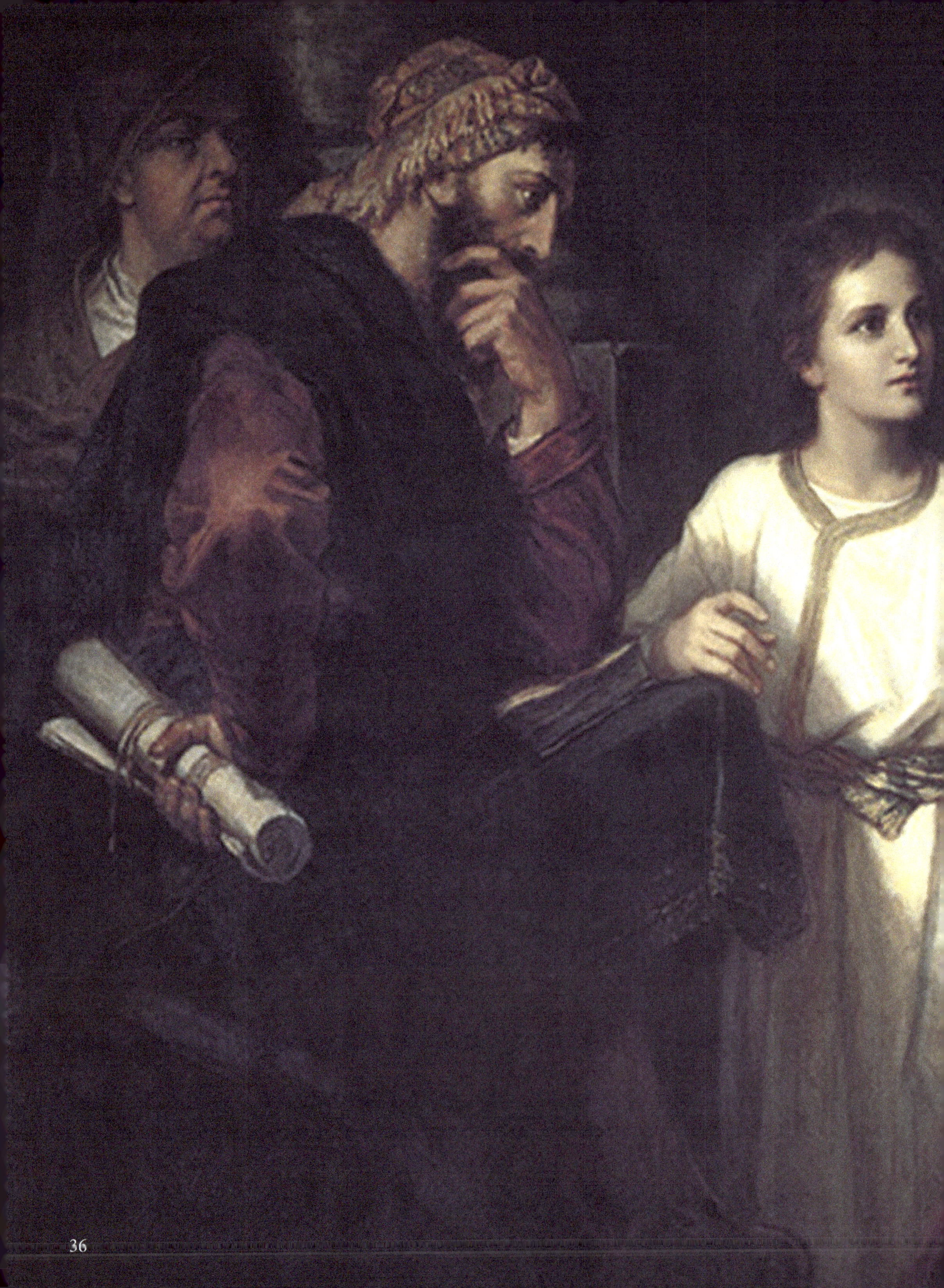

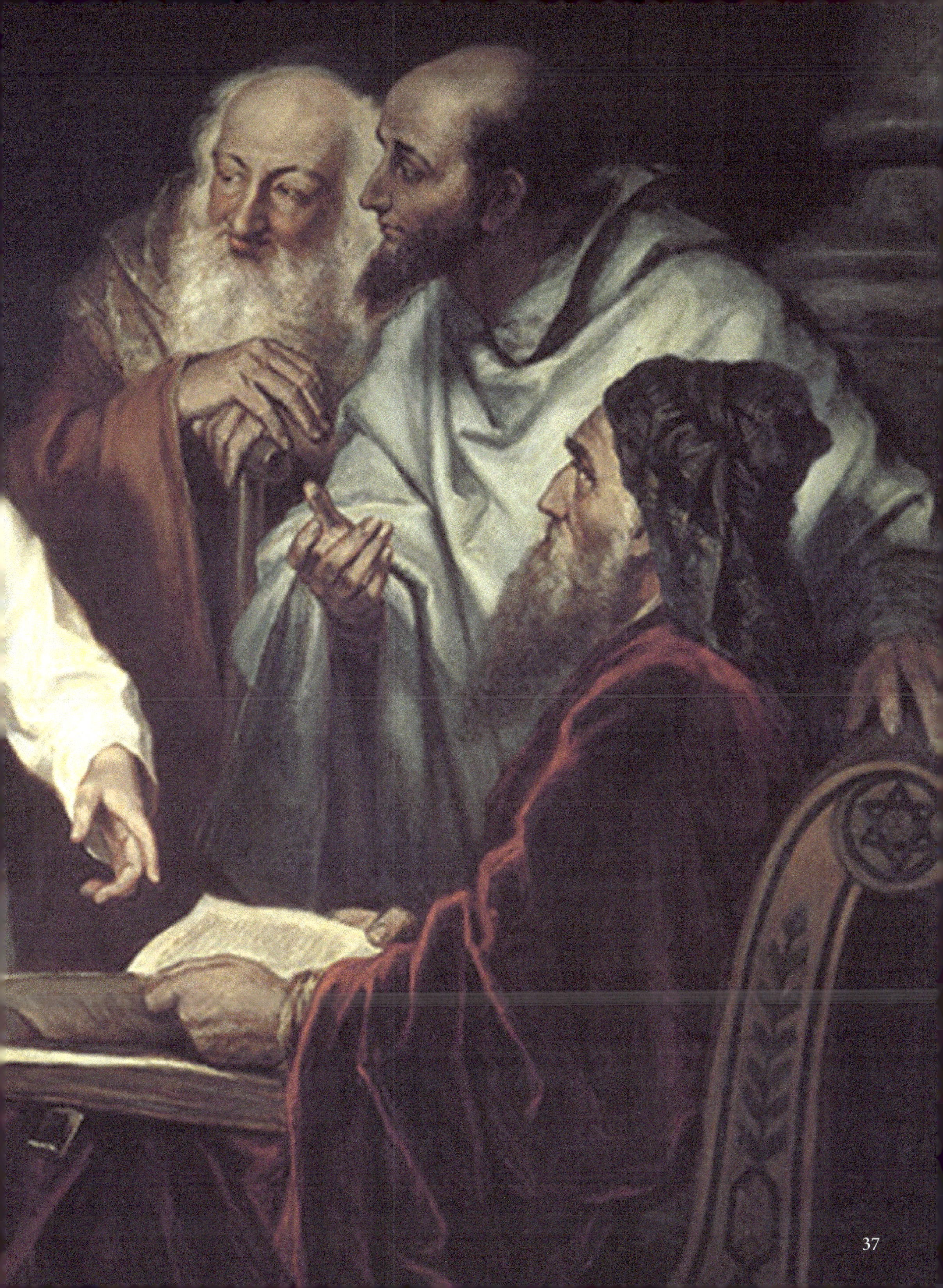

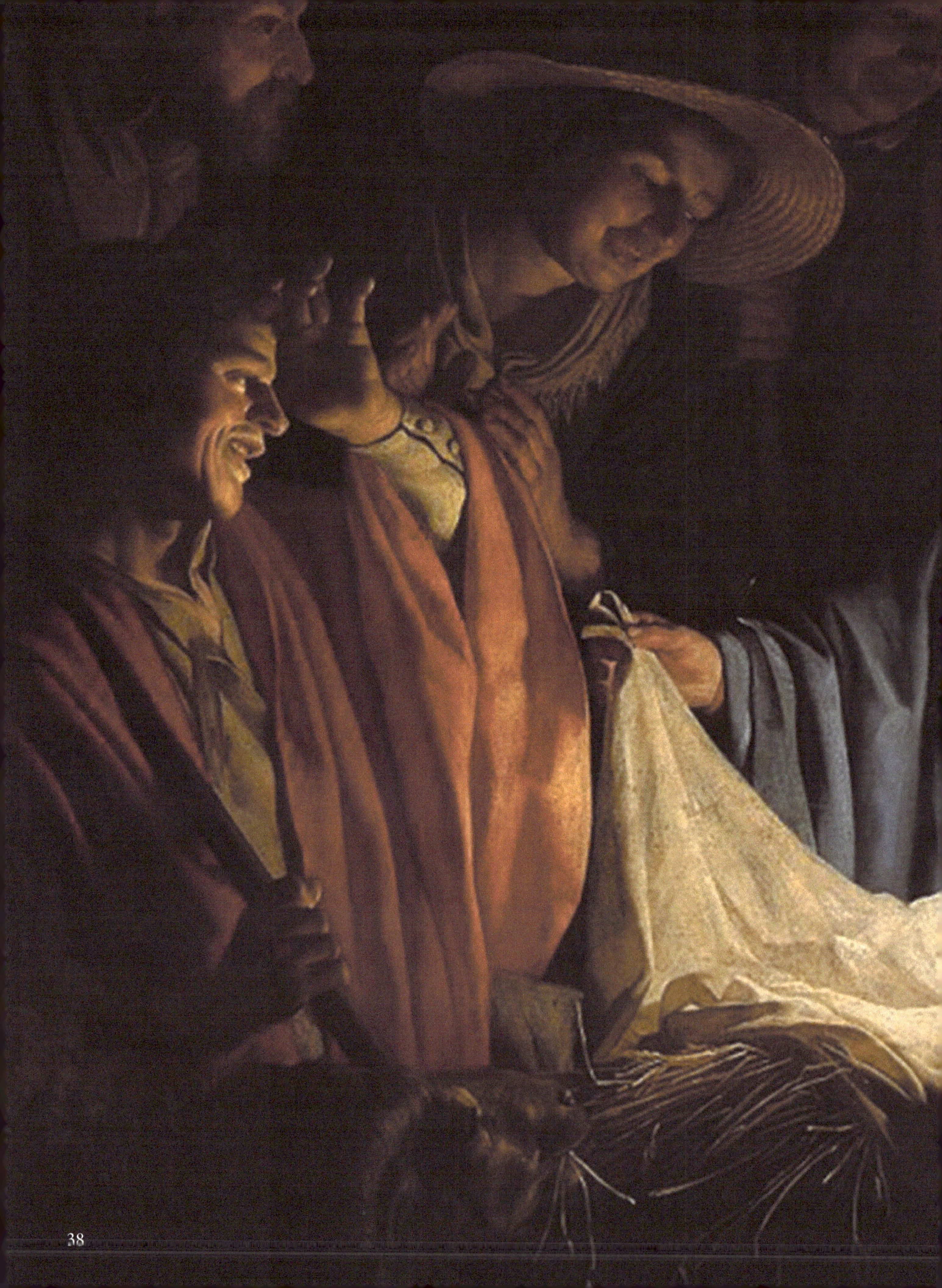

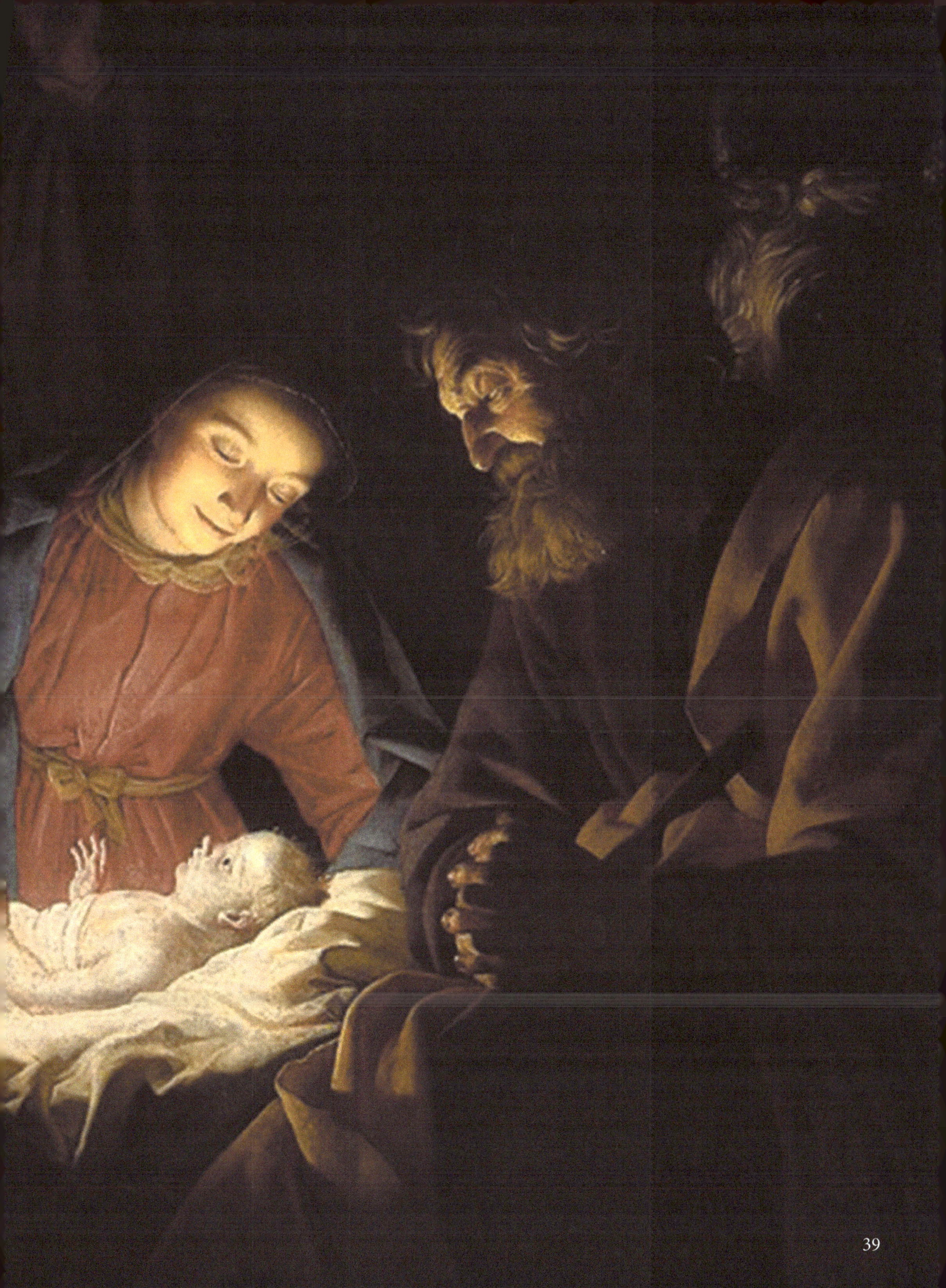

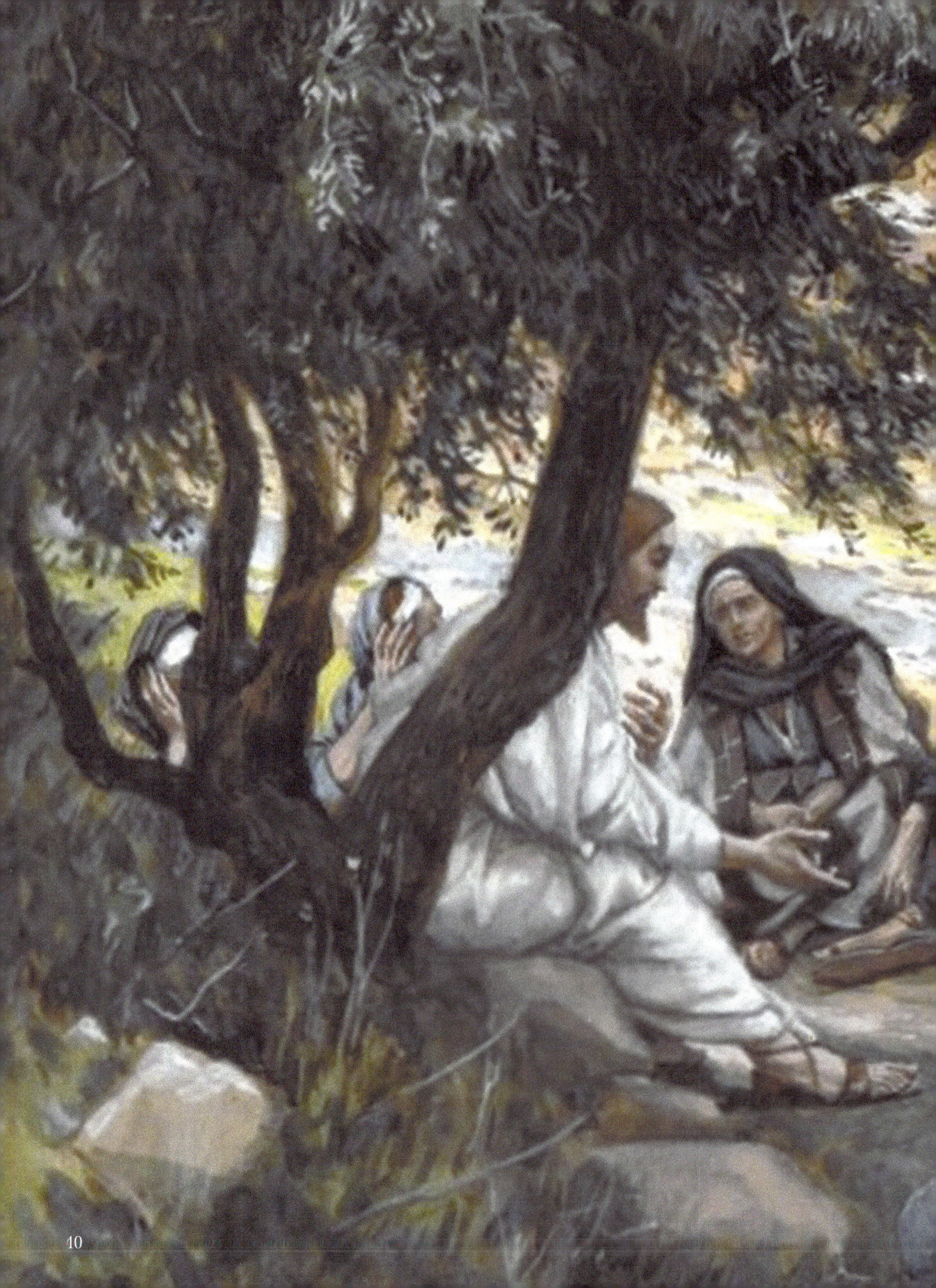

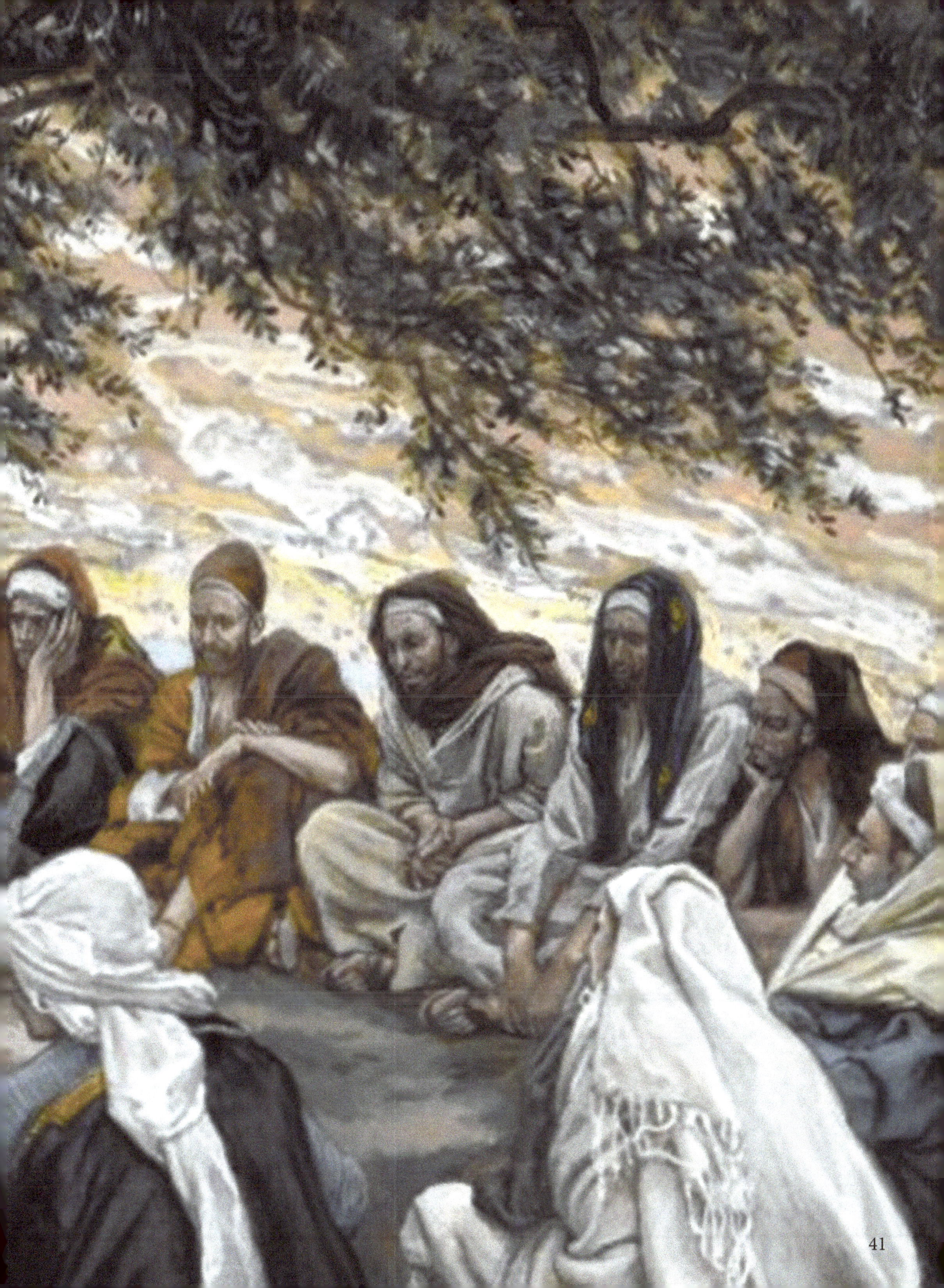

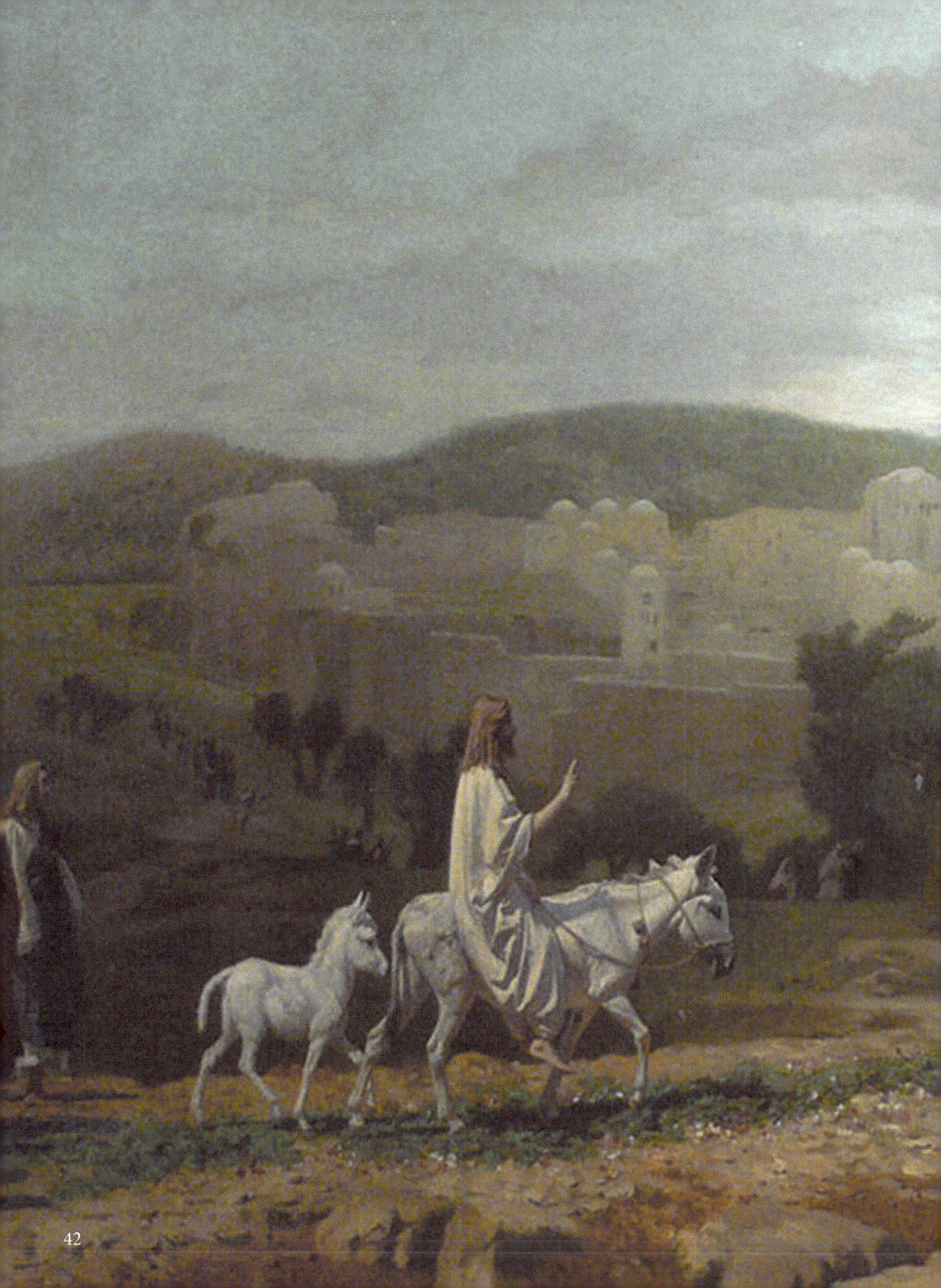

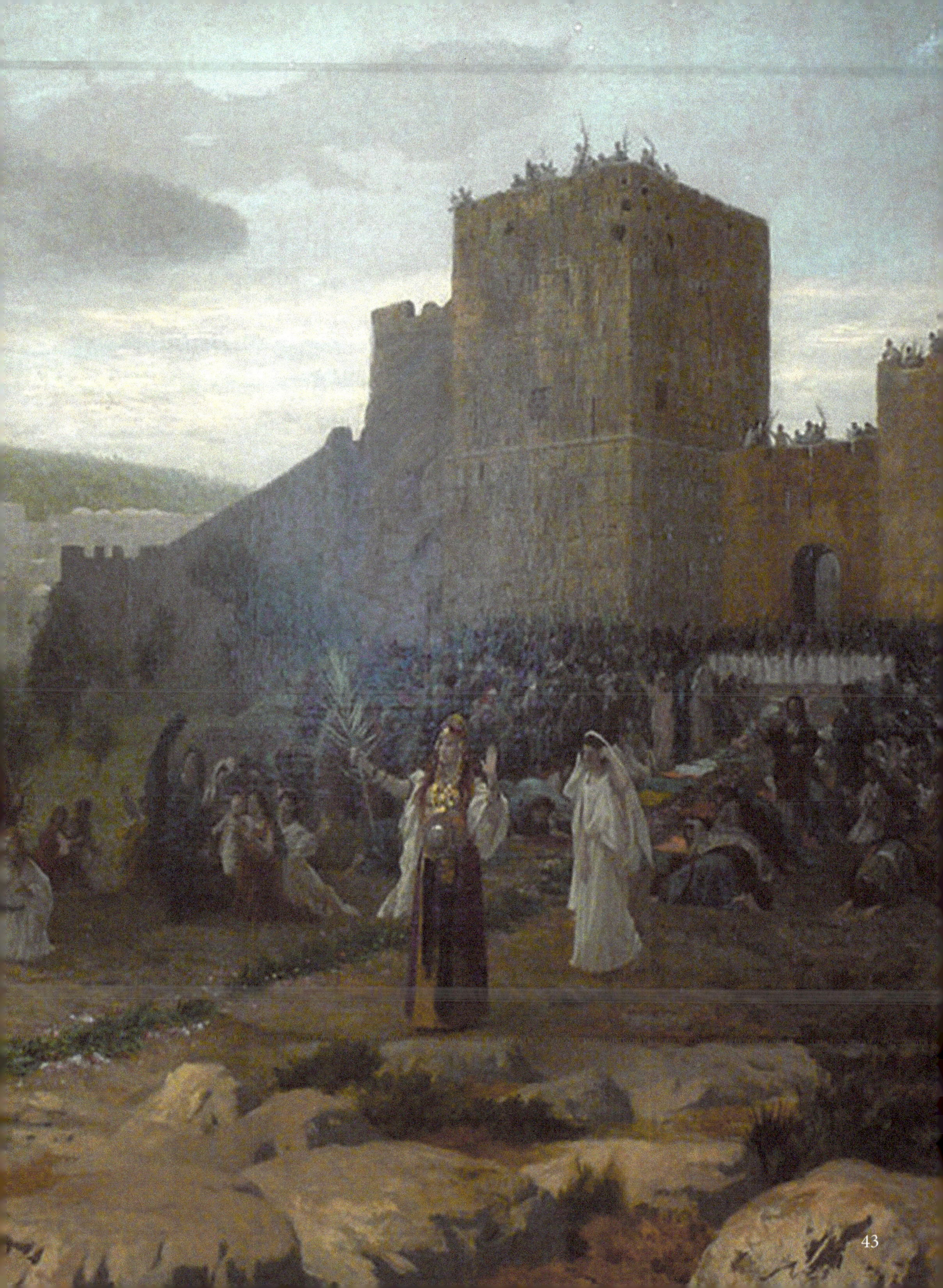

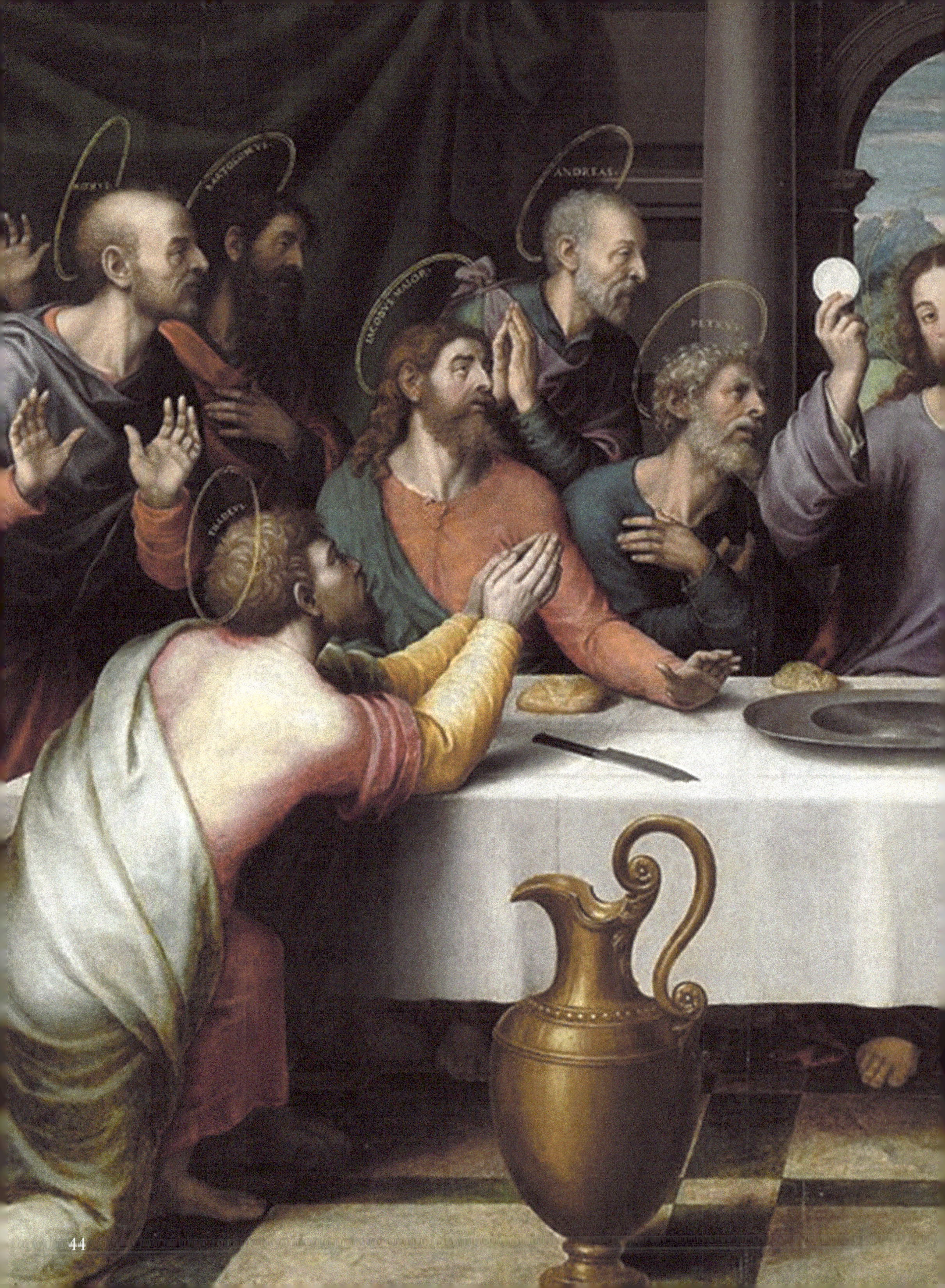

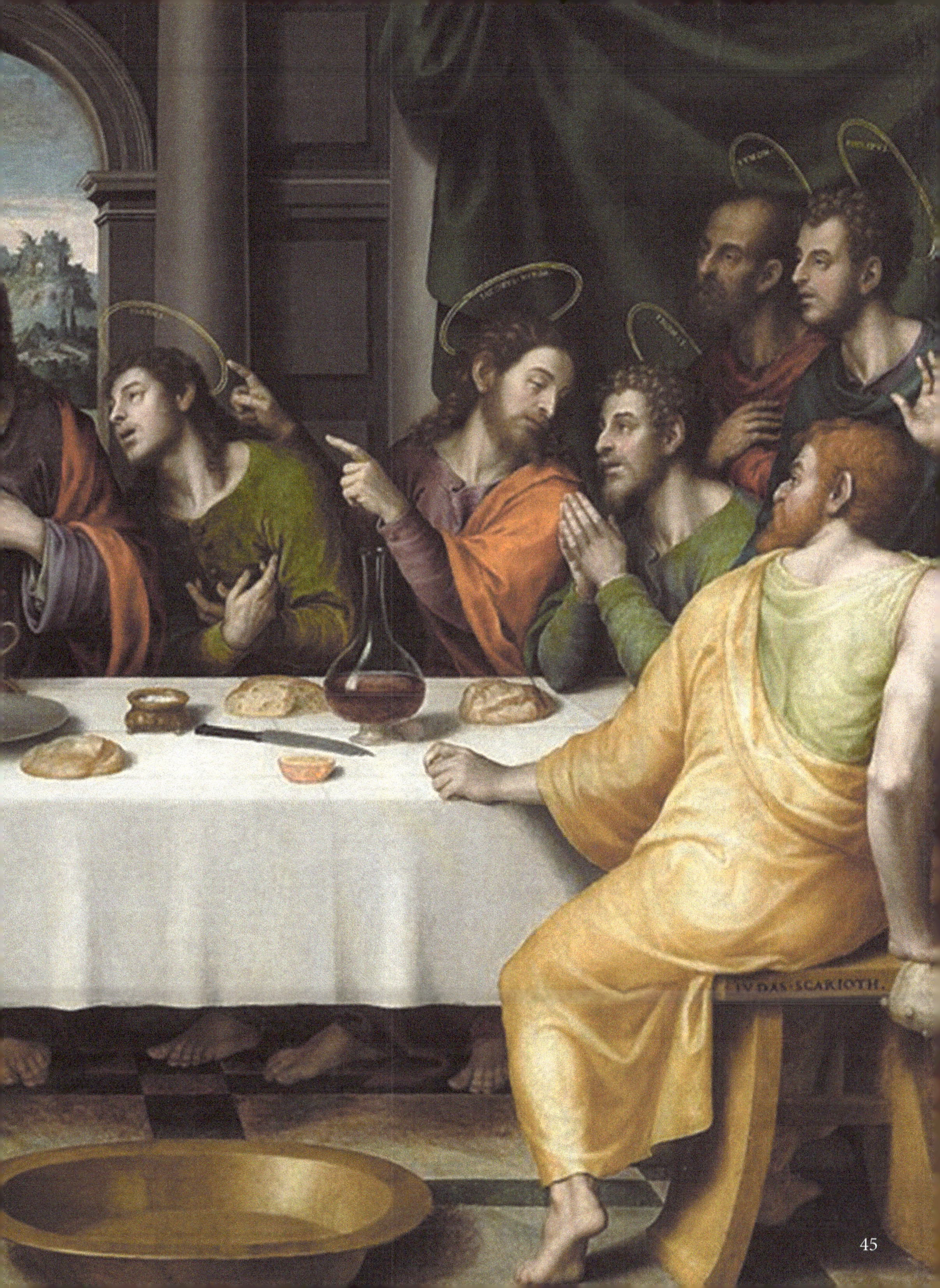

IVDAS·SCARIOTH·

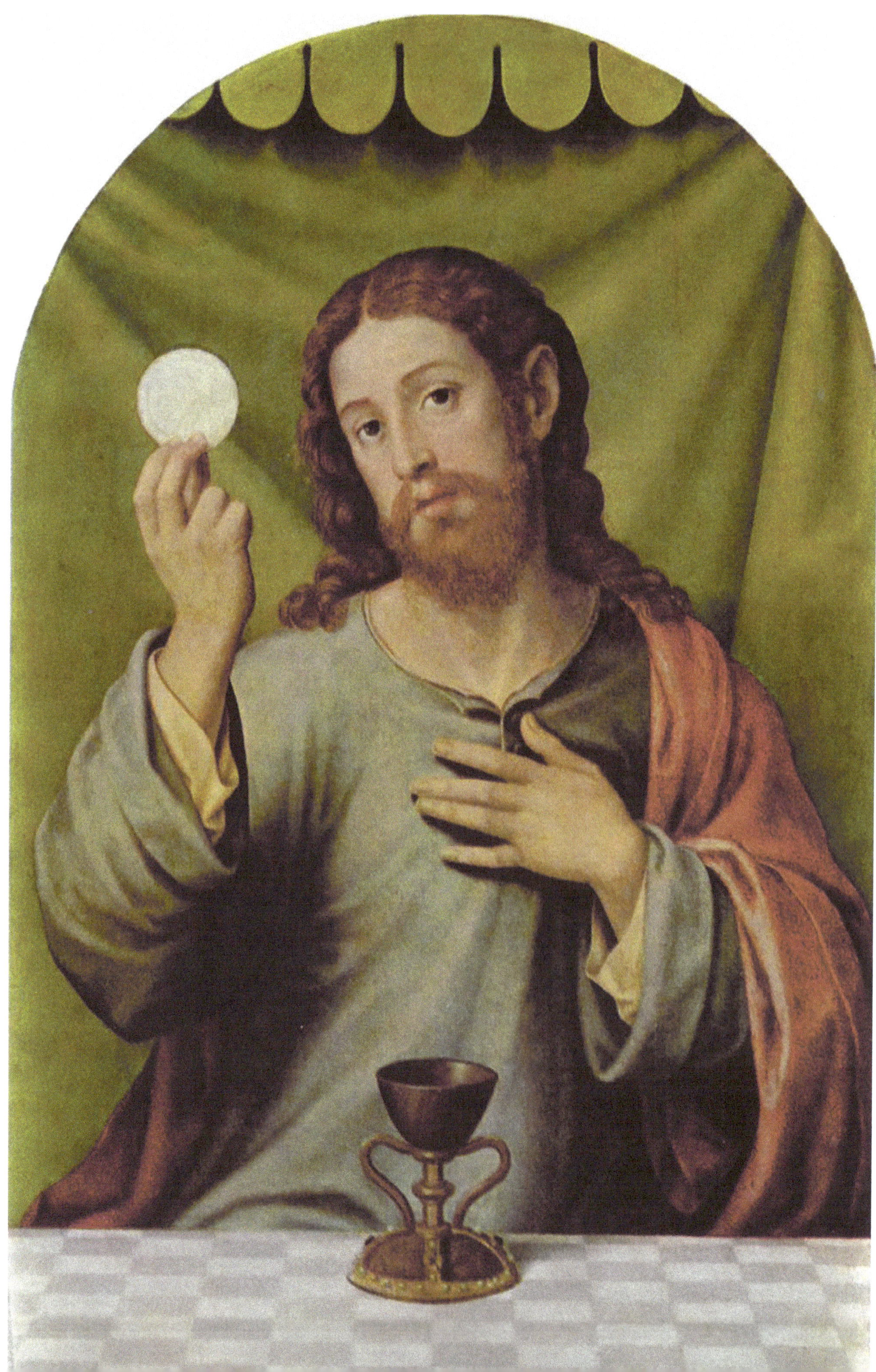

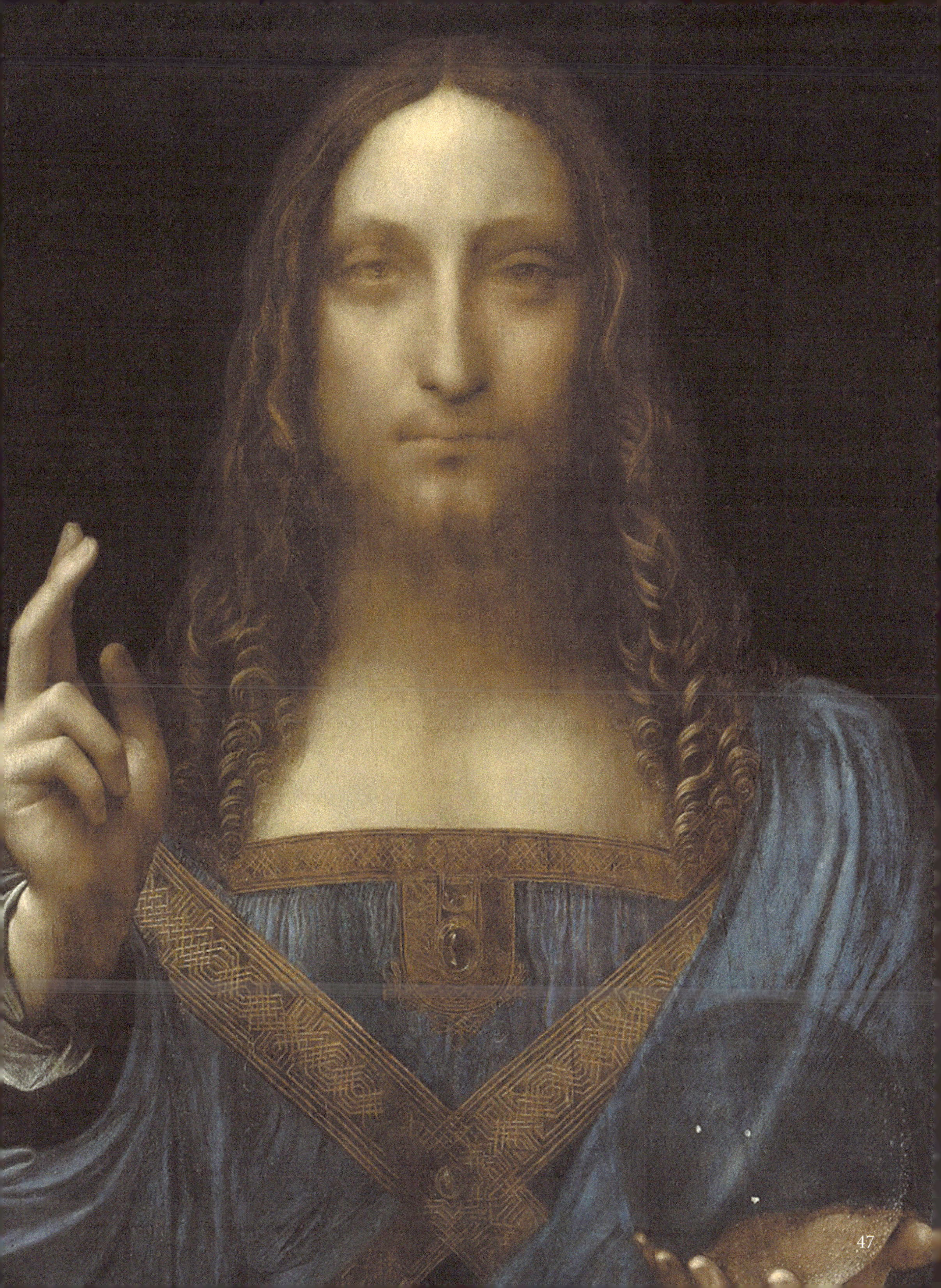

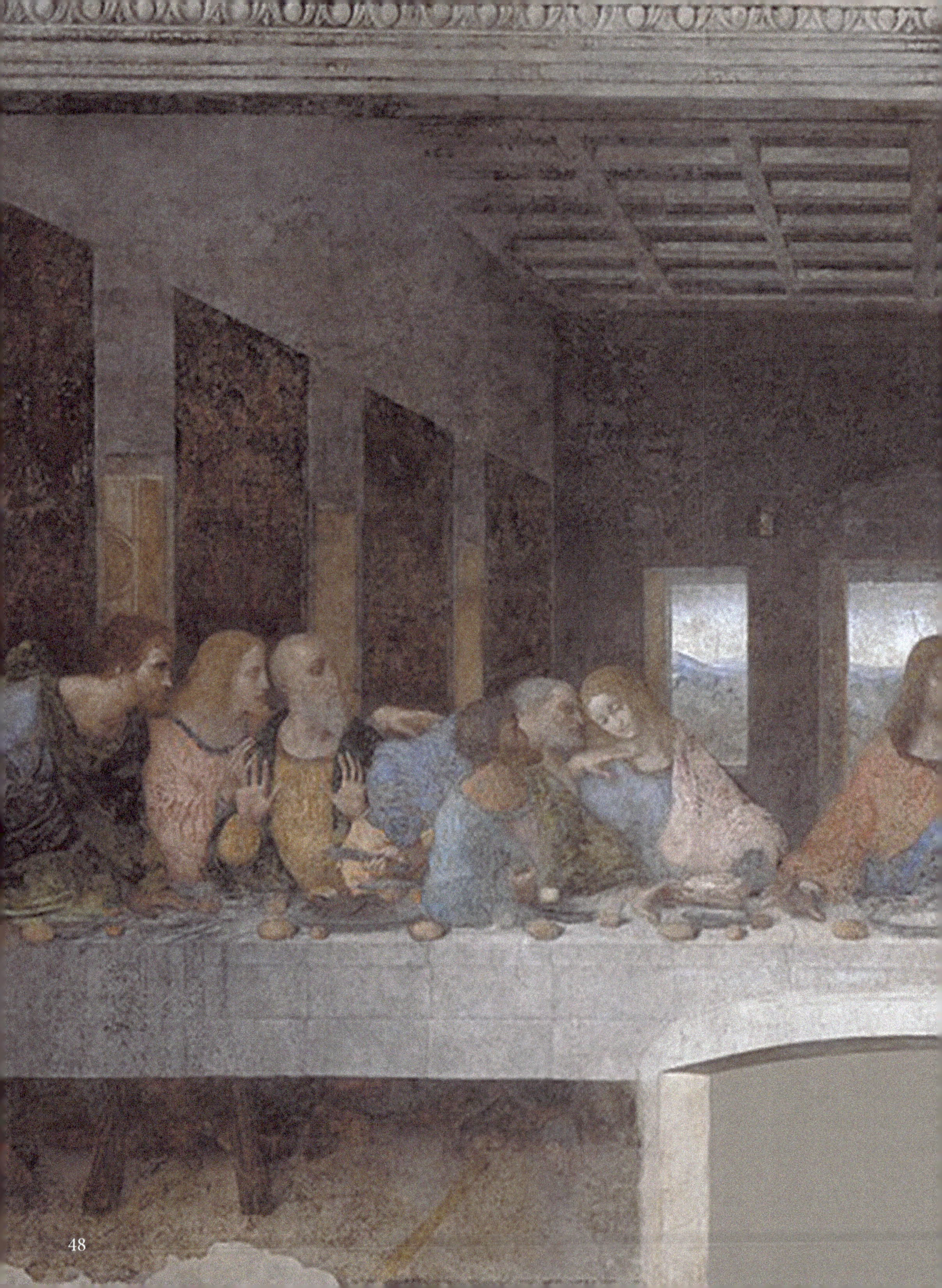

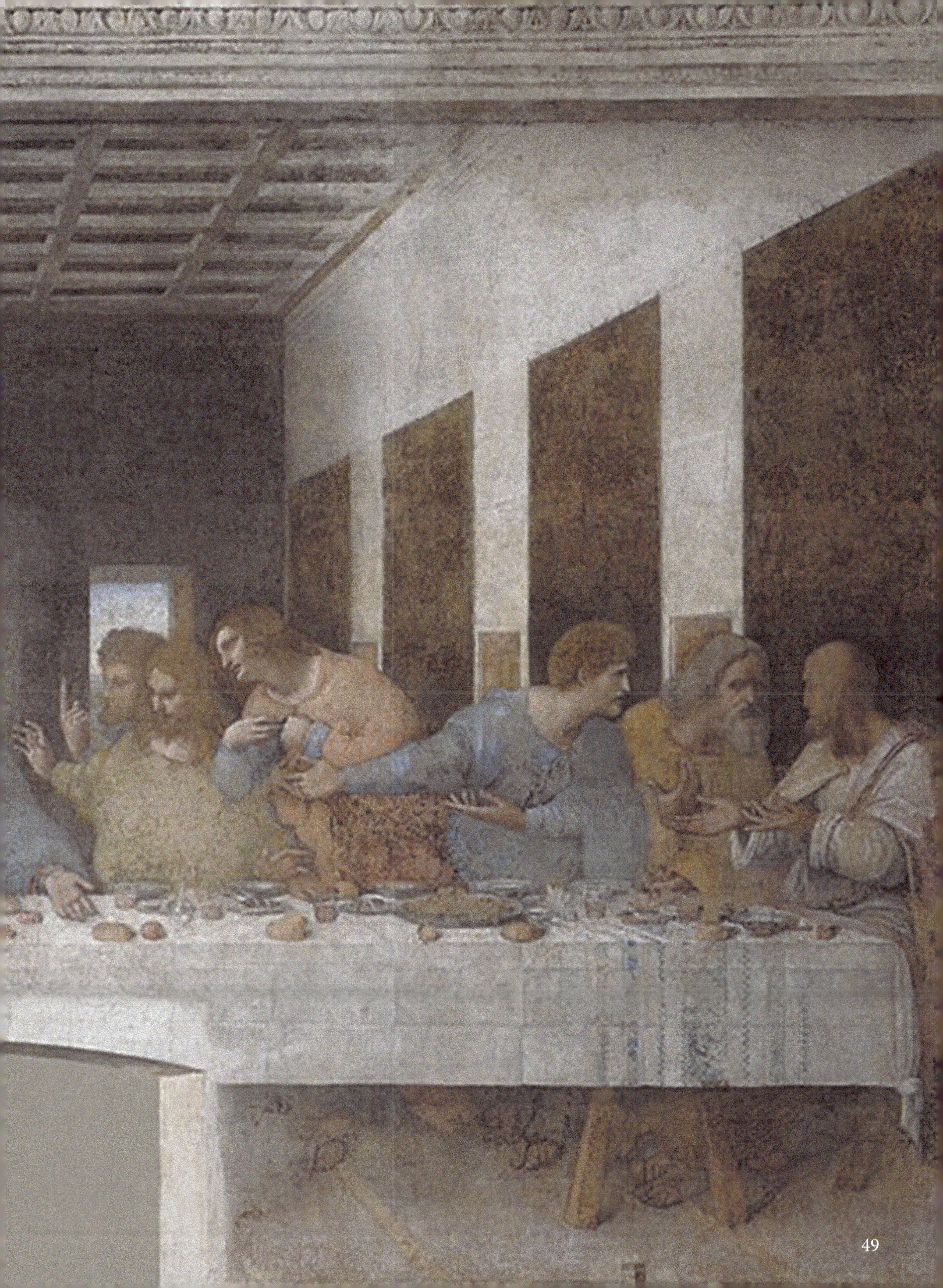

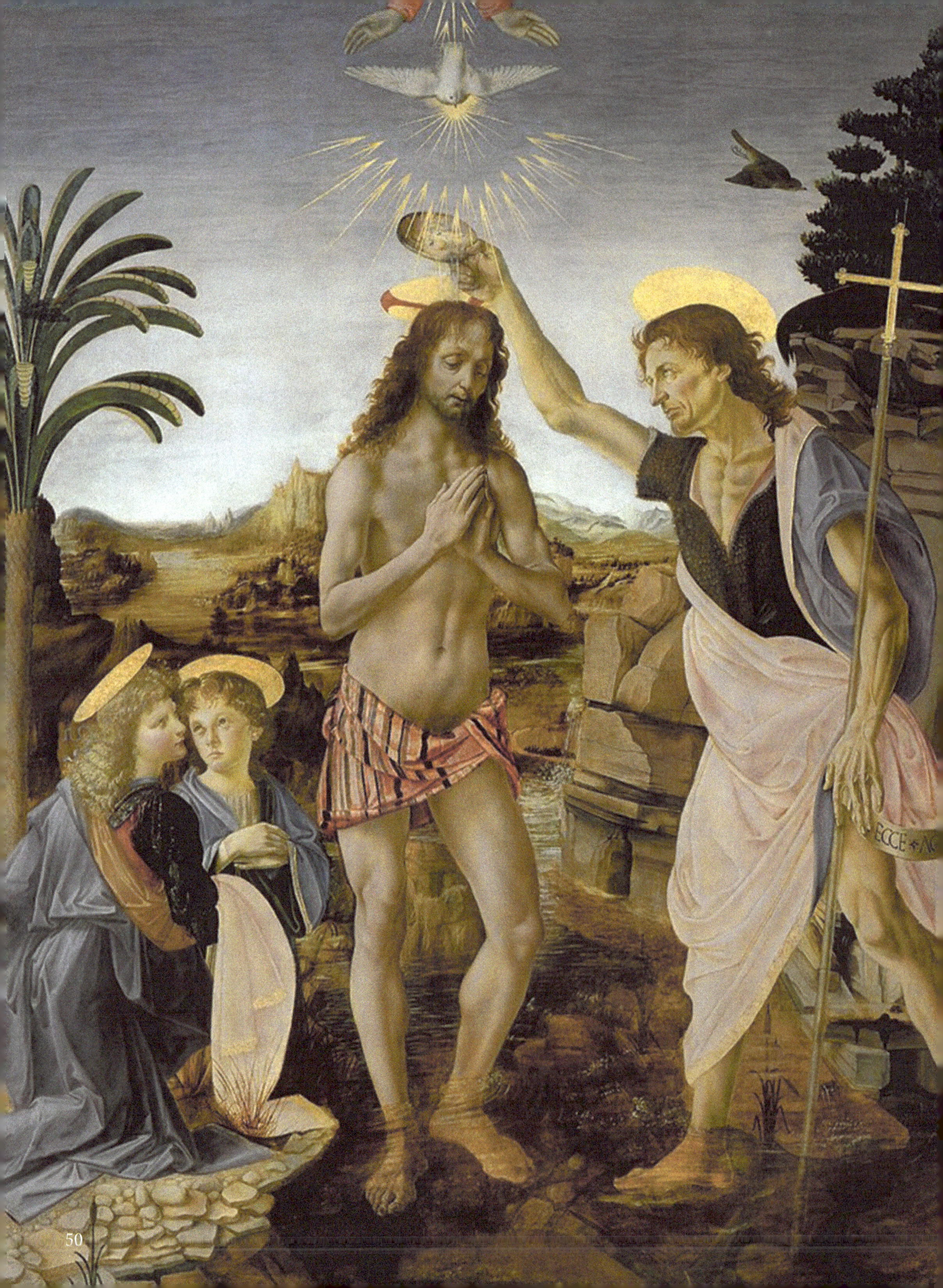

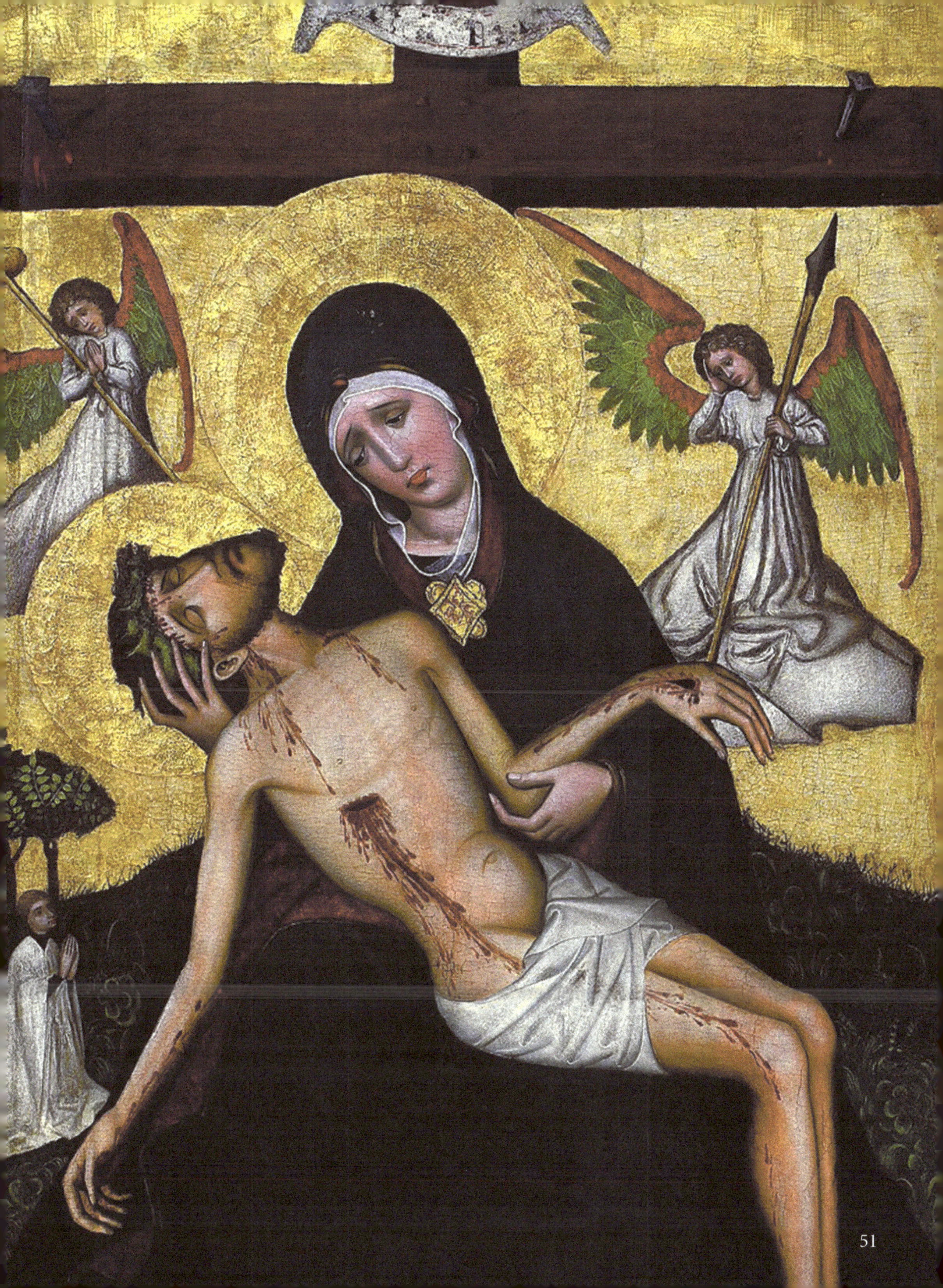

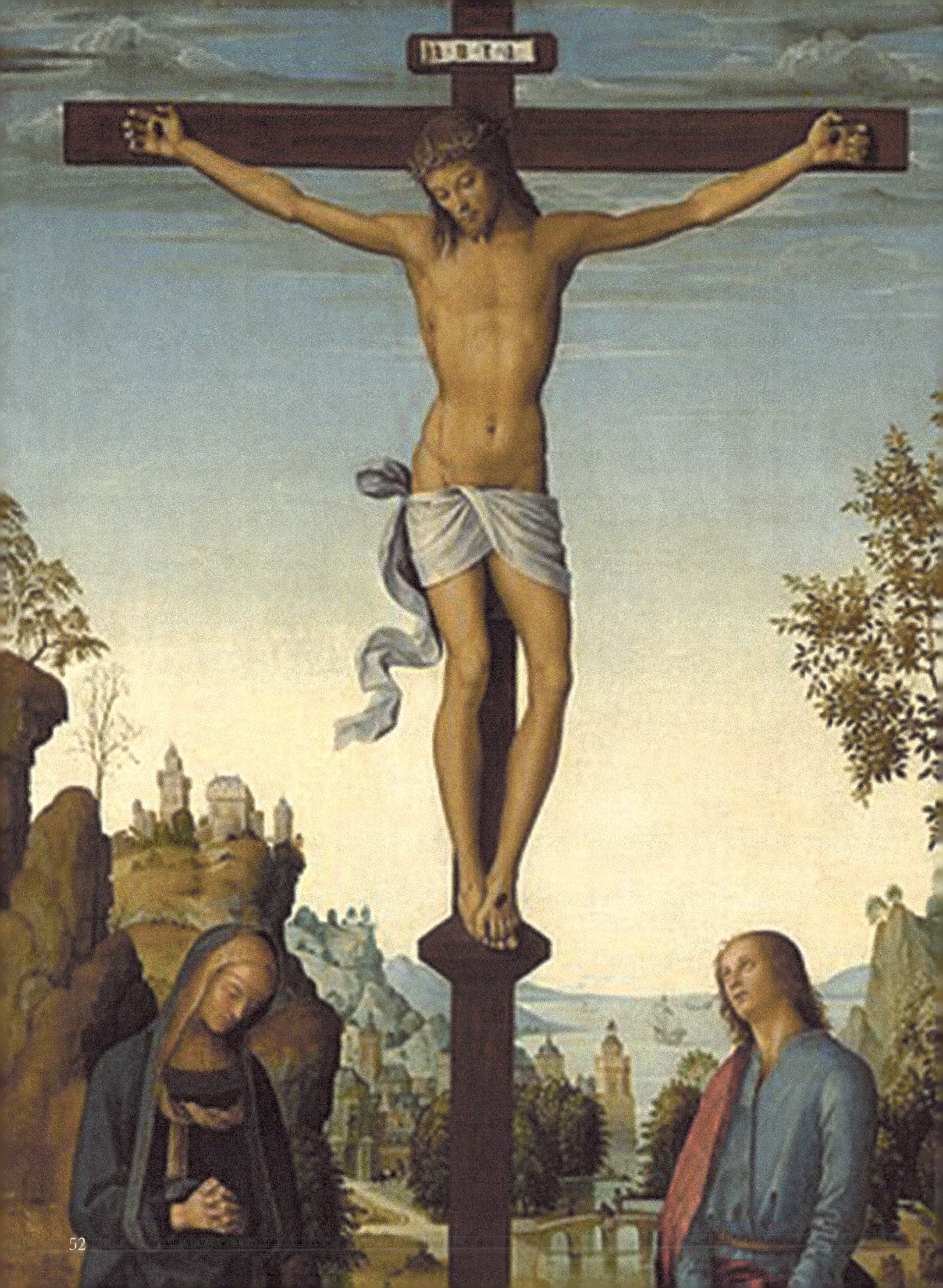

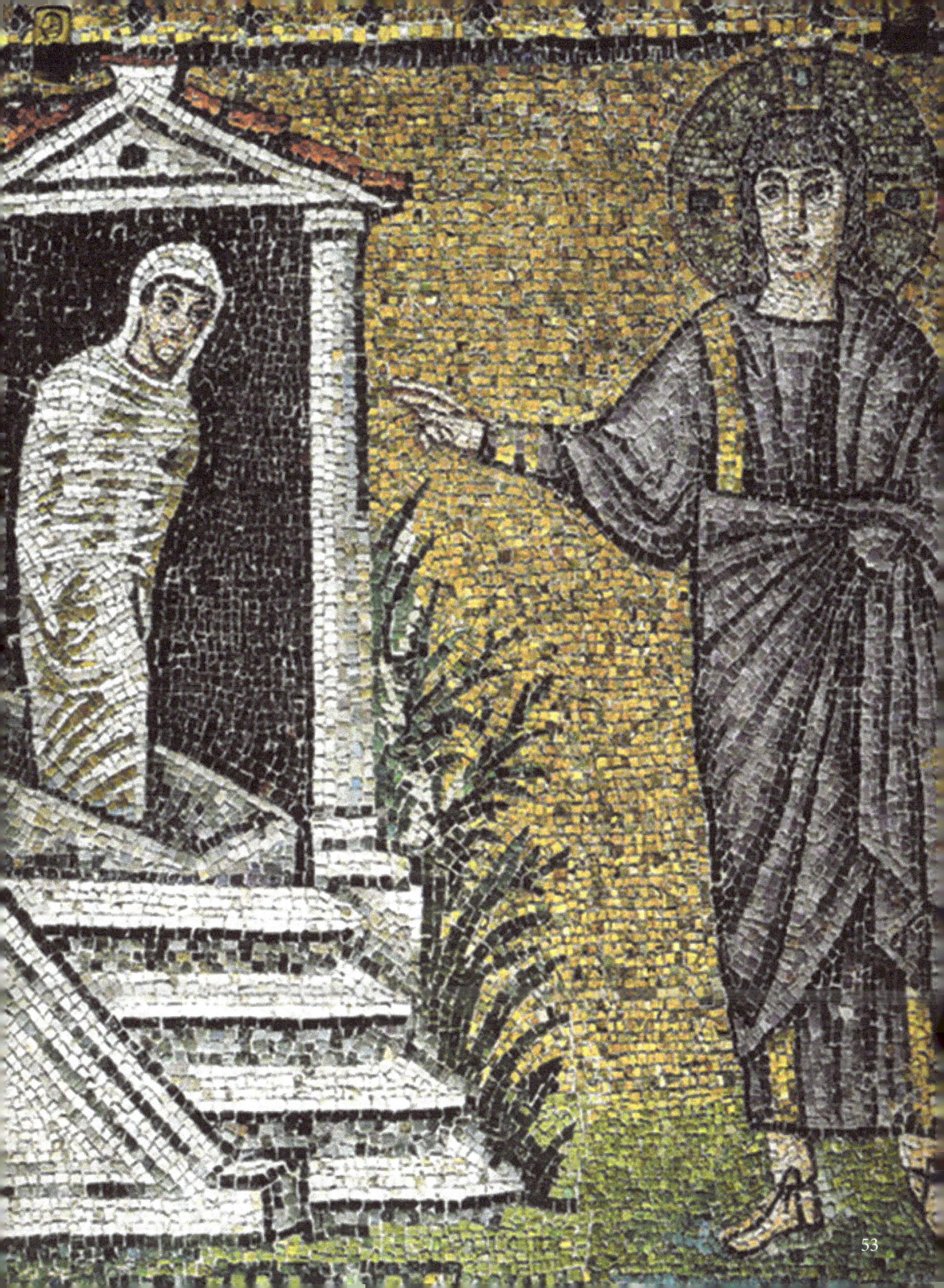

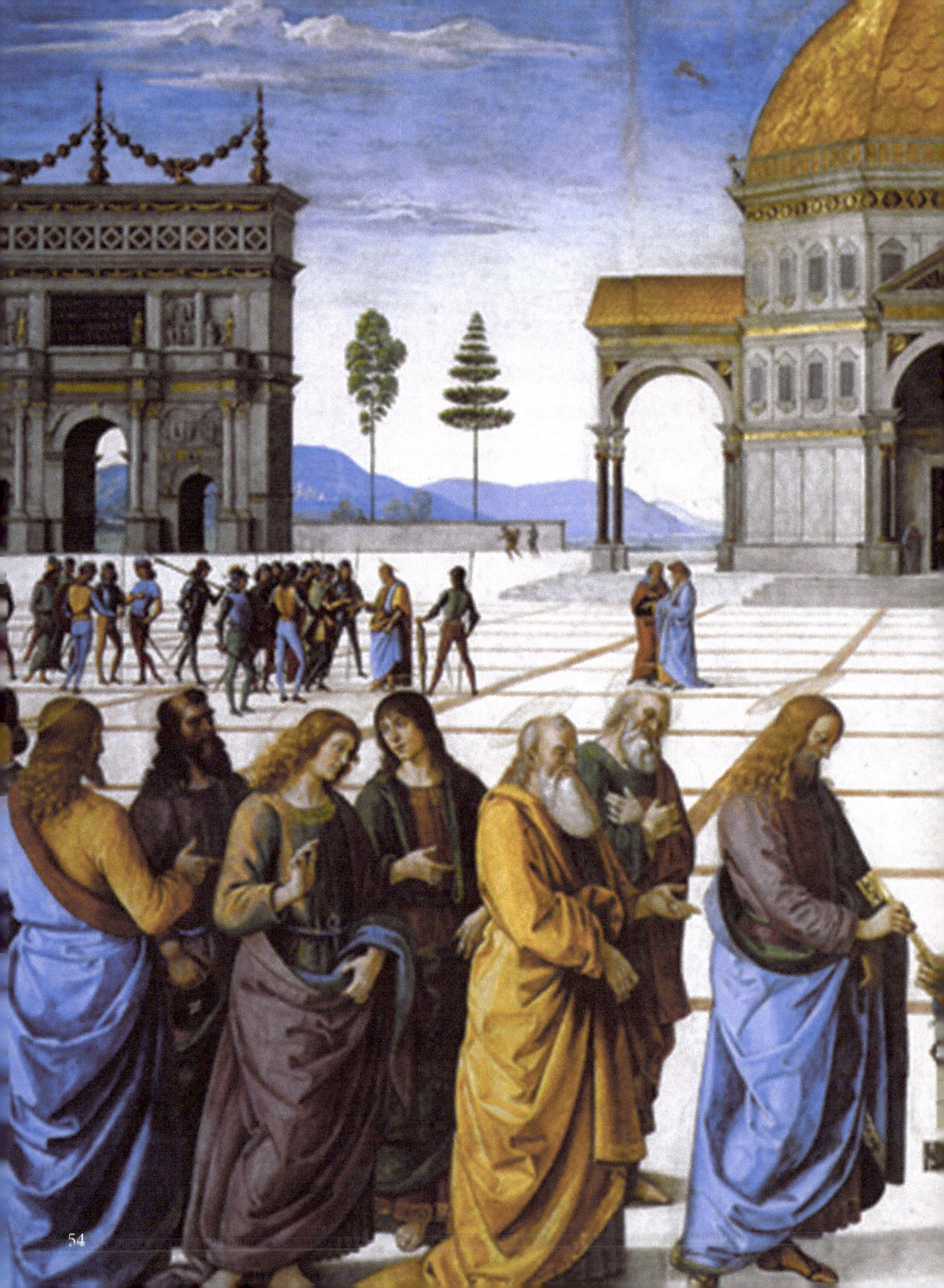

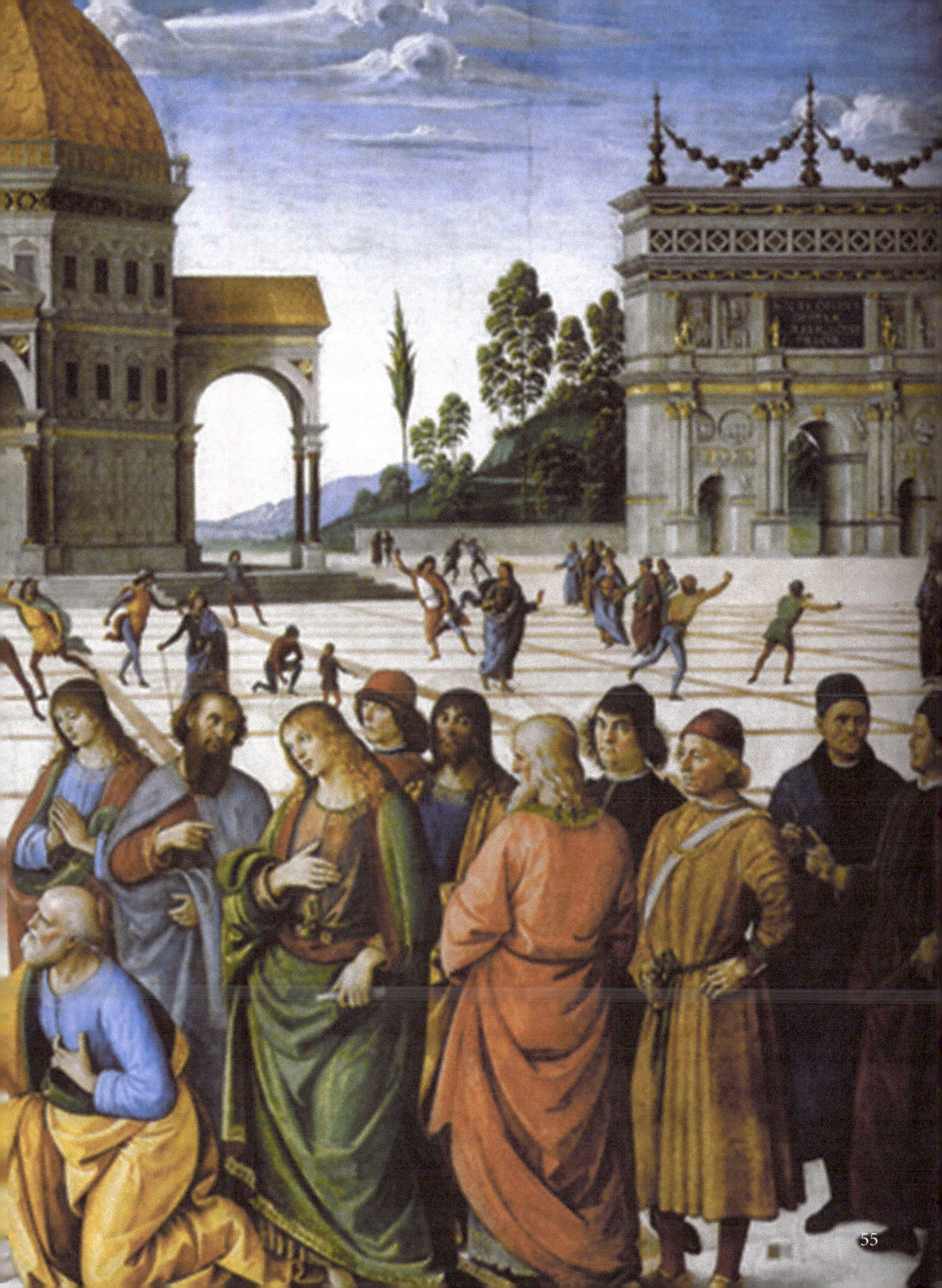

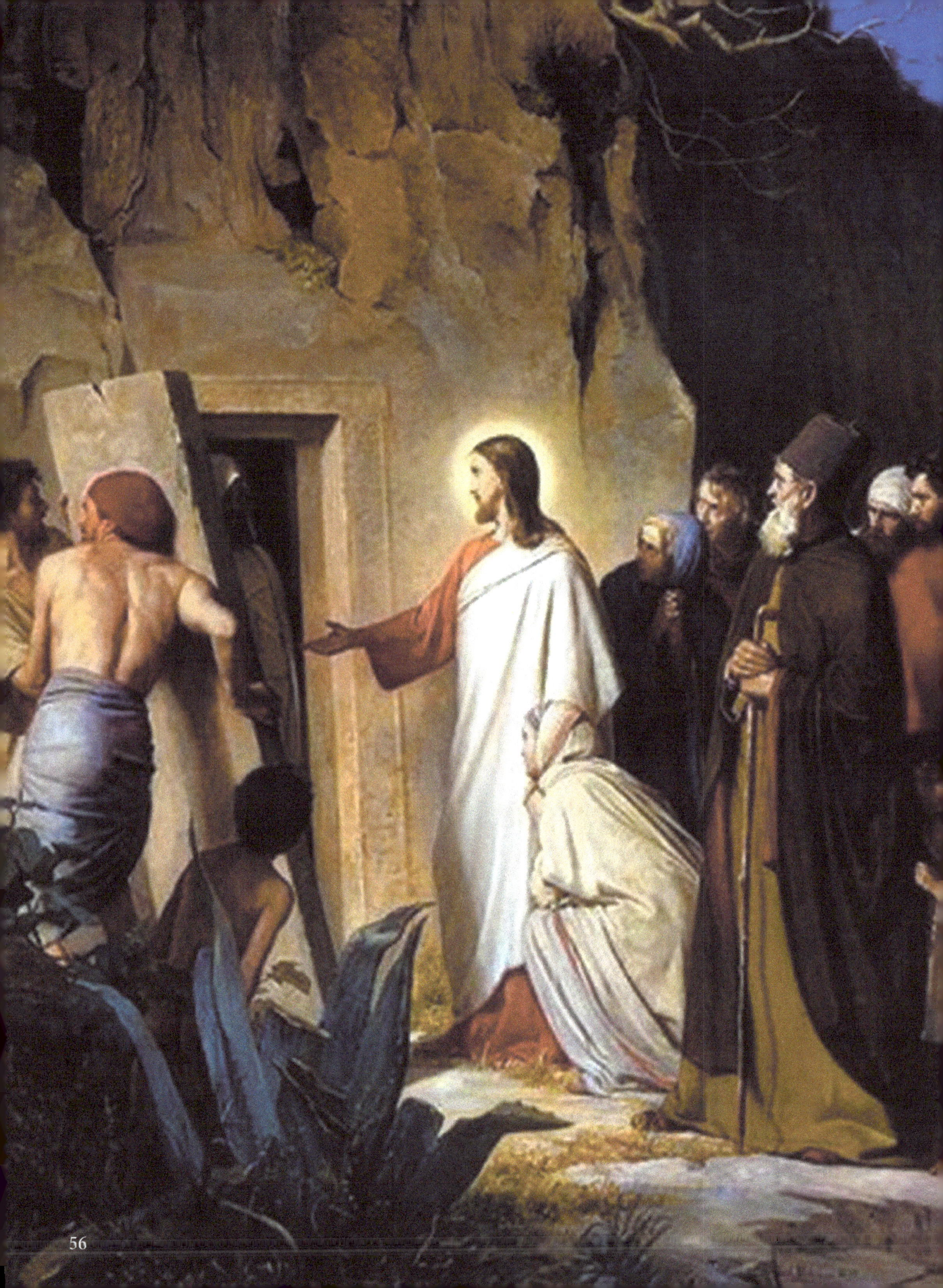

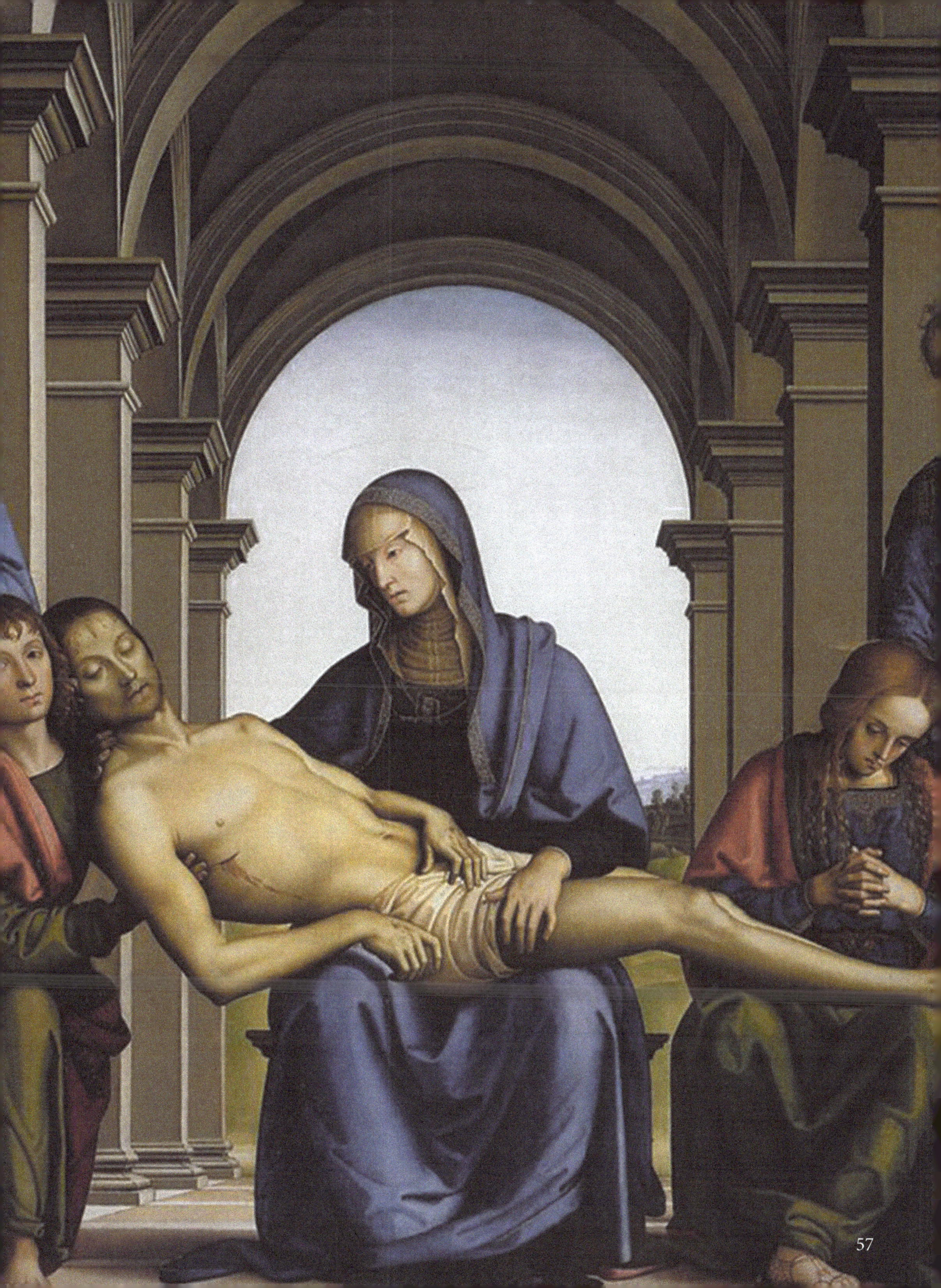

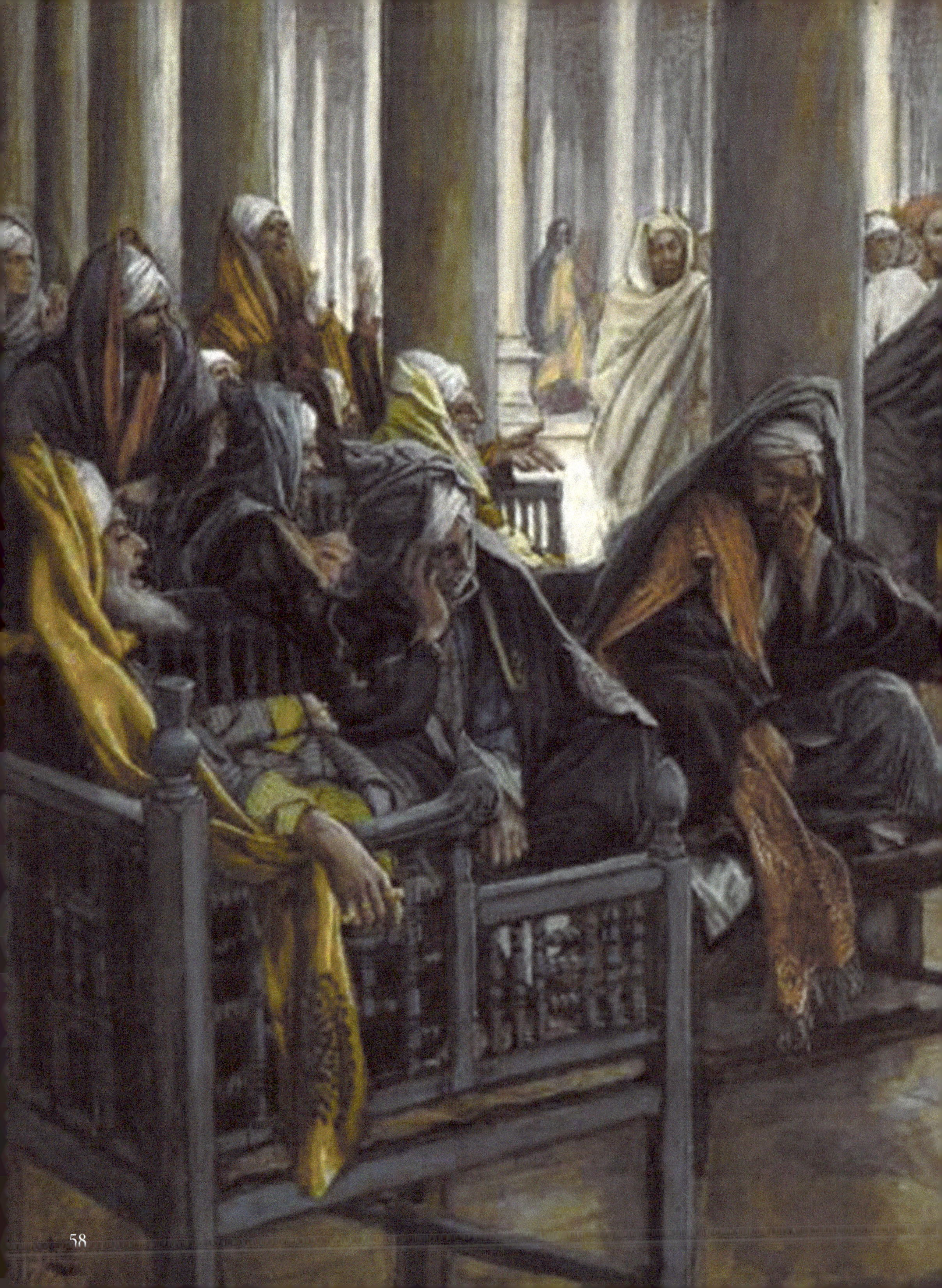

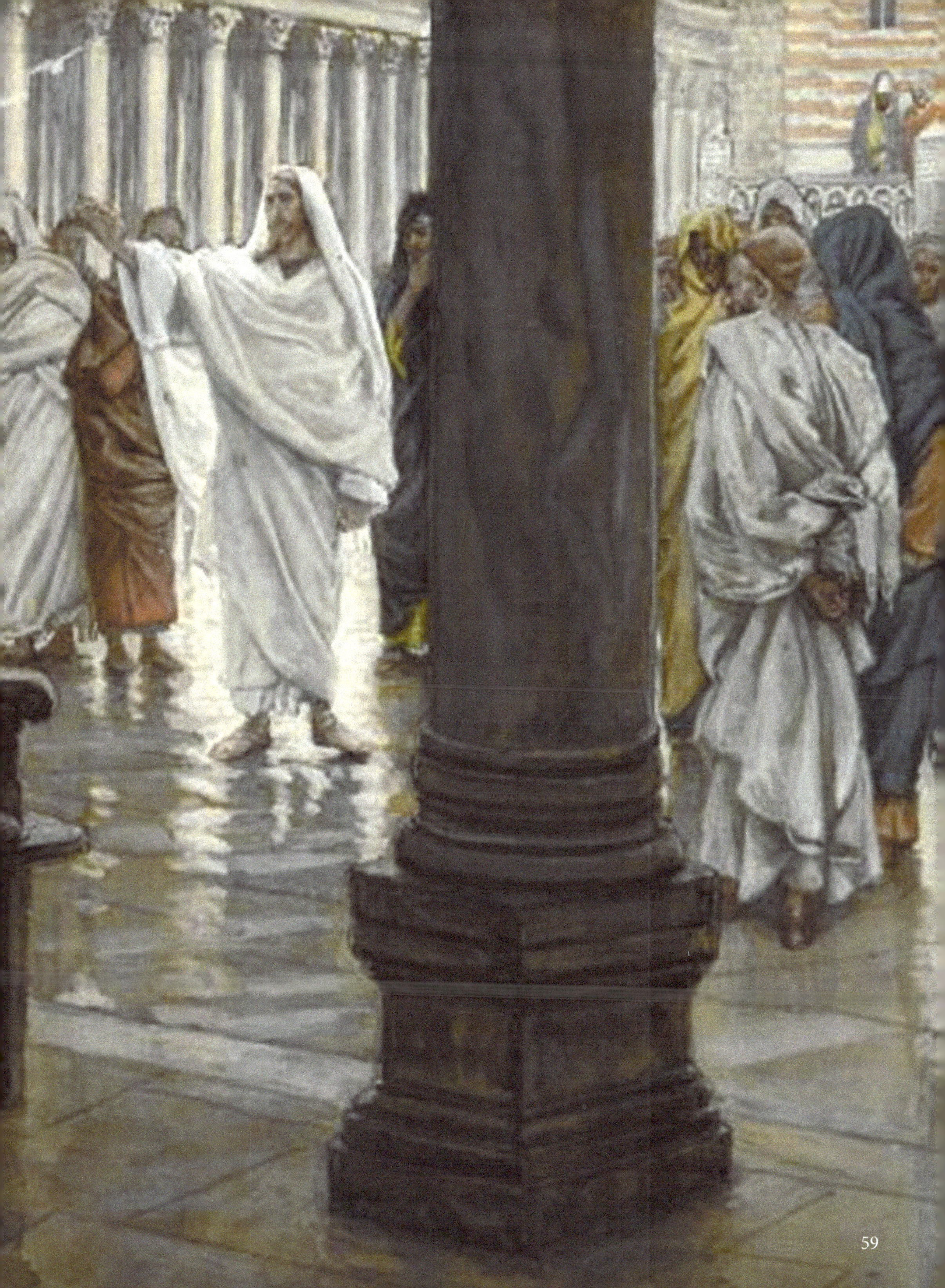

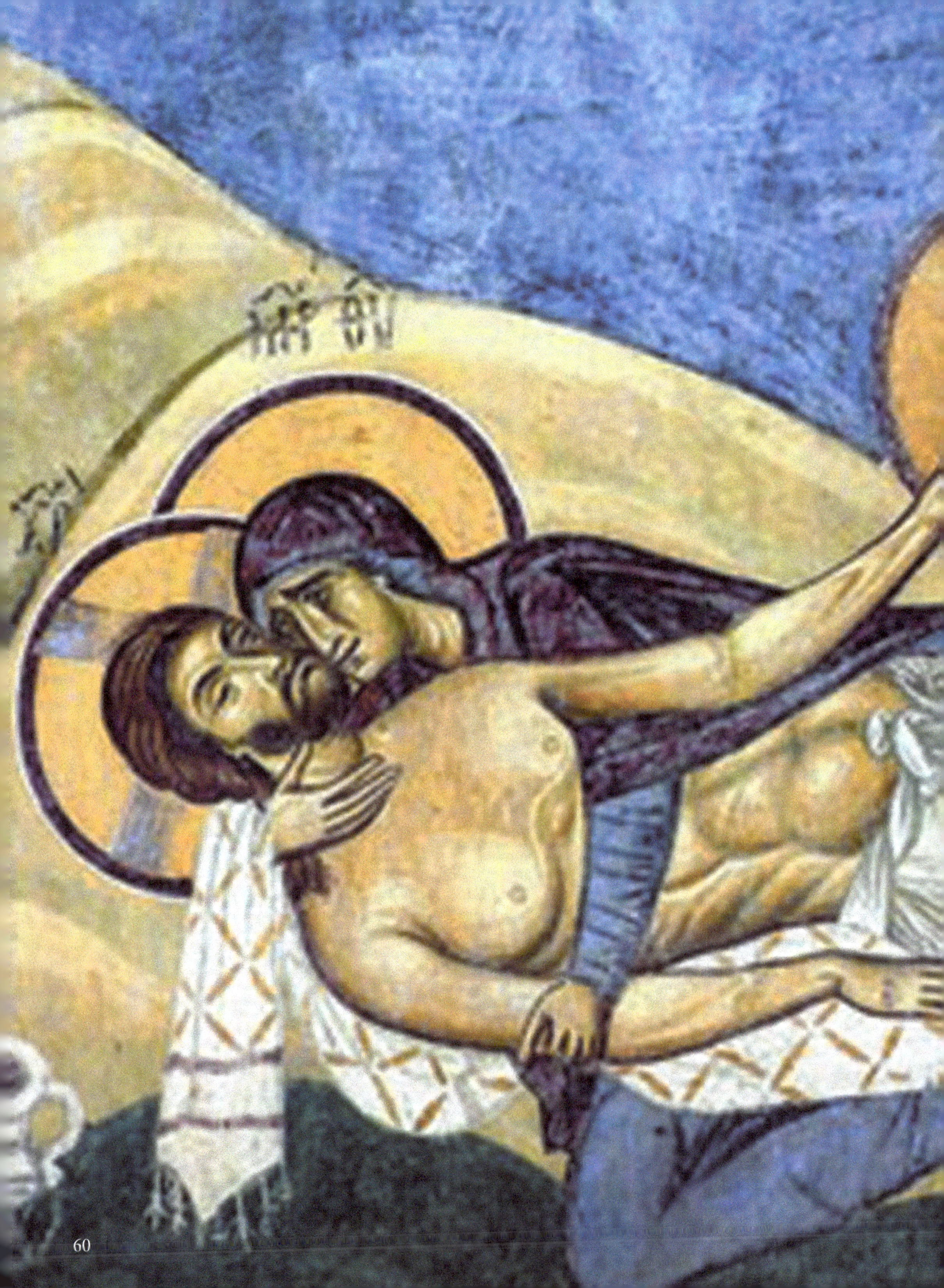
ΜΡ ΘΥ

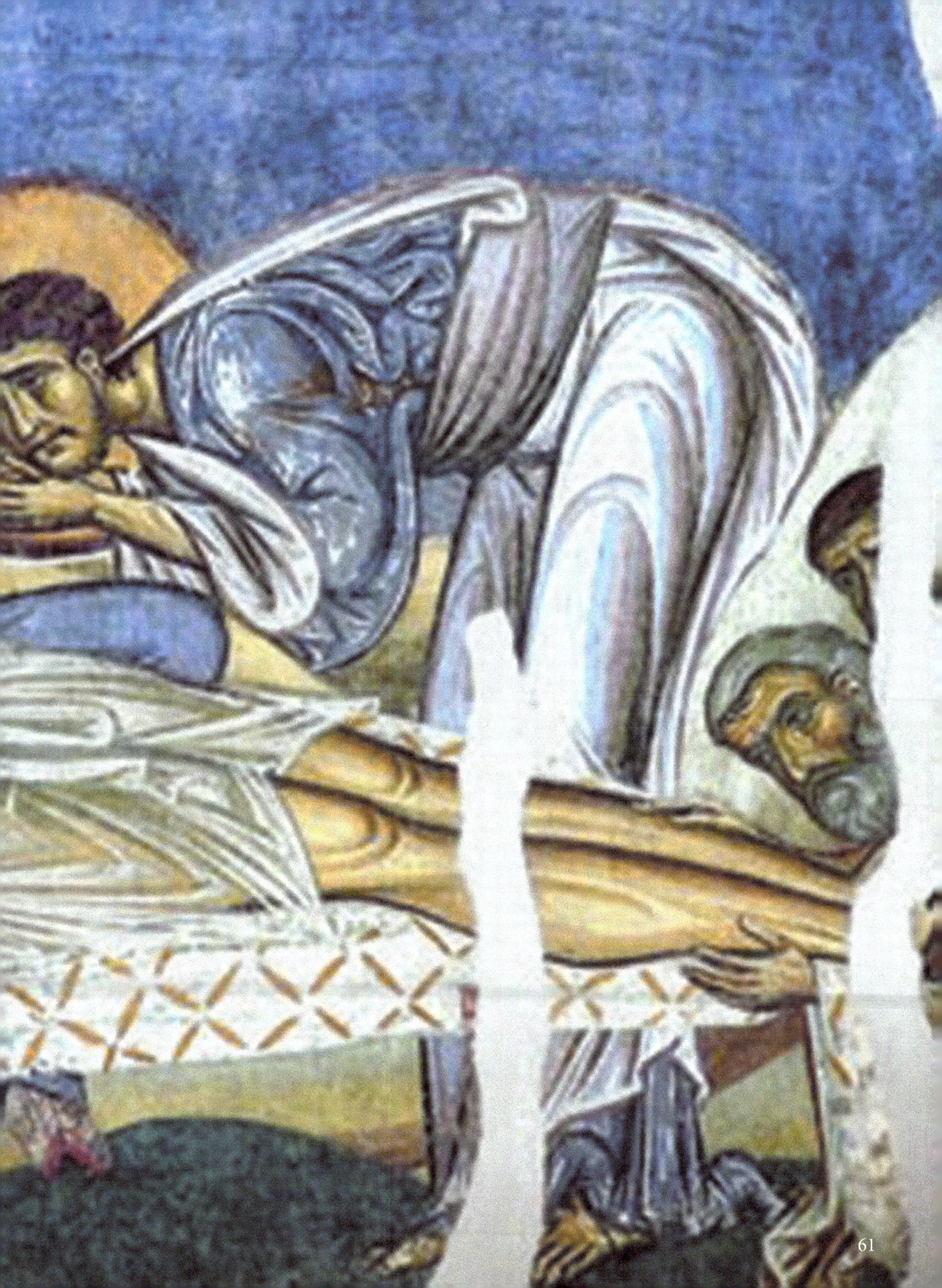

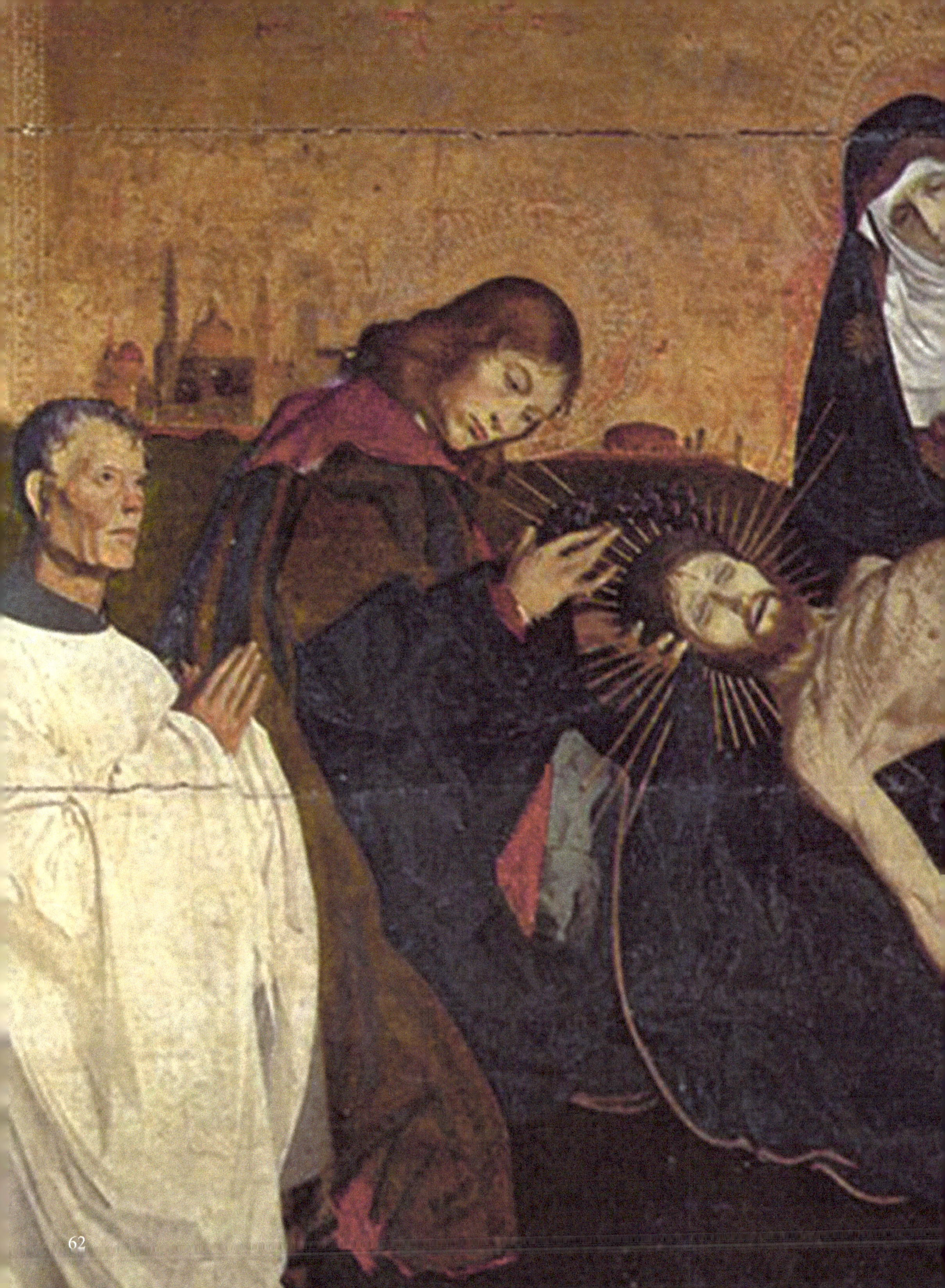

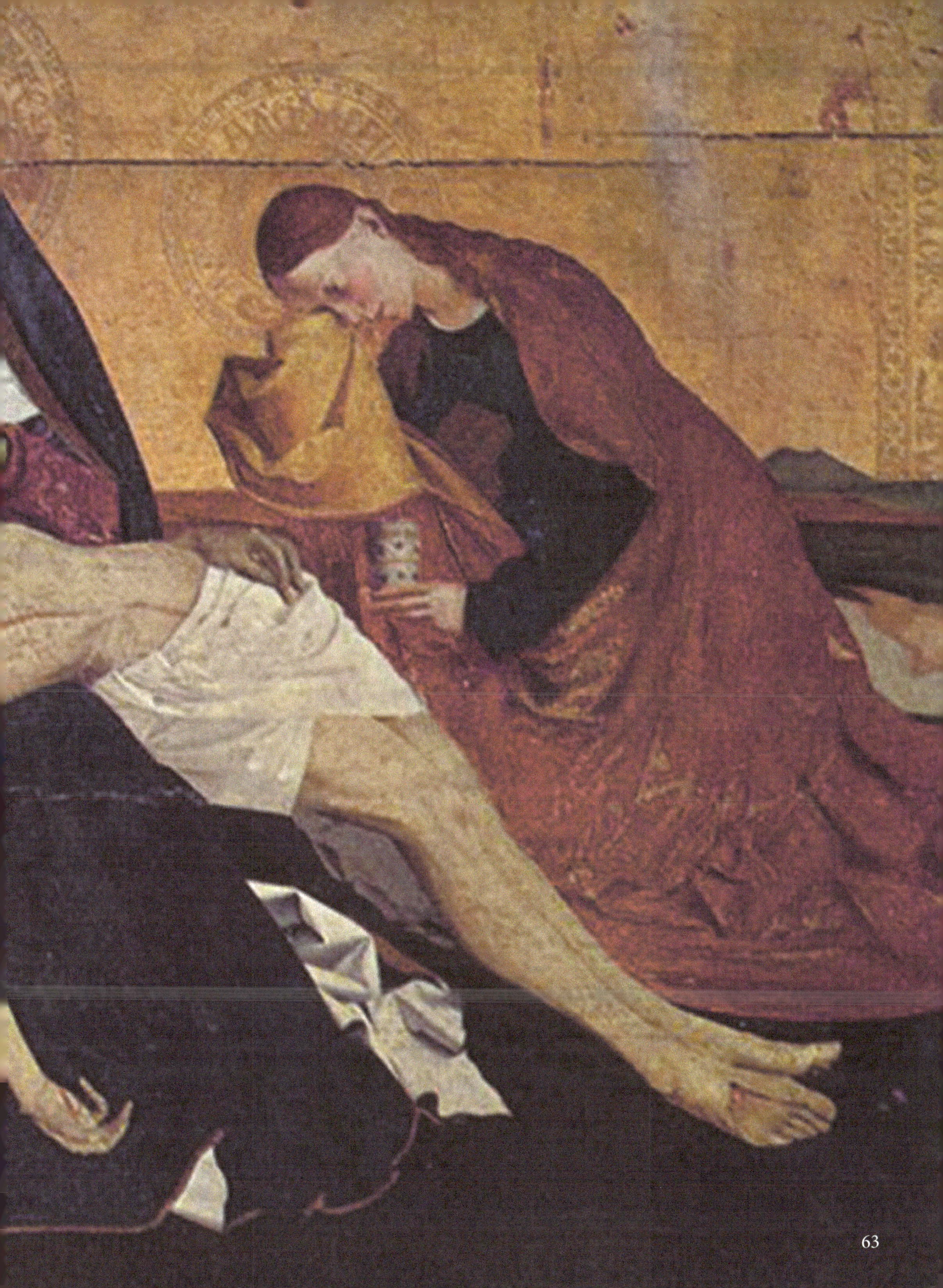

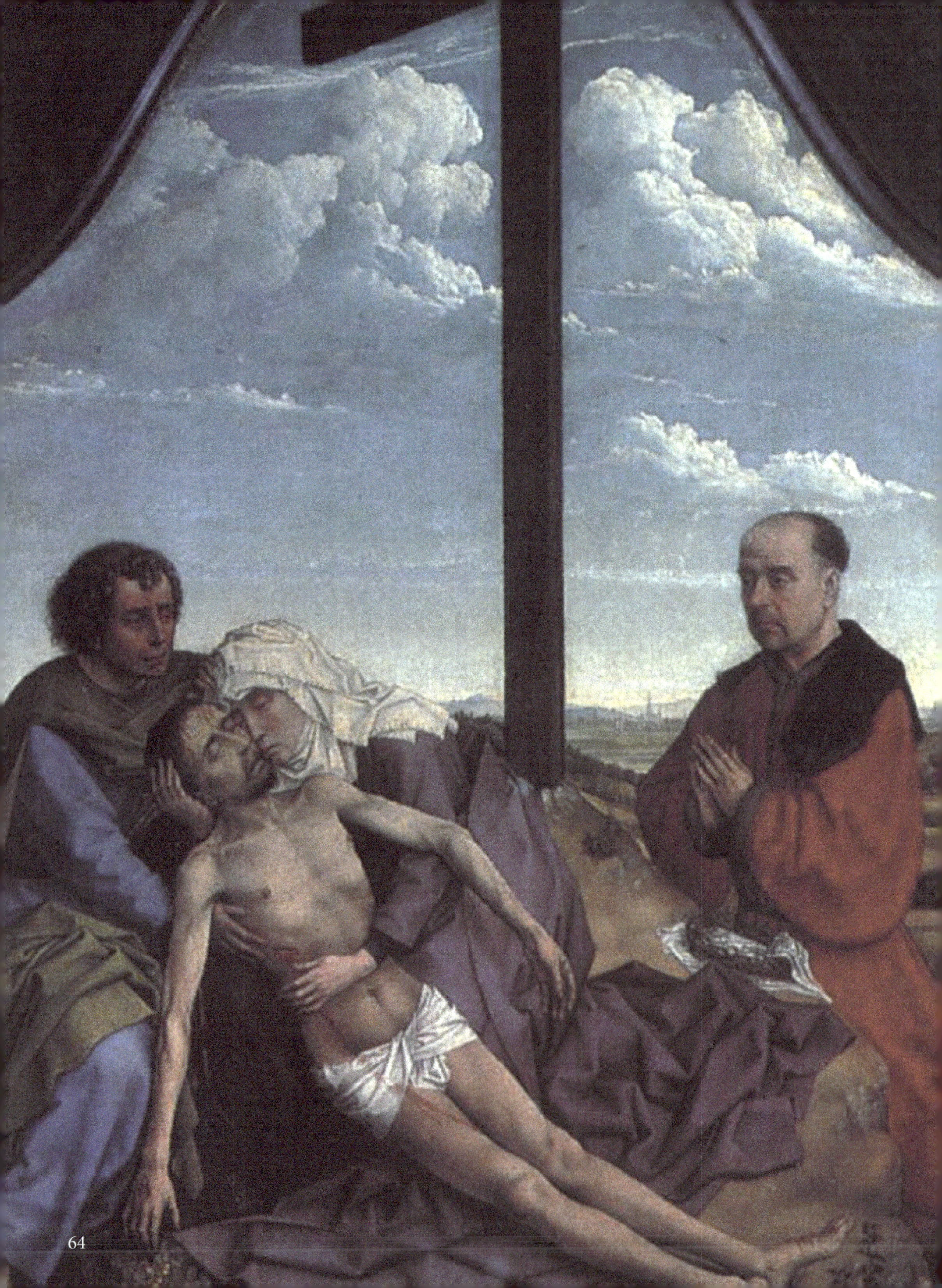

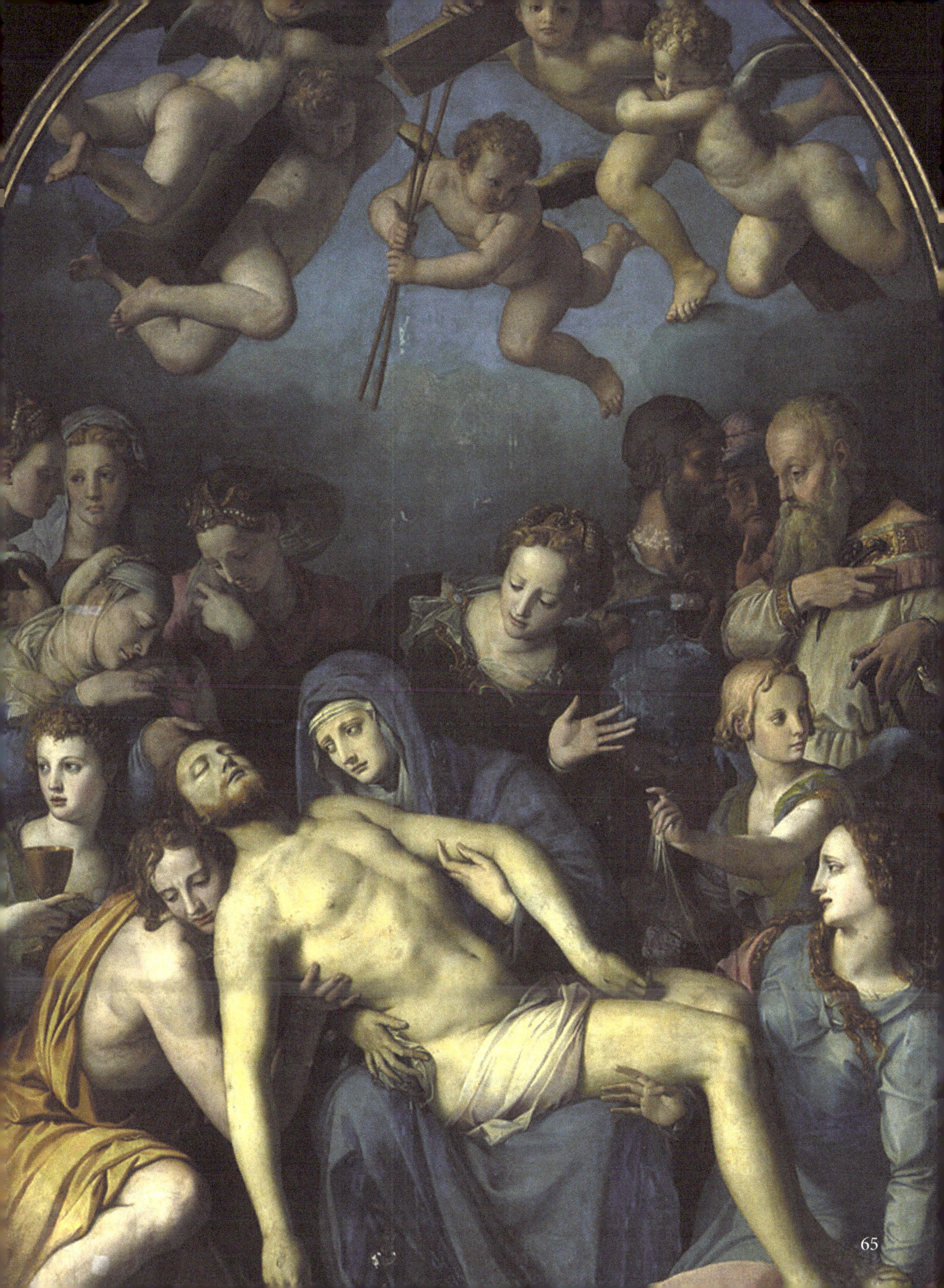

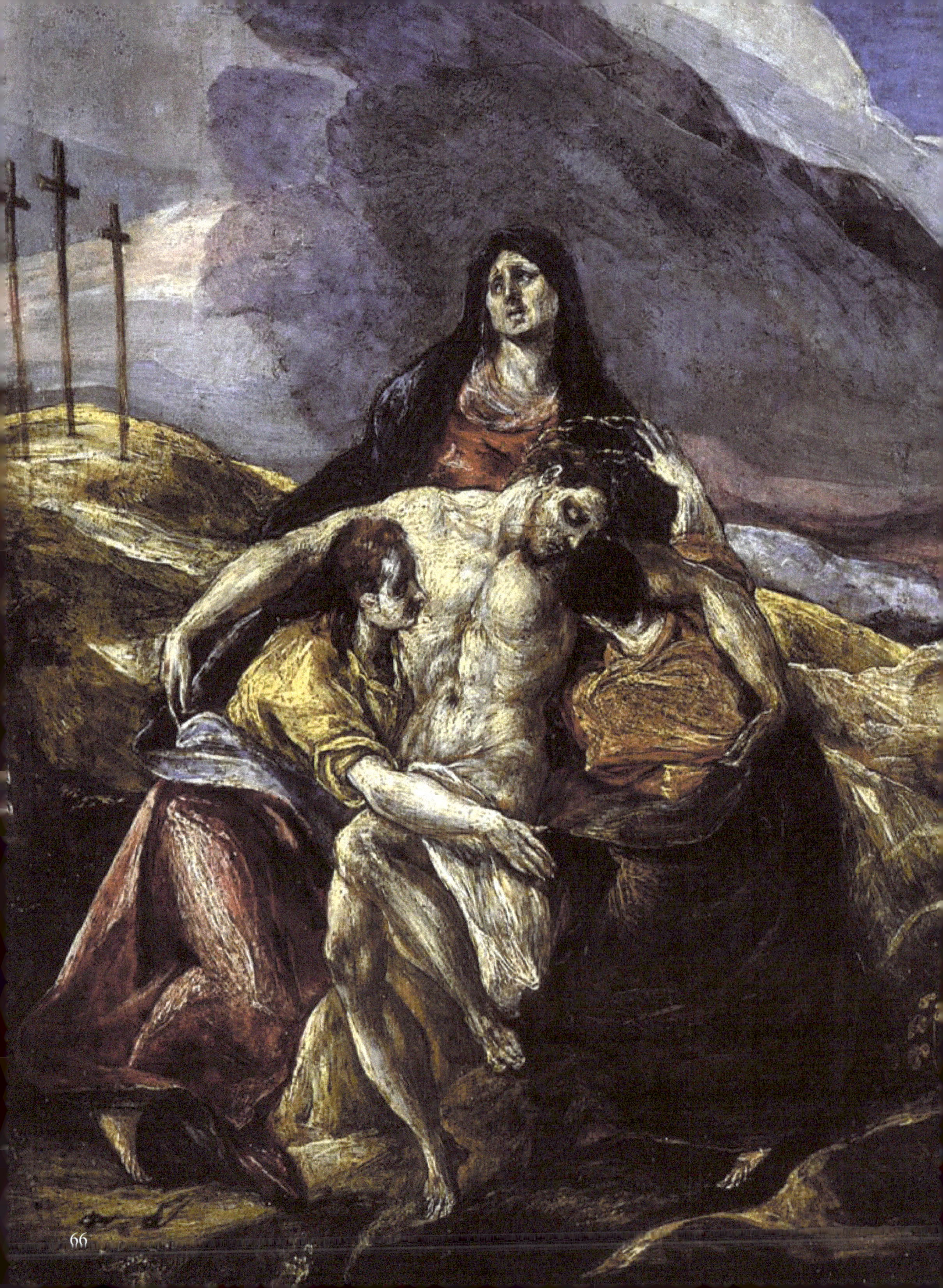

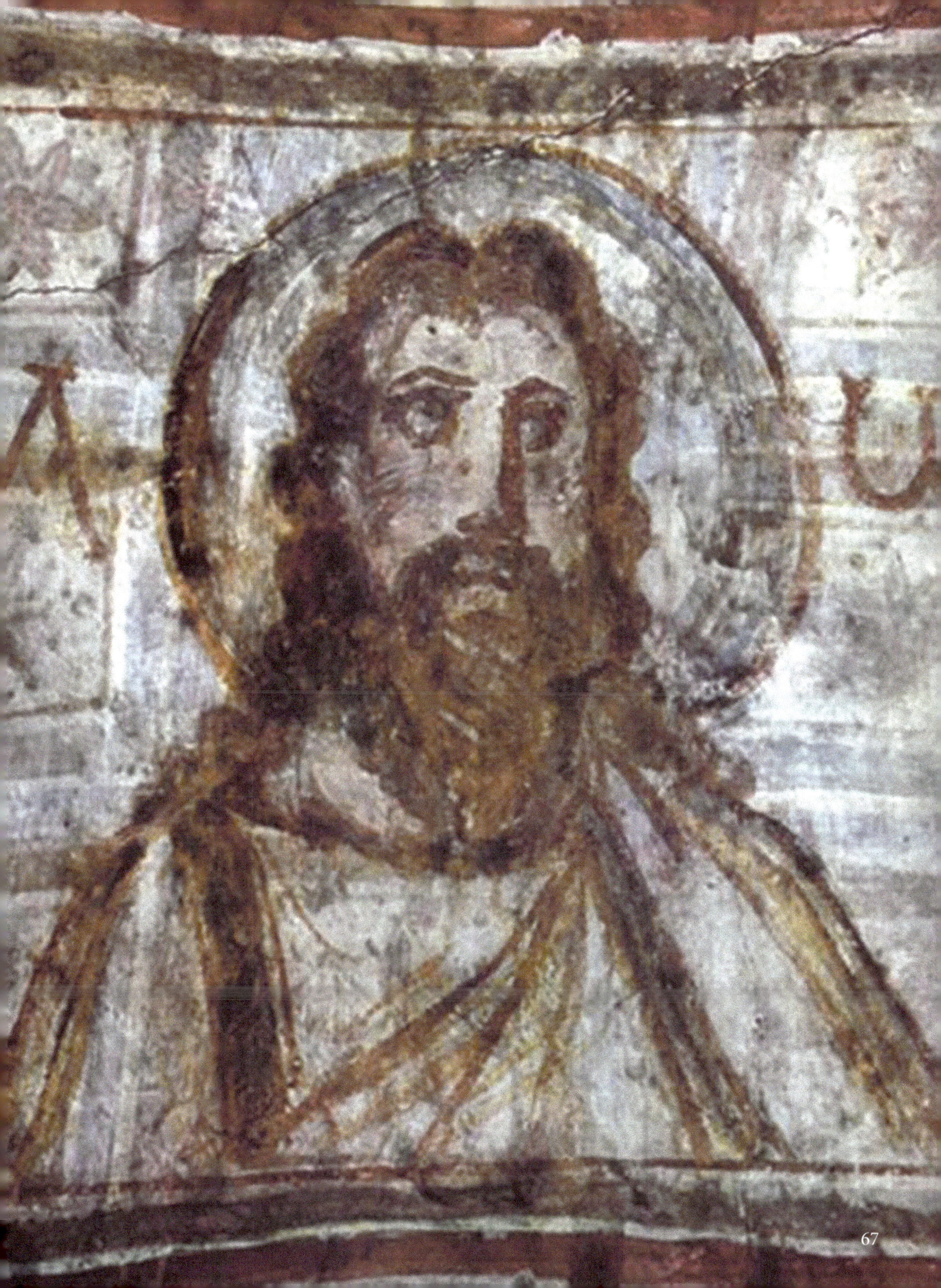

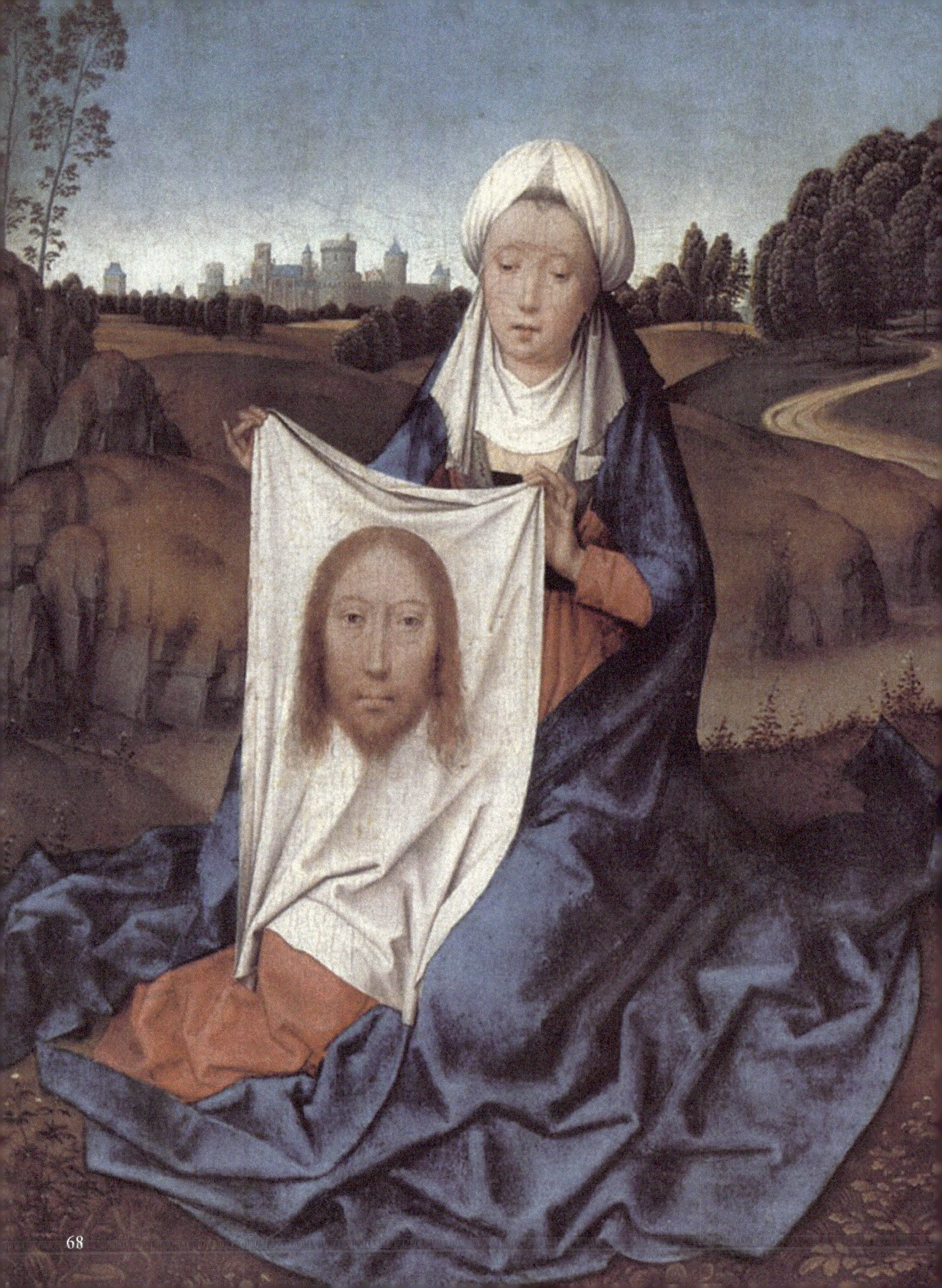

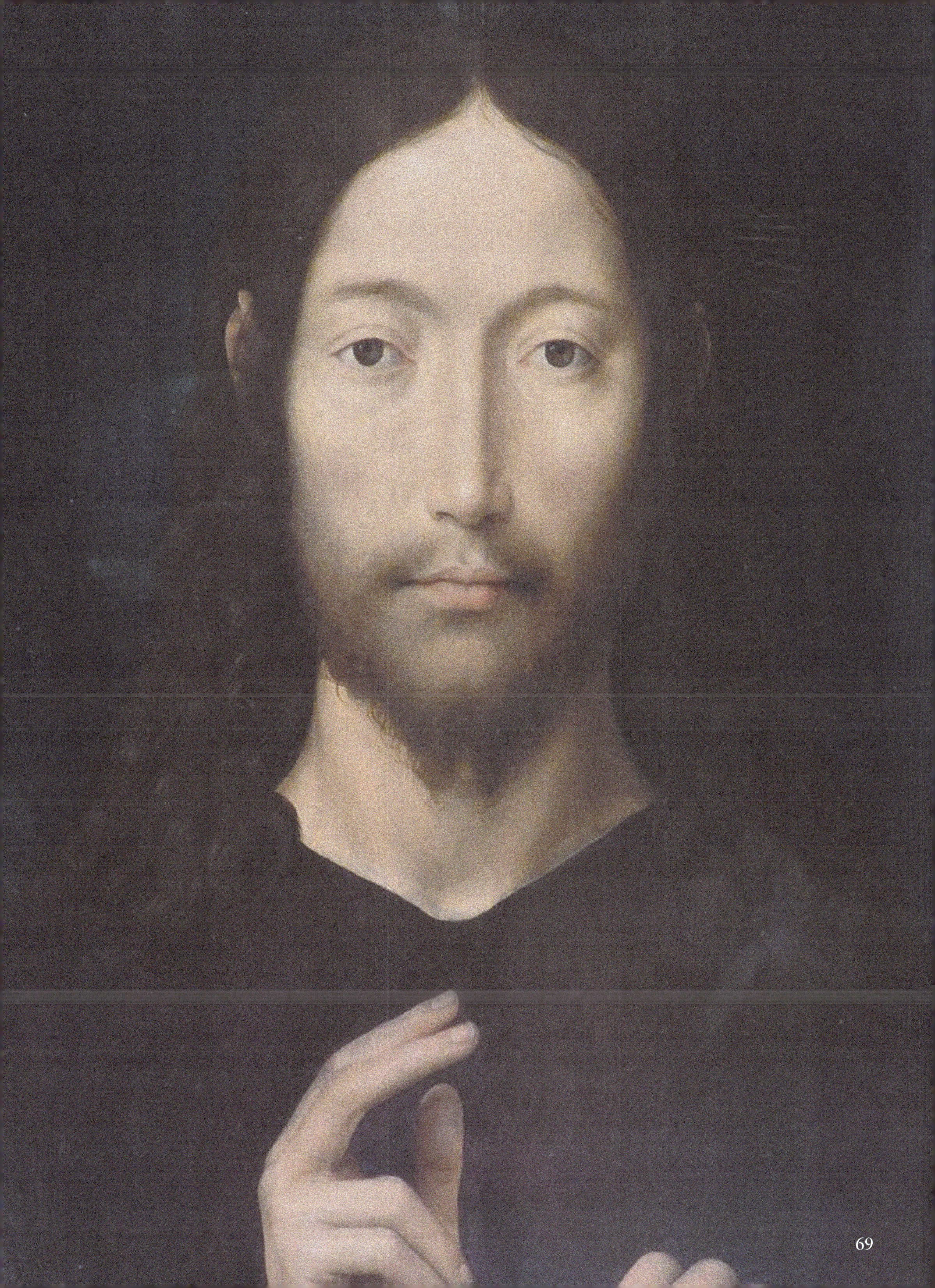

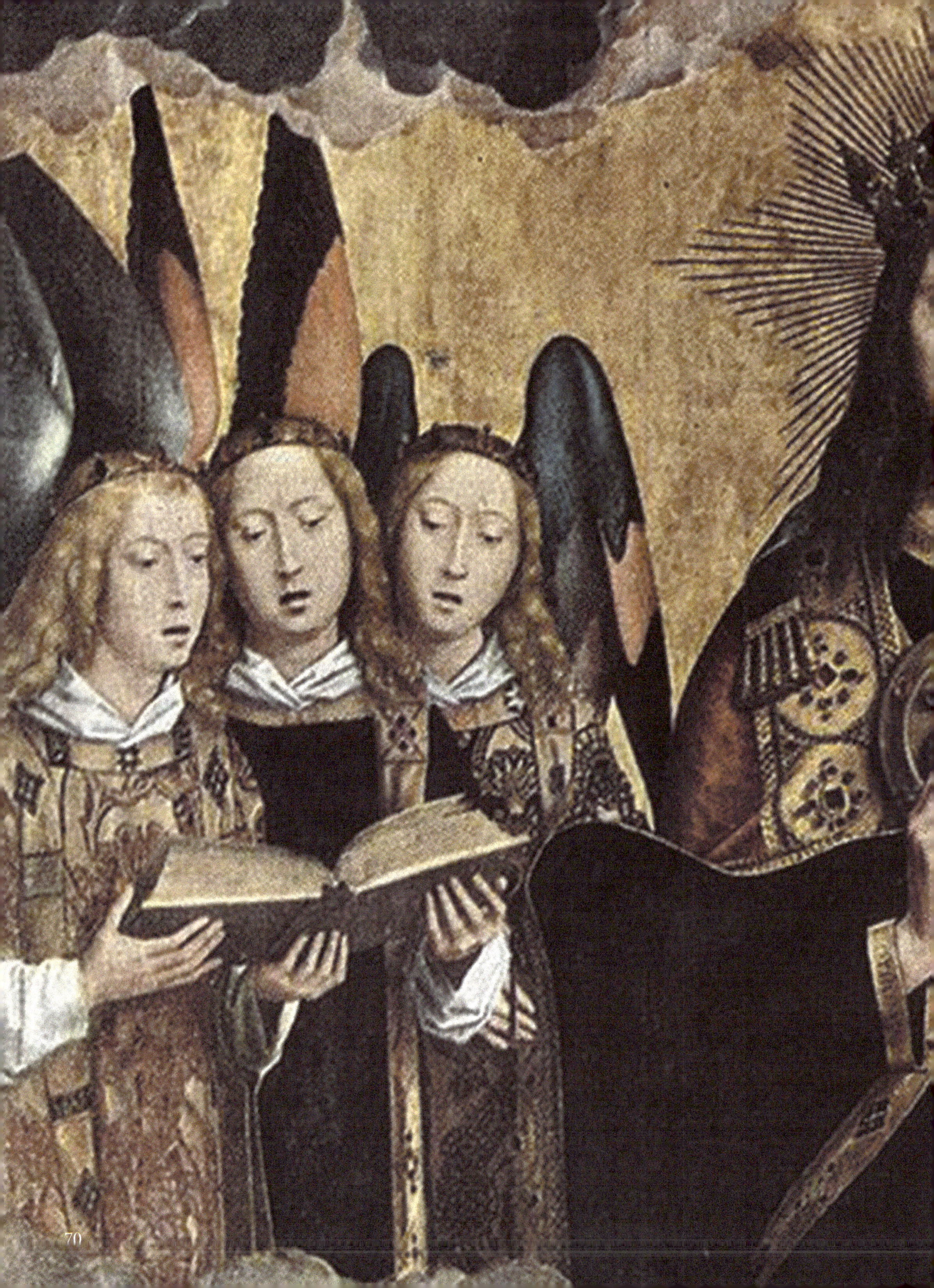

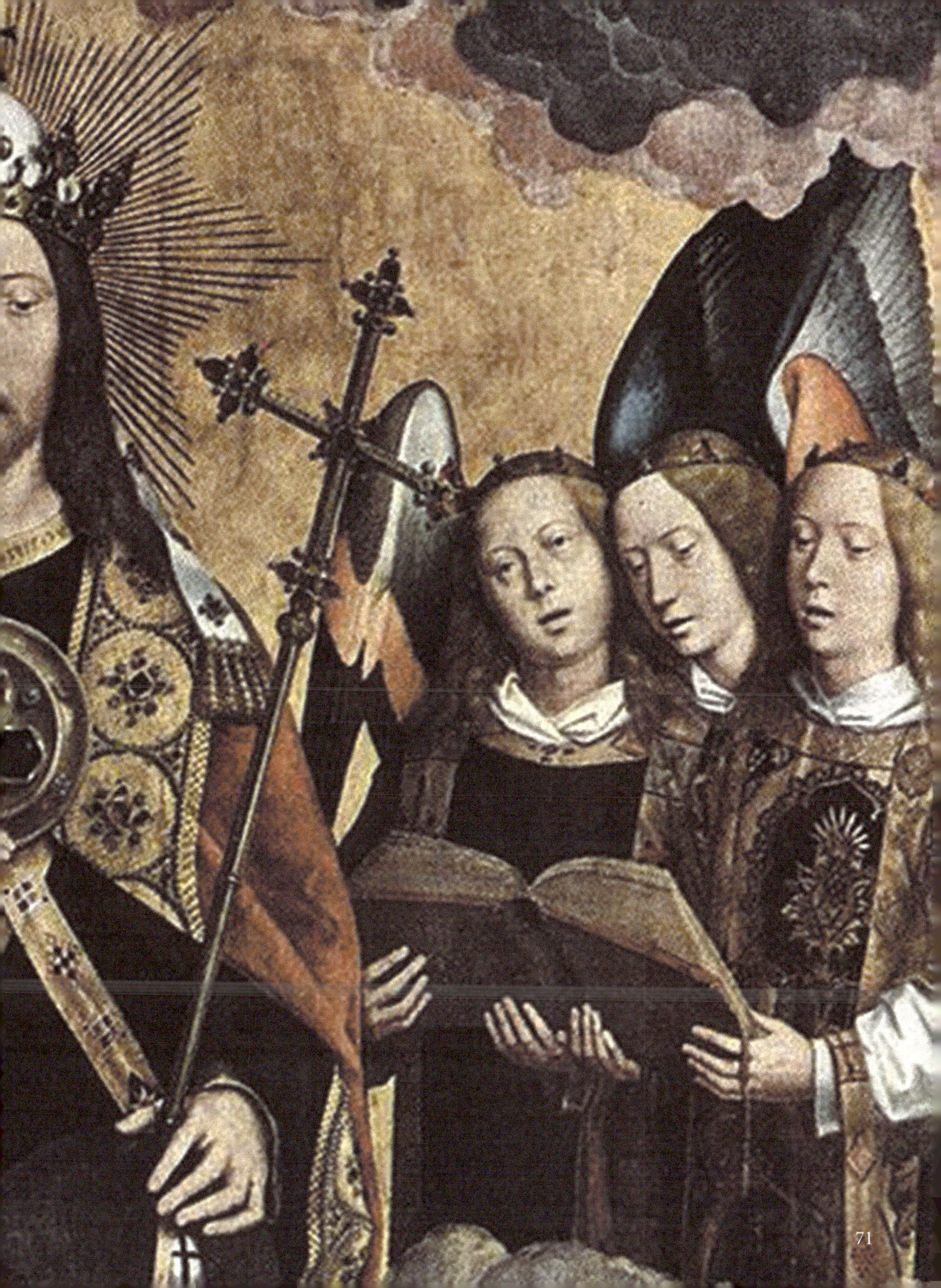

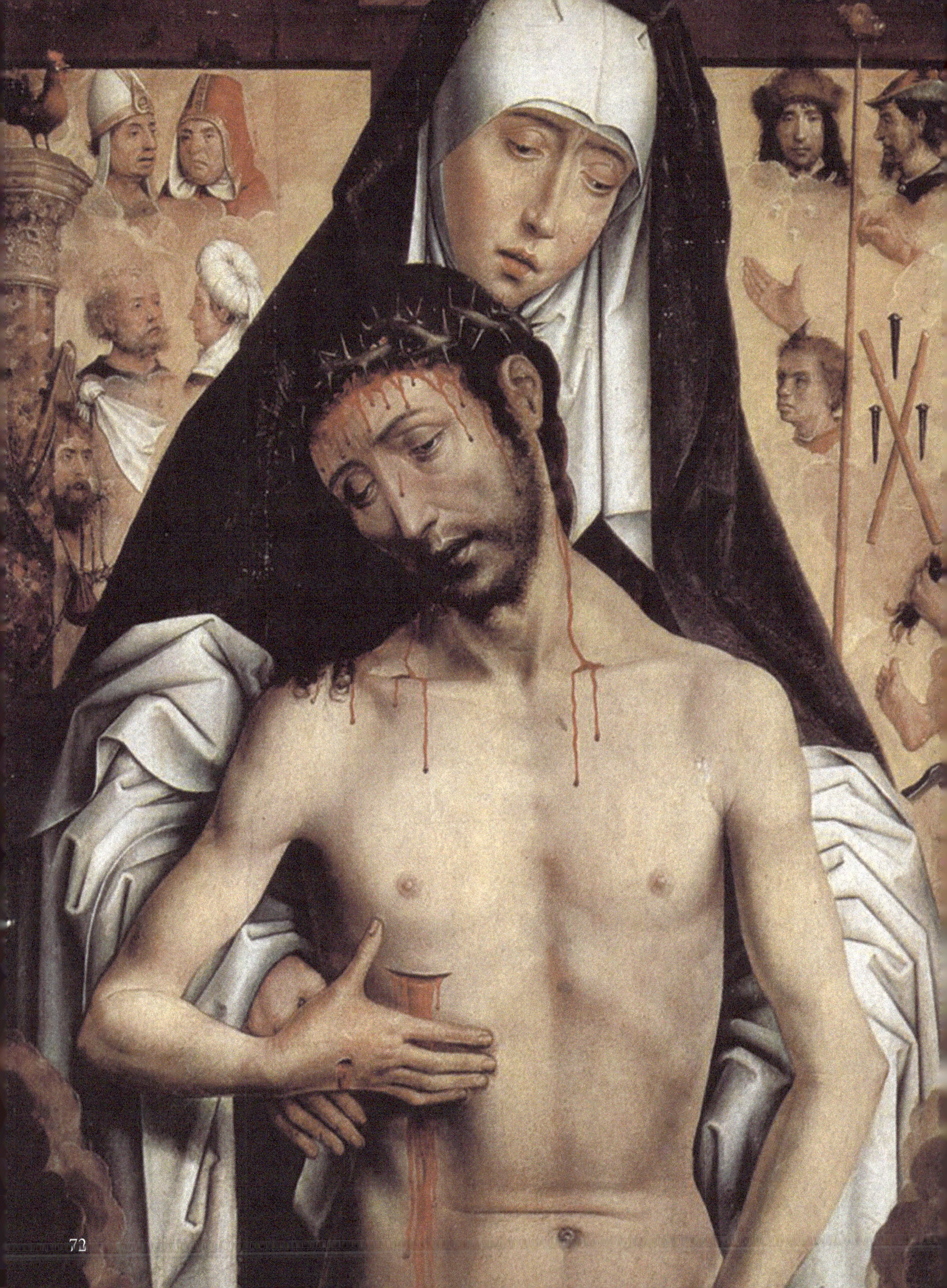

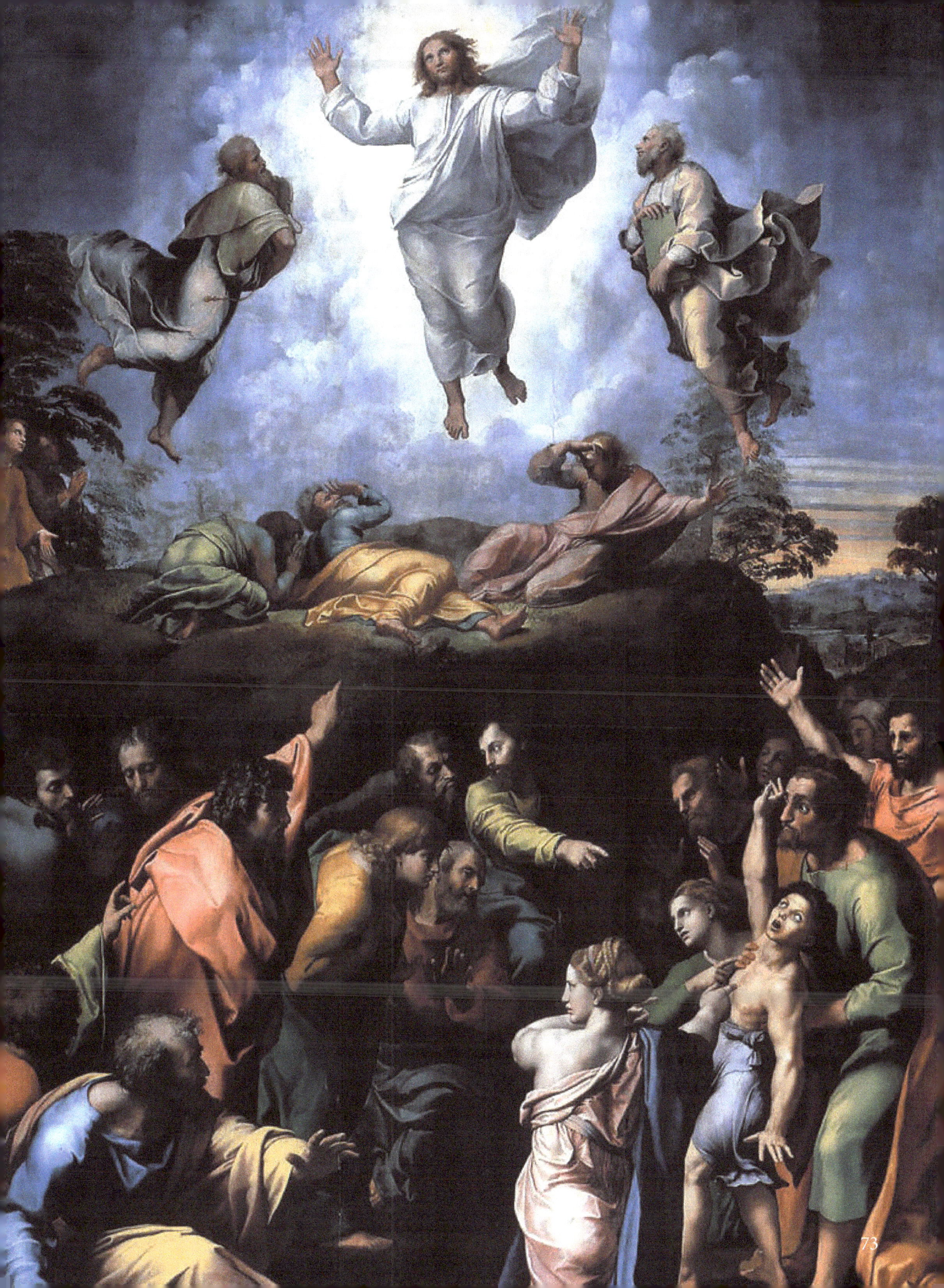

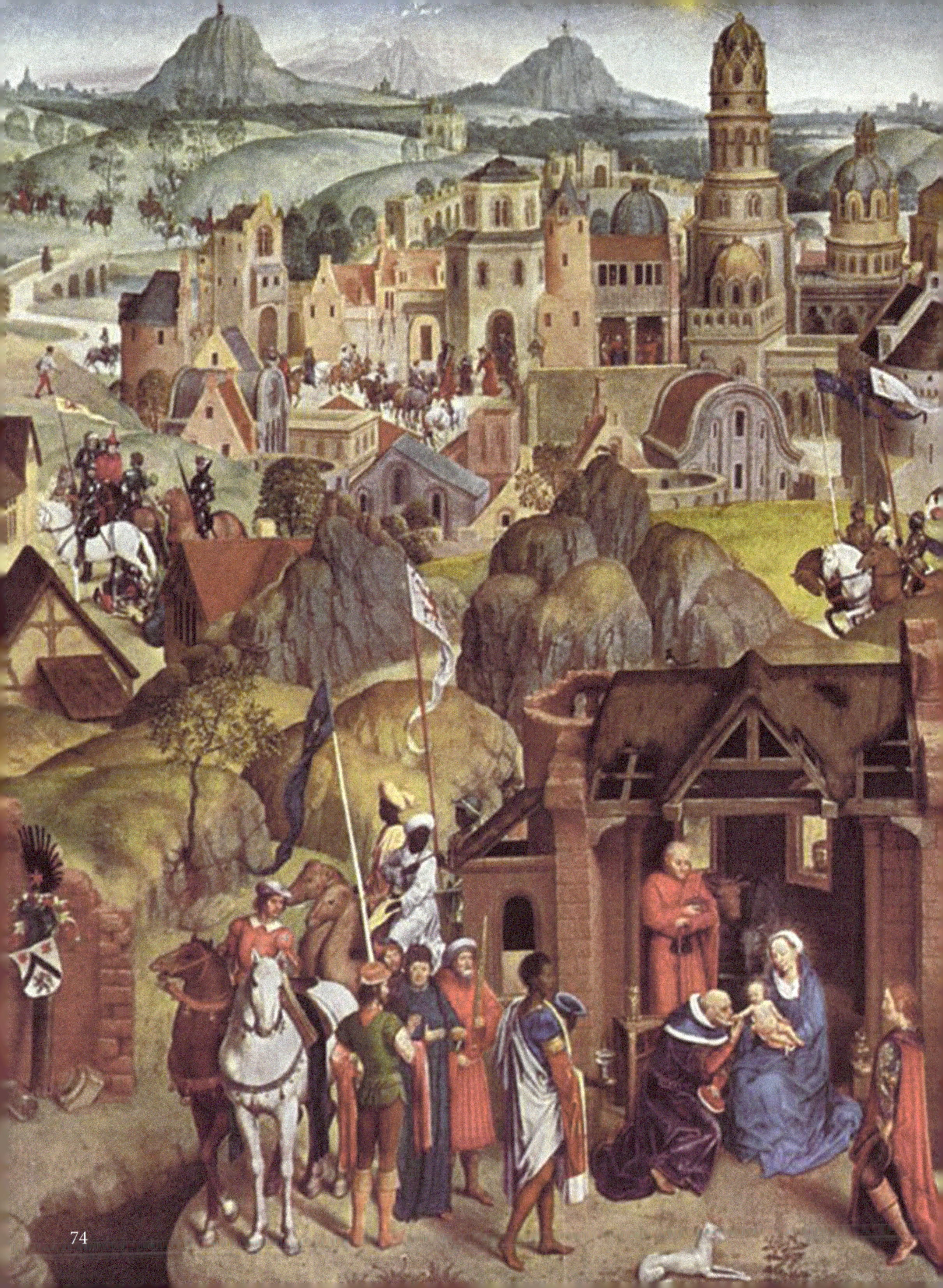

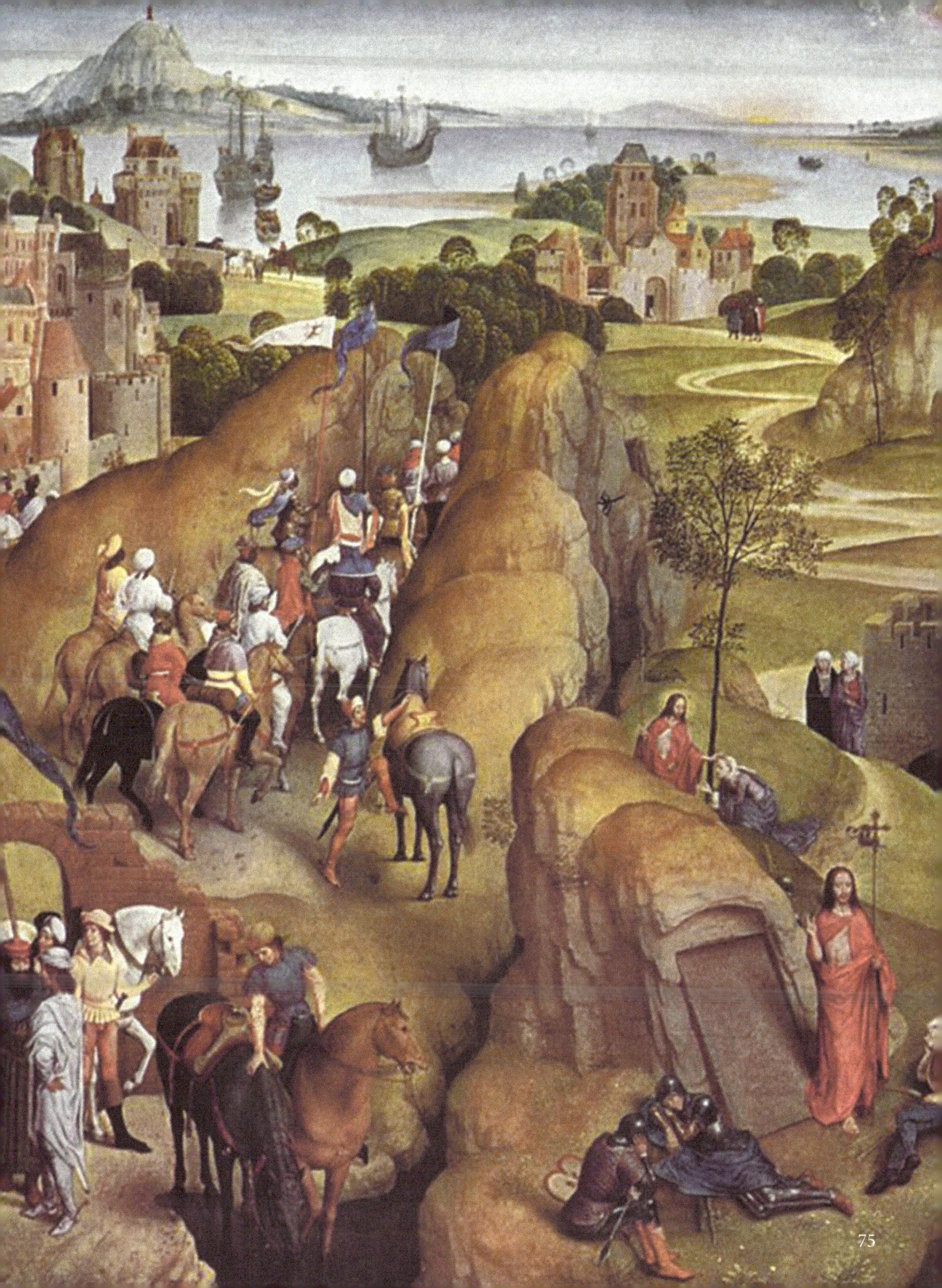

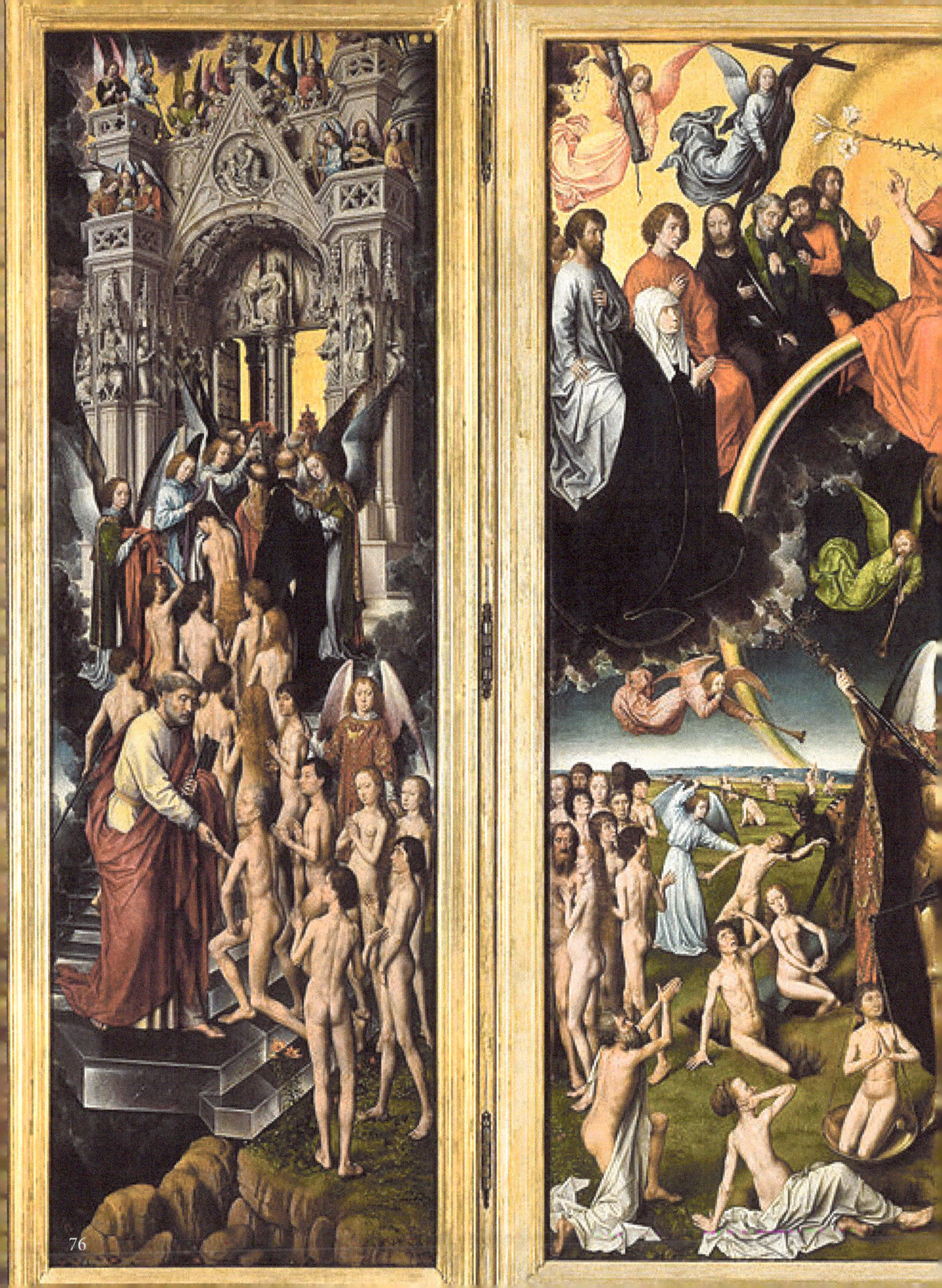

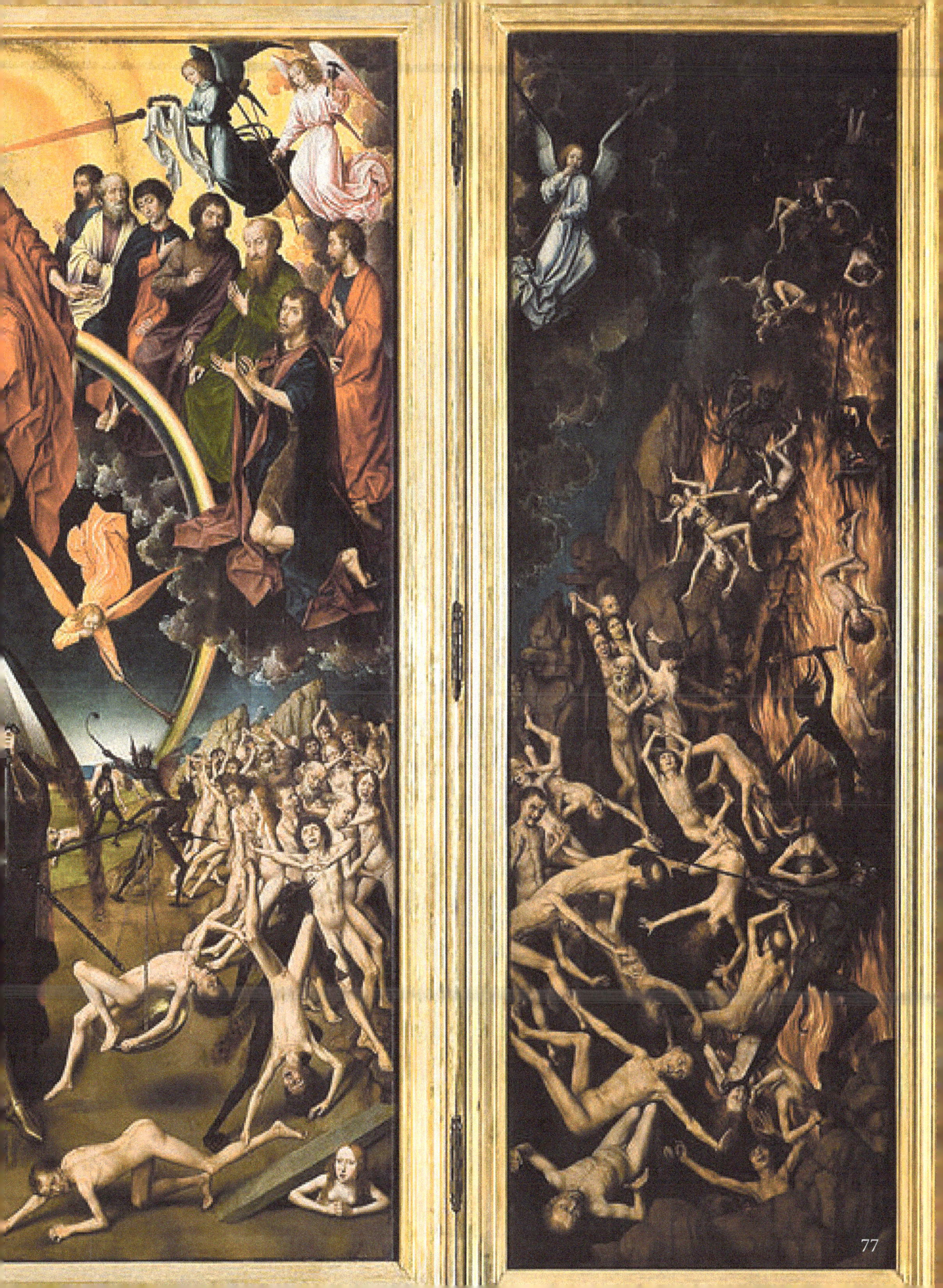

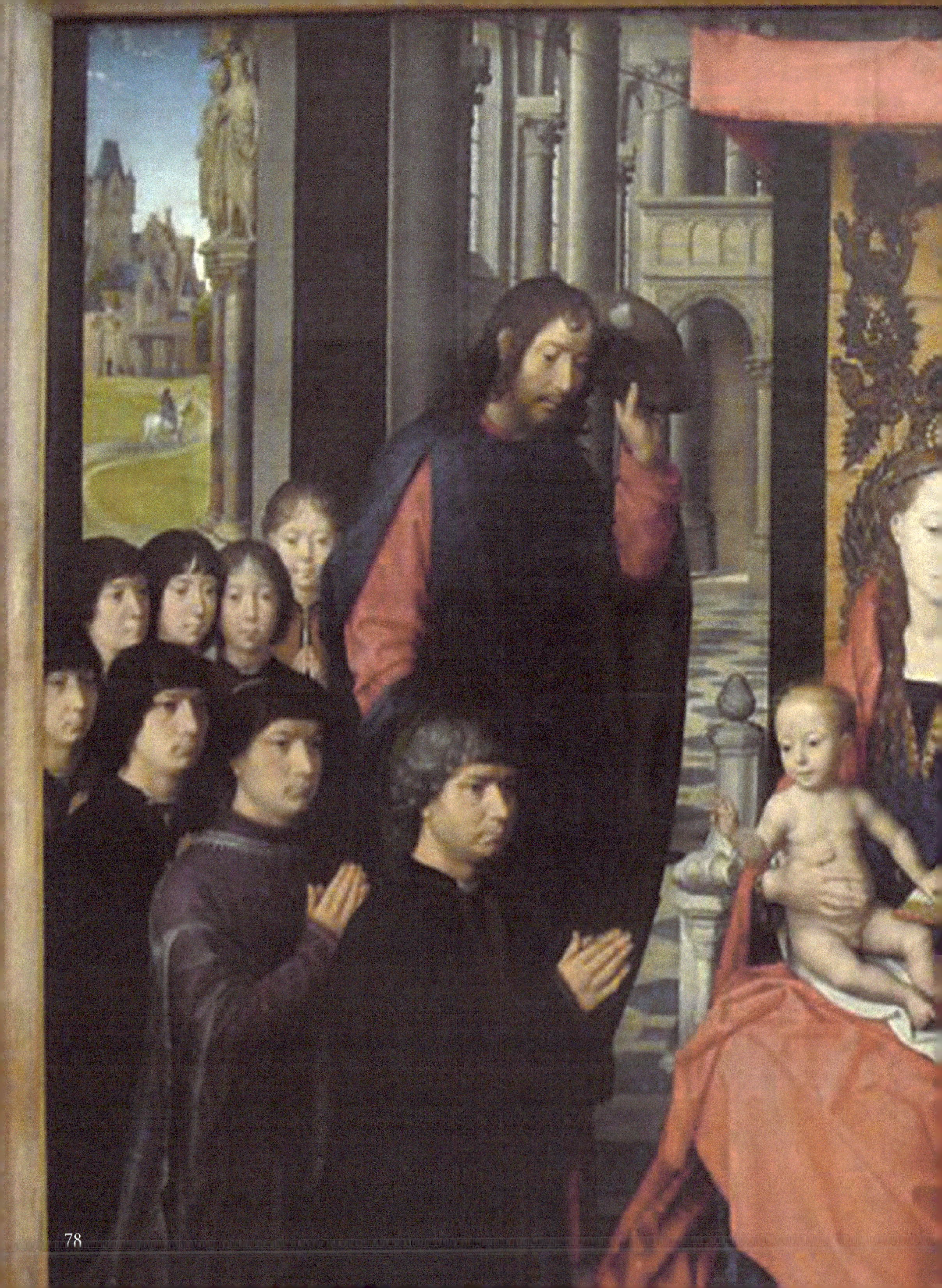

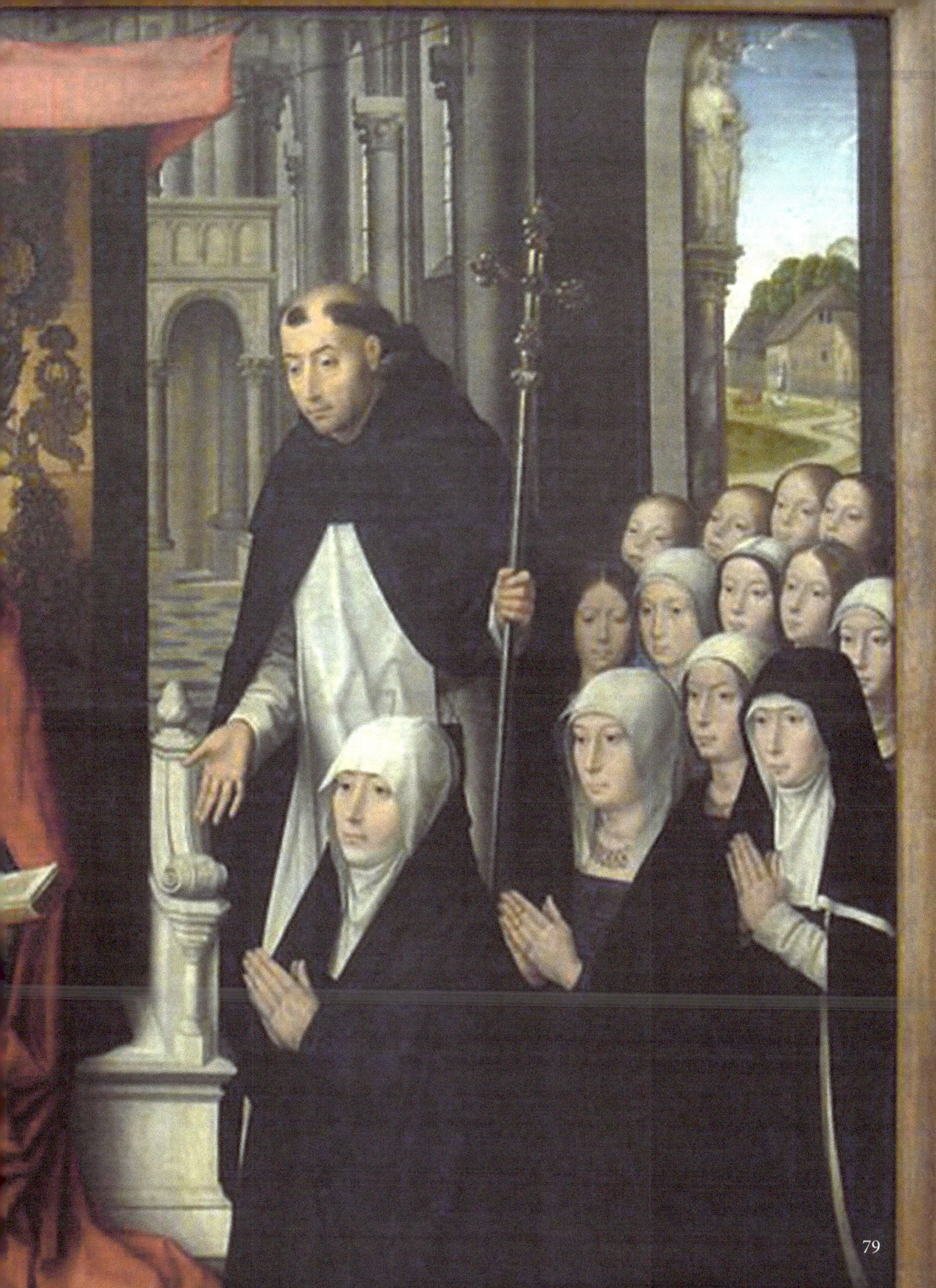

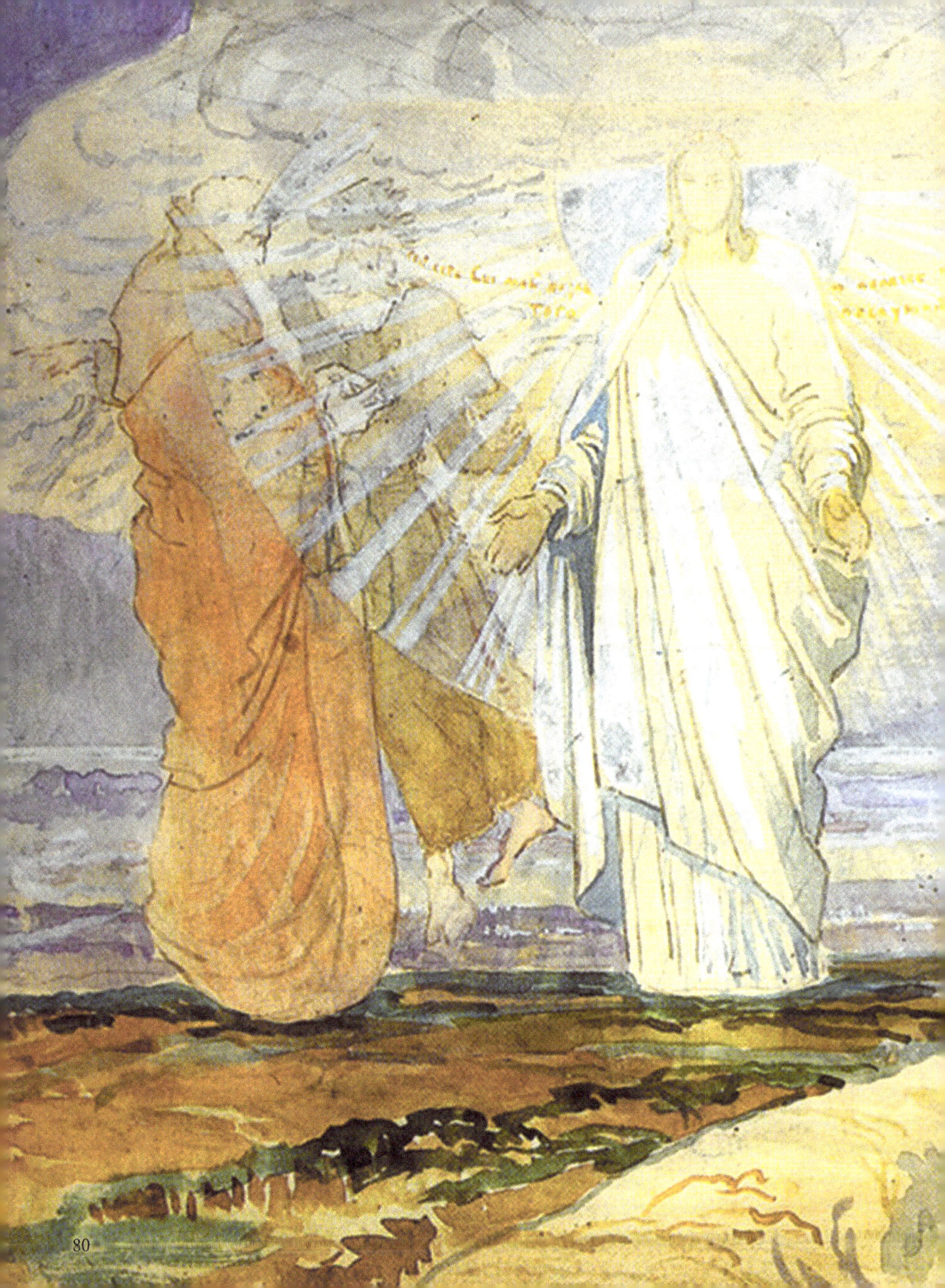

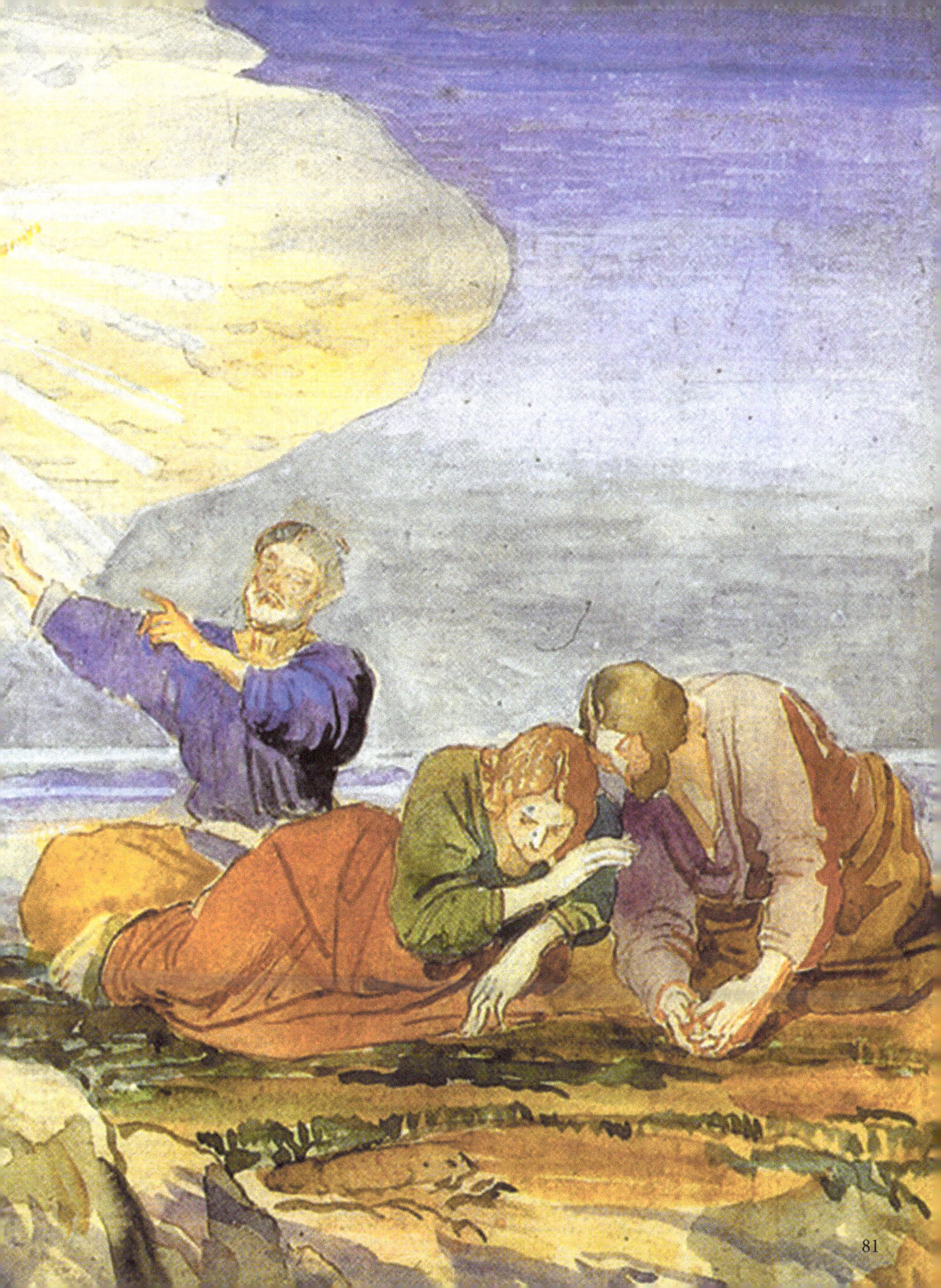

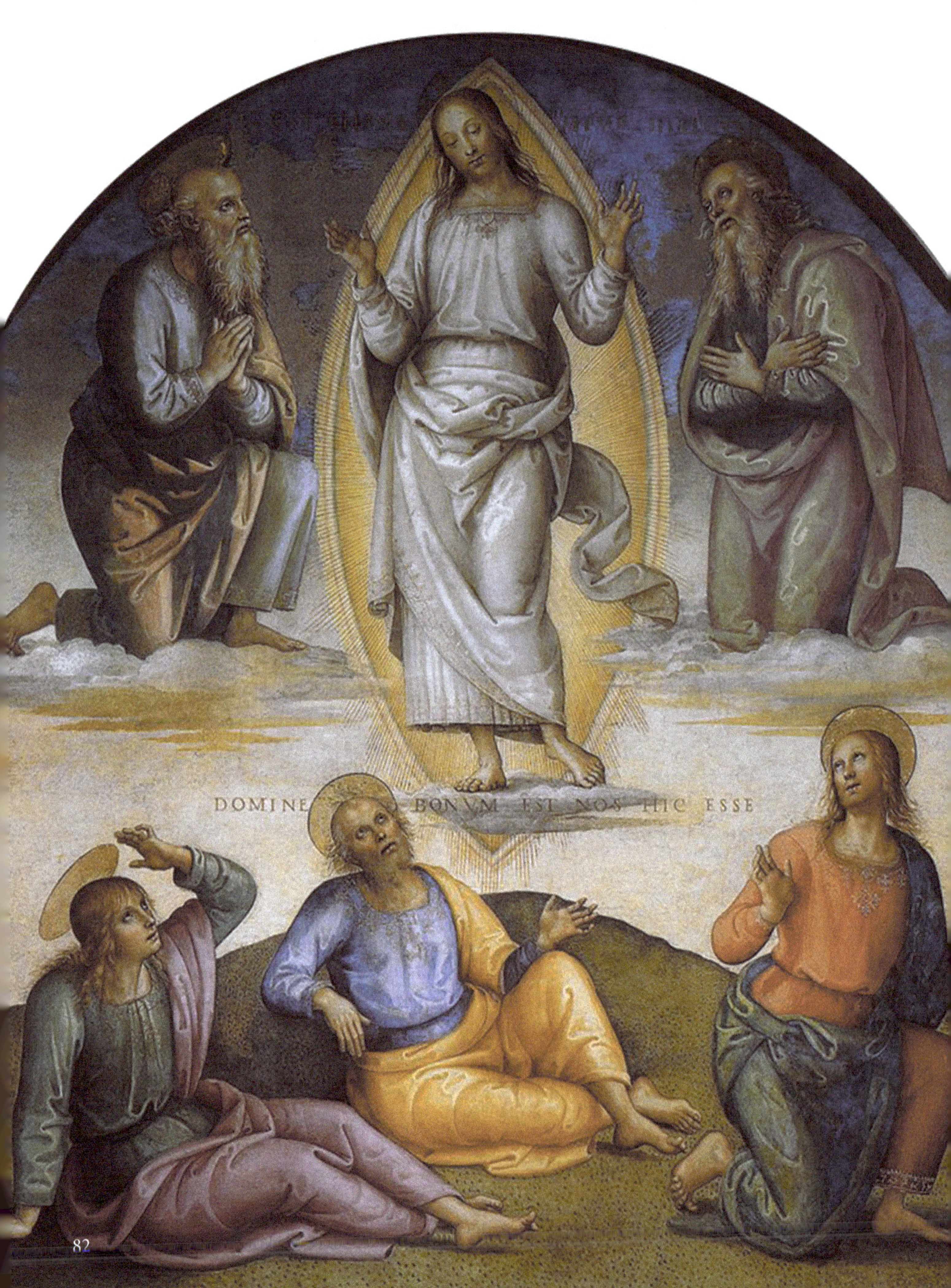

DOMINE BONVM EST NOS HIC ESSE

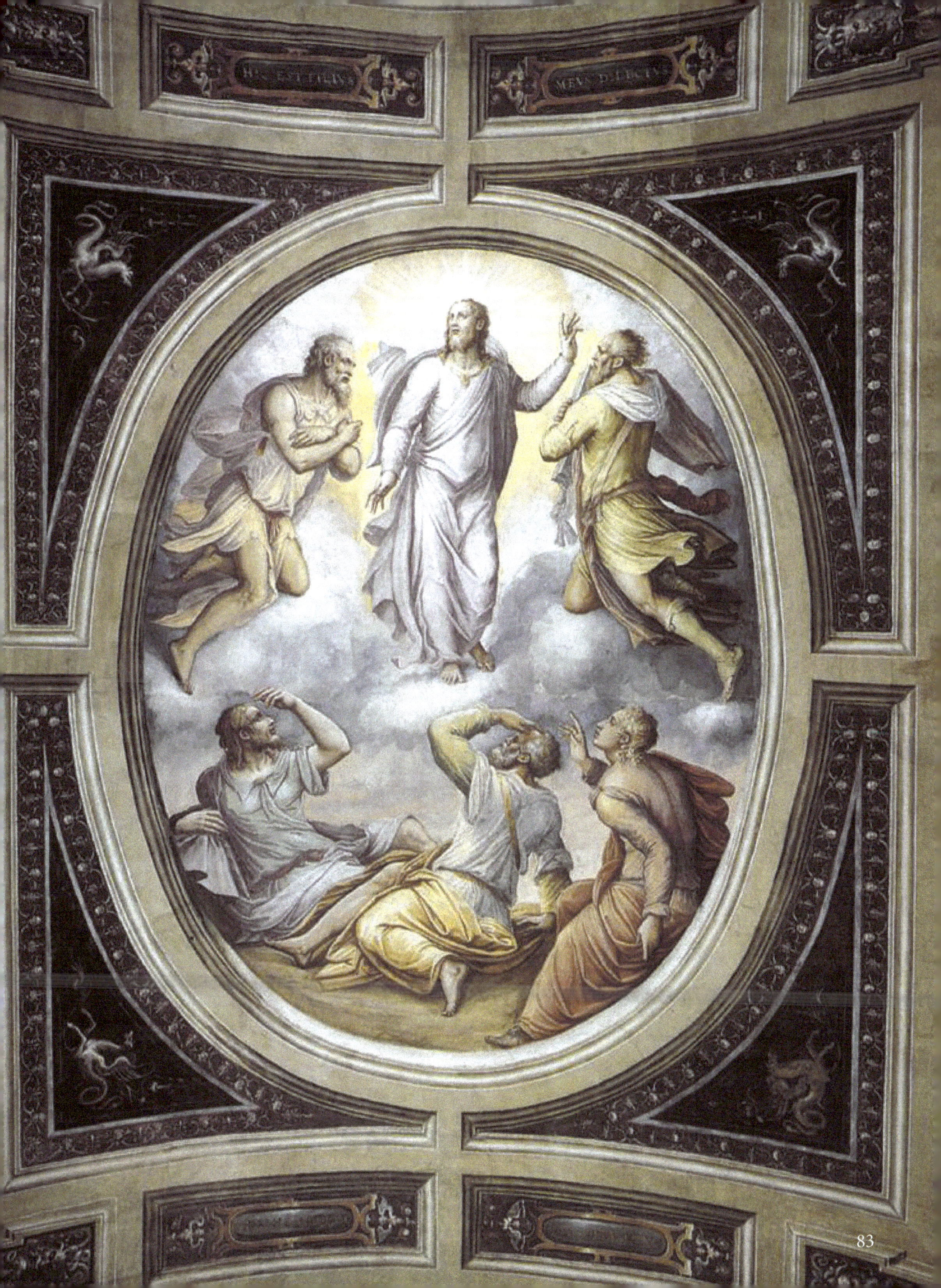

HIC EST FILIVS
MEVS DILECTVS

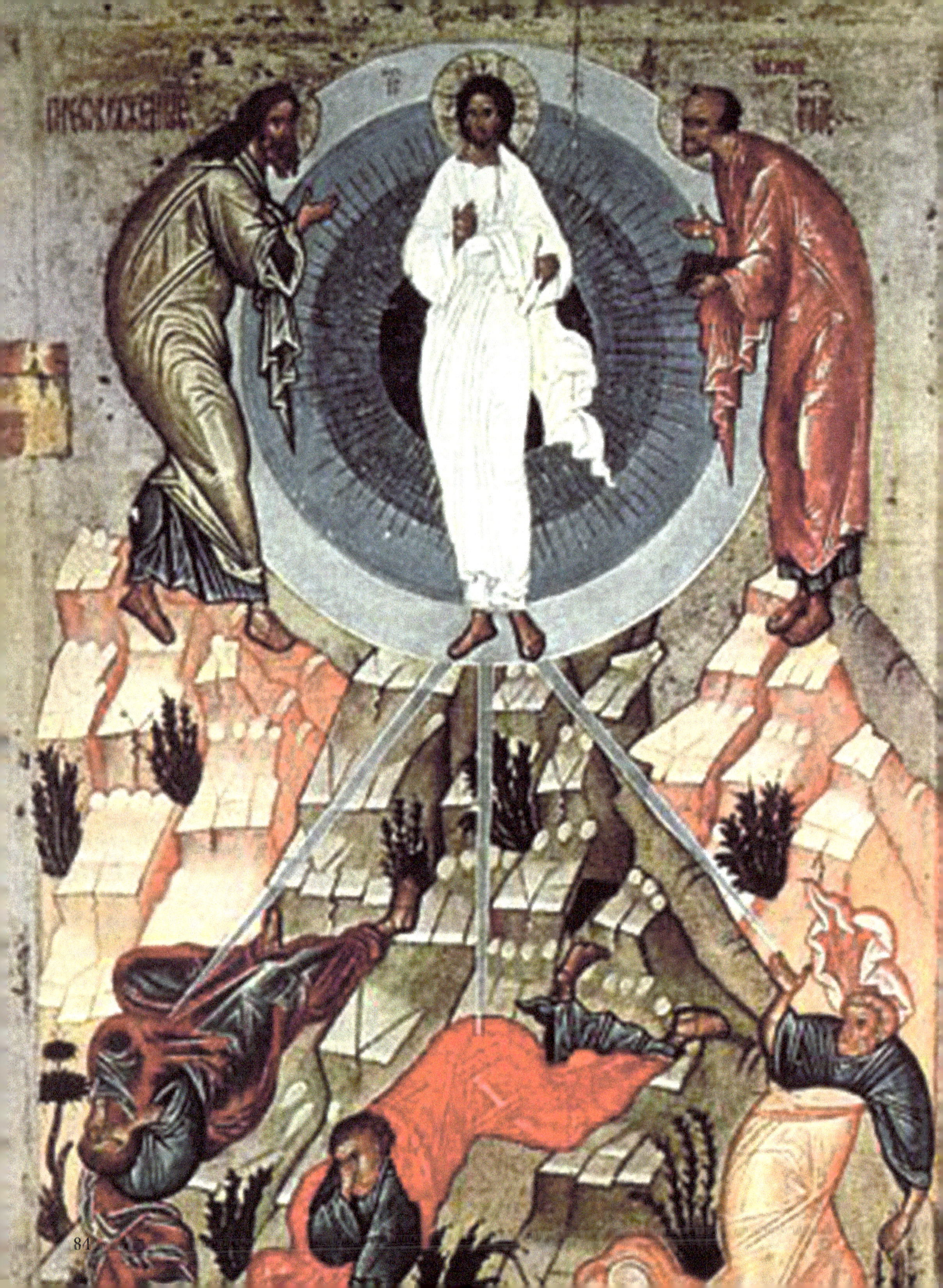
ПРЕѠБРАЖЕНИЕ

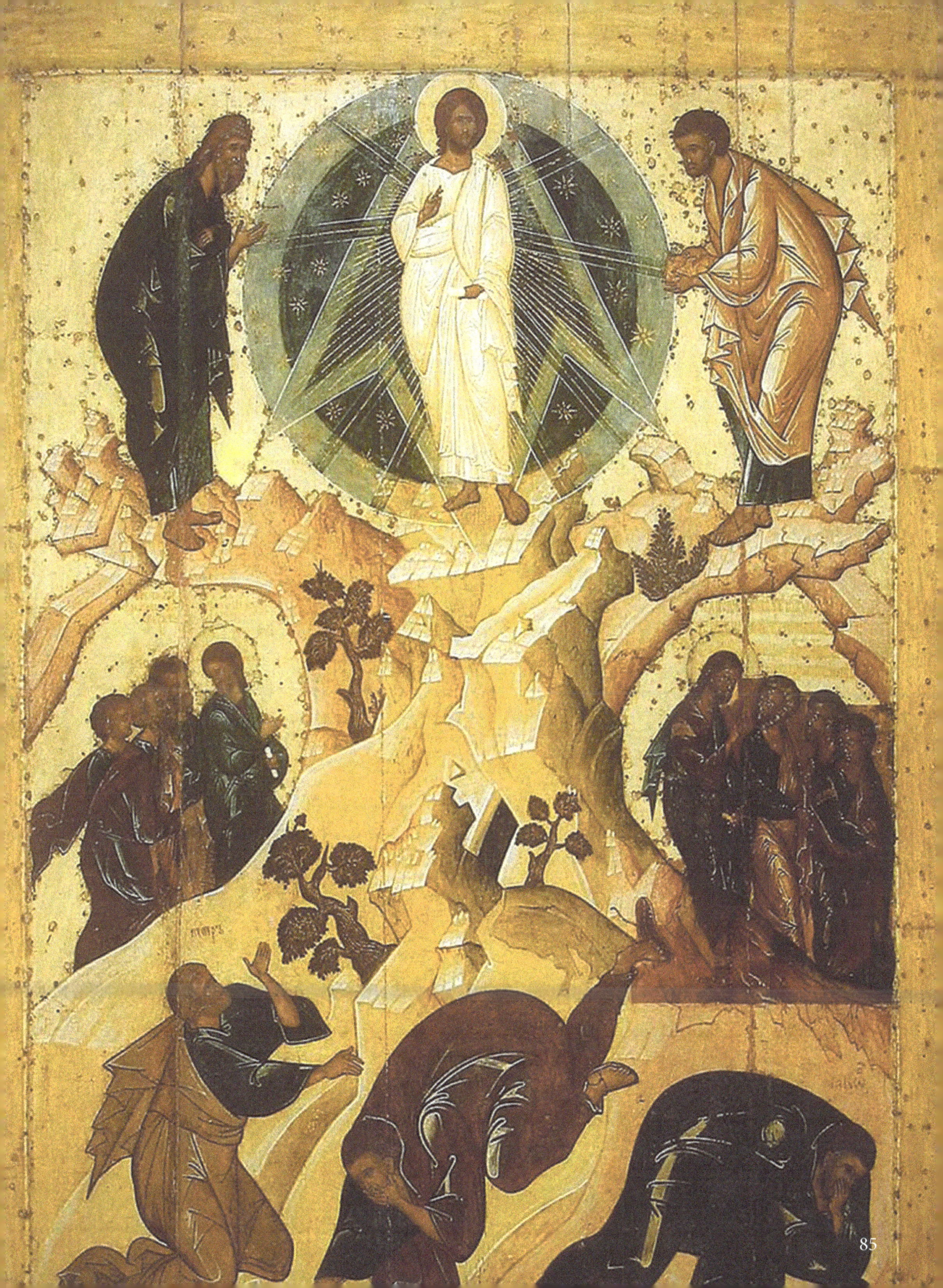

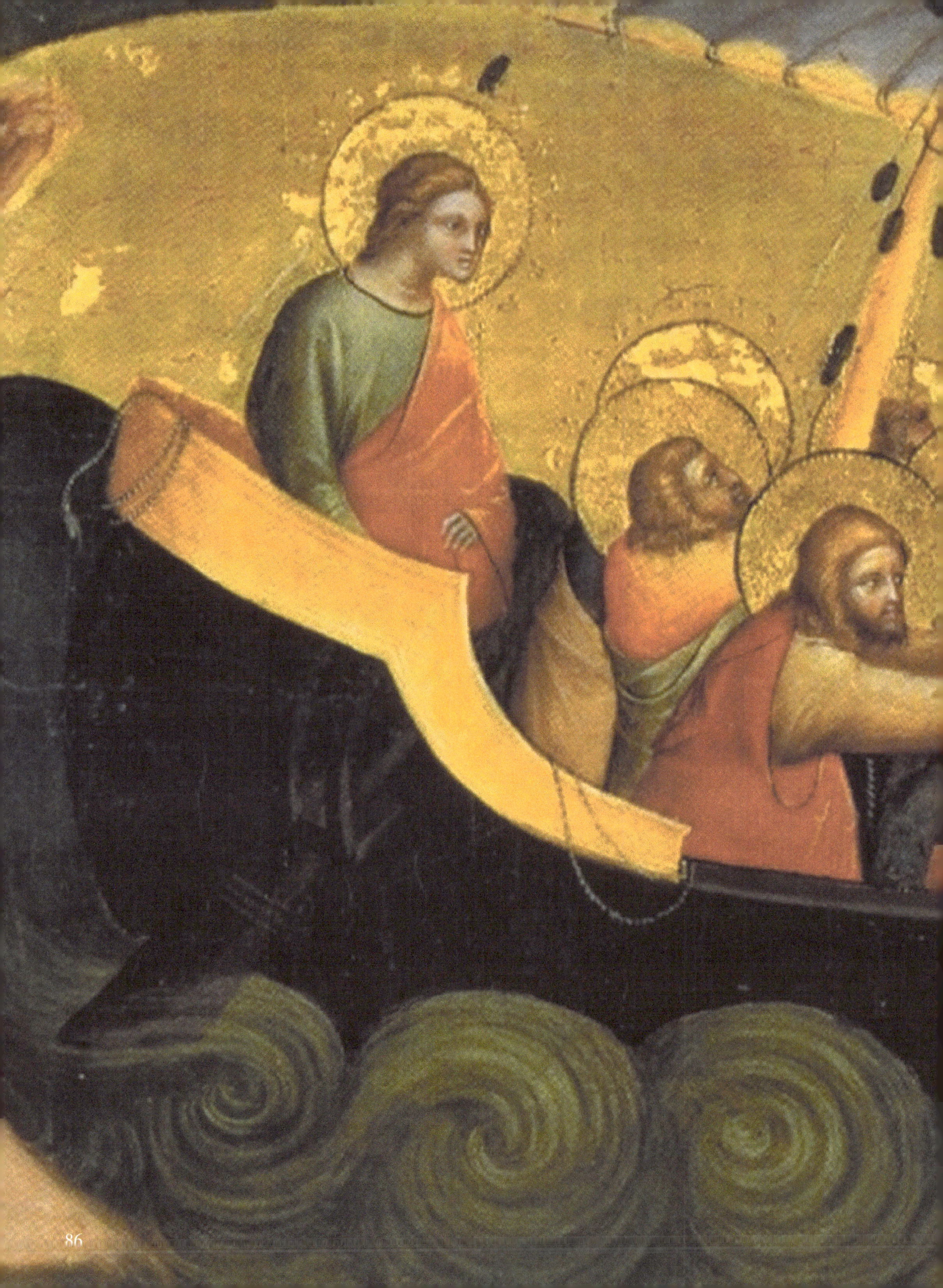

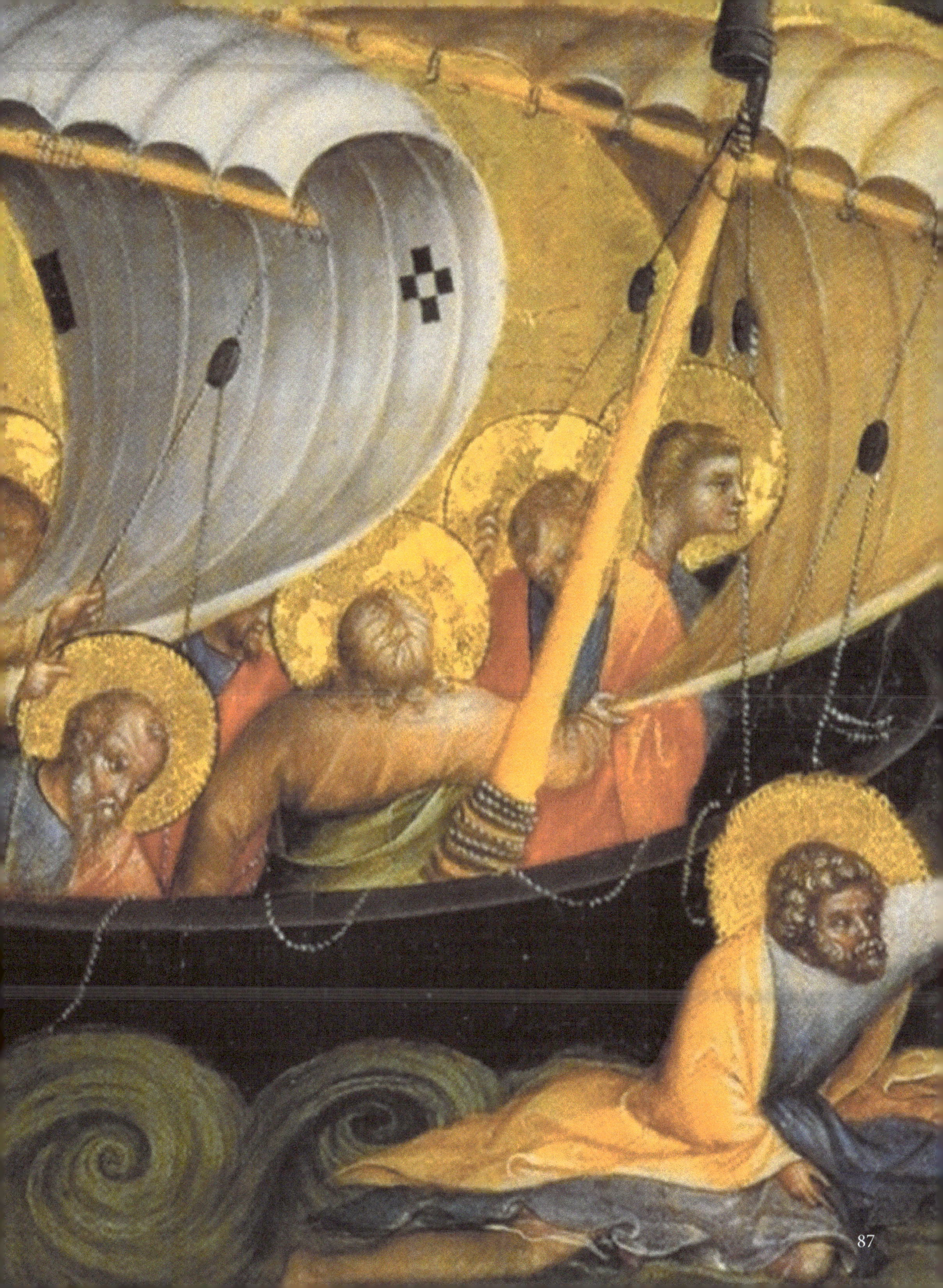

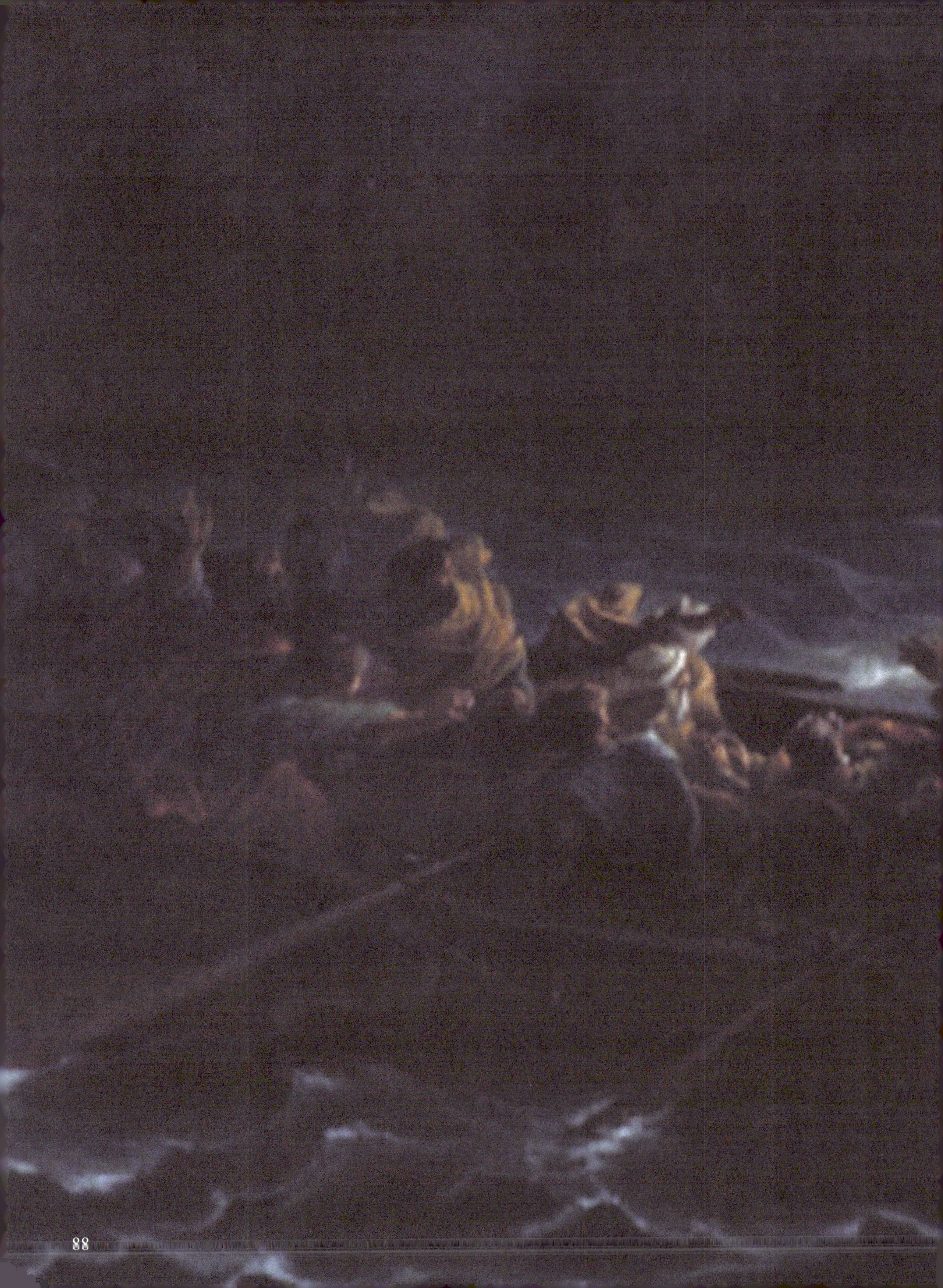

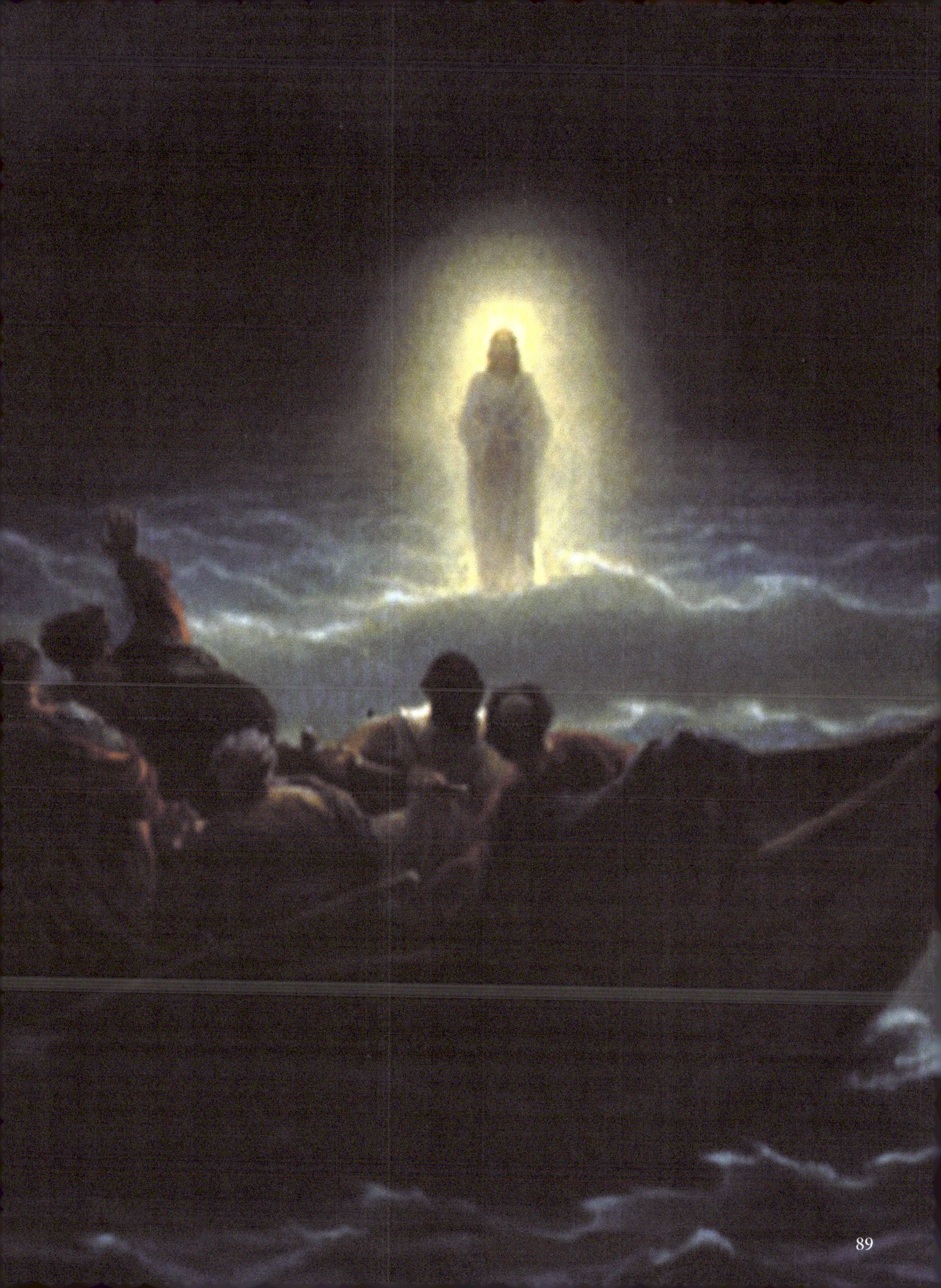

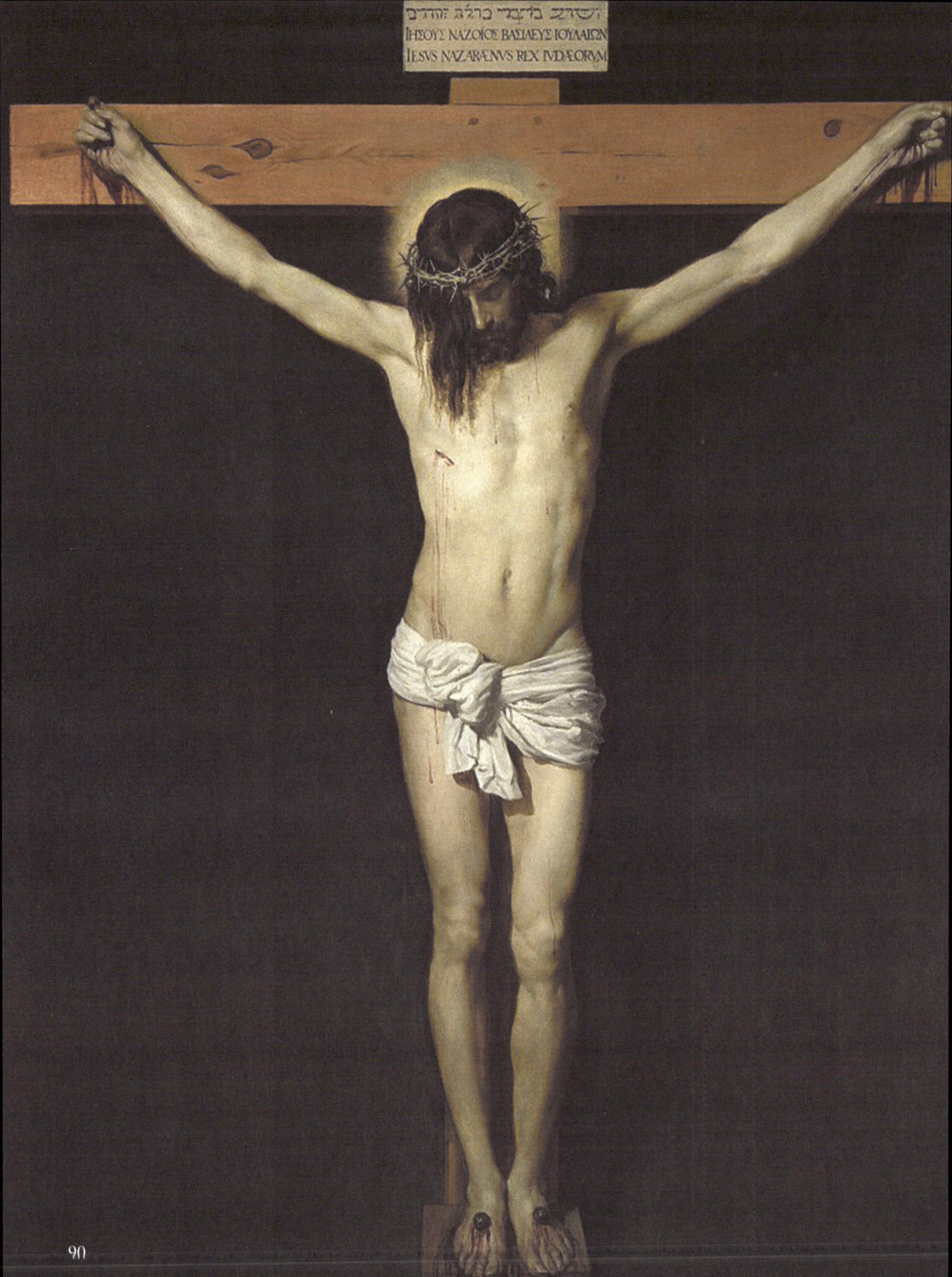

ישוע הנצרי מלך היהודים
ΙΗΣΟΥΣ ΝΑΖΩΡΑΙΟΣ ΒΑΣΙΛΕΥΣ ΙΟΥΛΑΙΩΝ
IESVS NAZARÆNVS REX IVDÆORVM

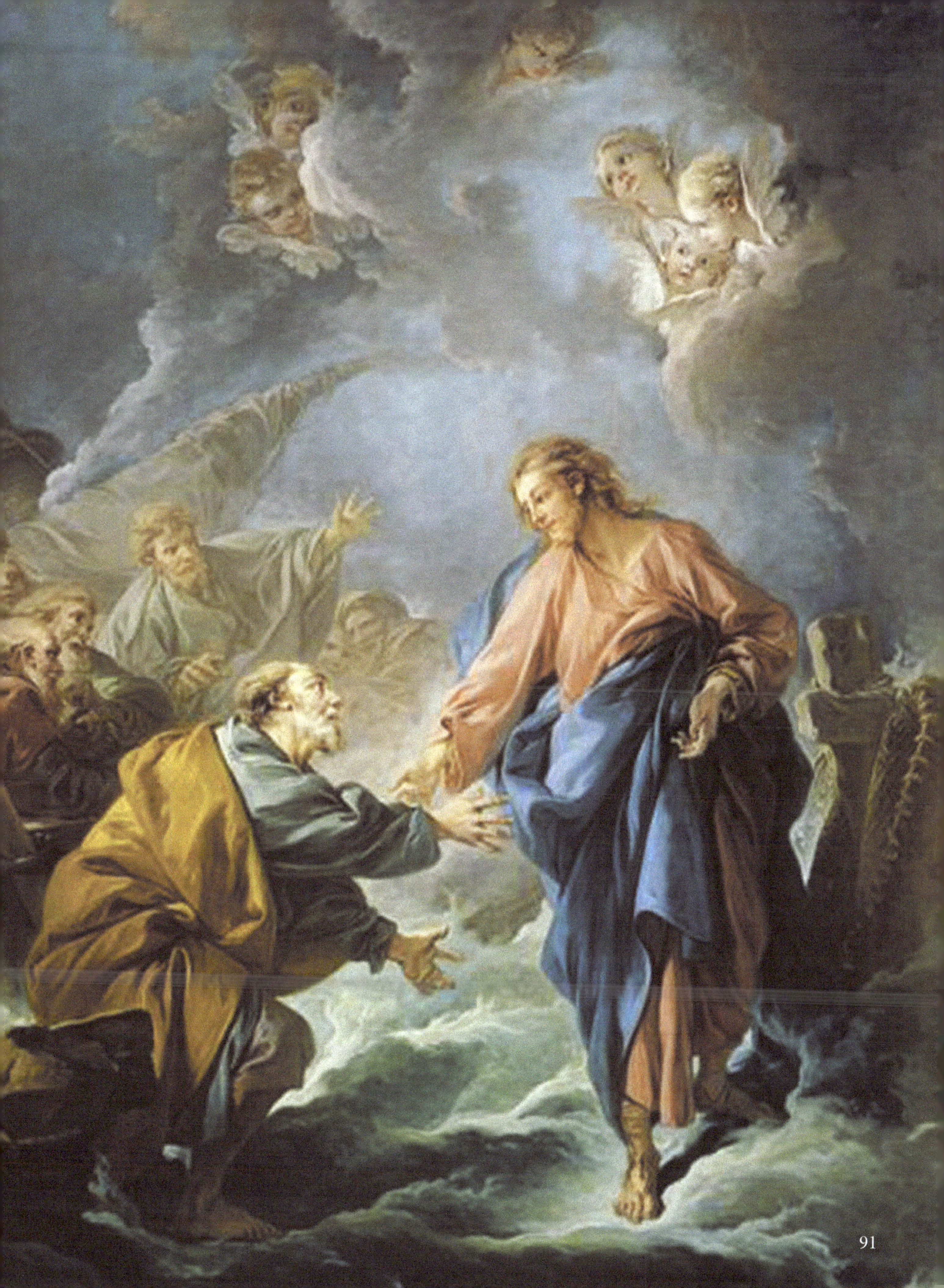

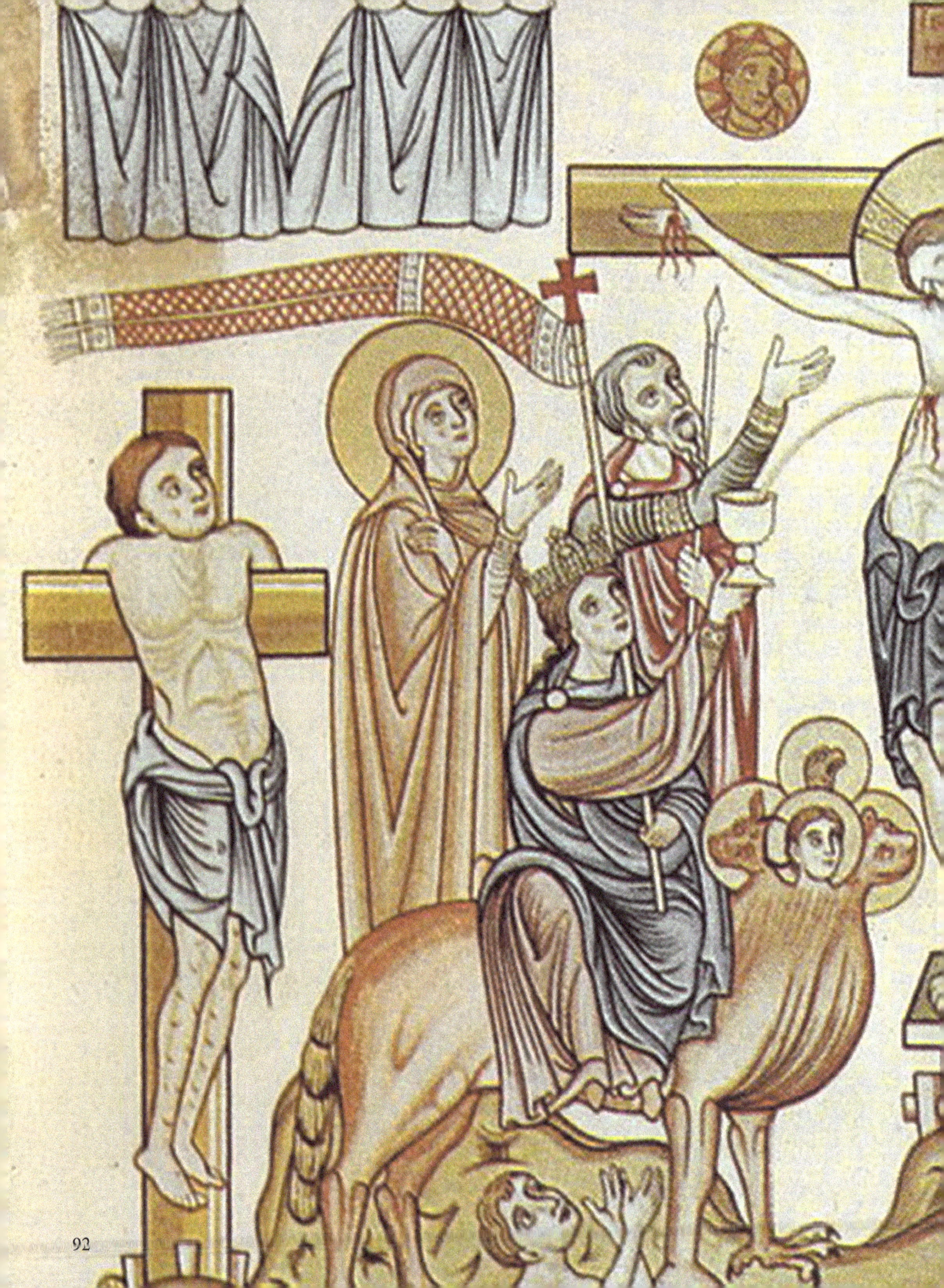

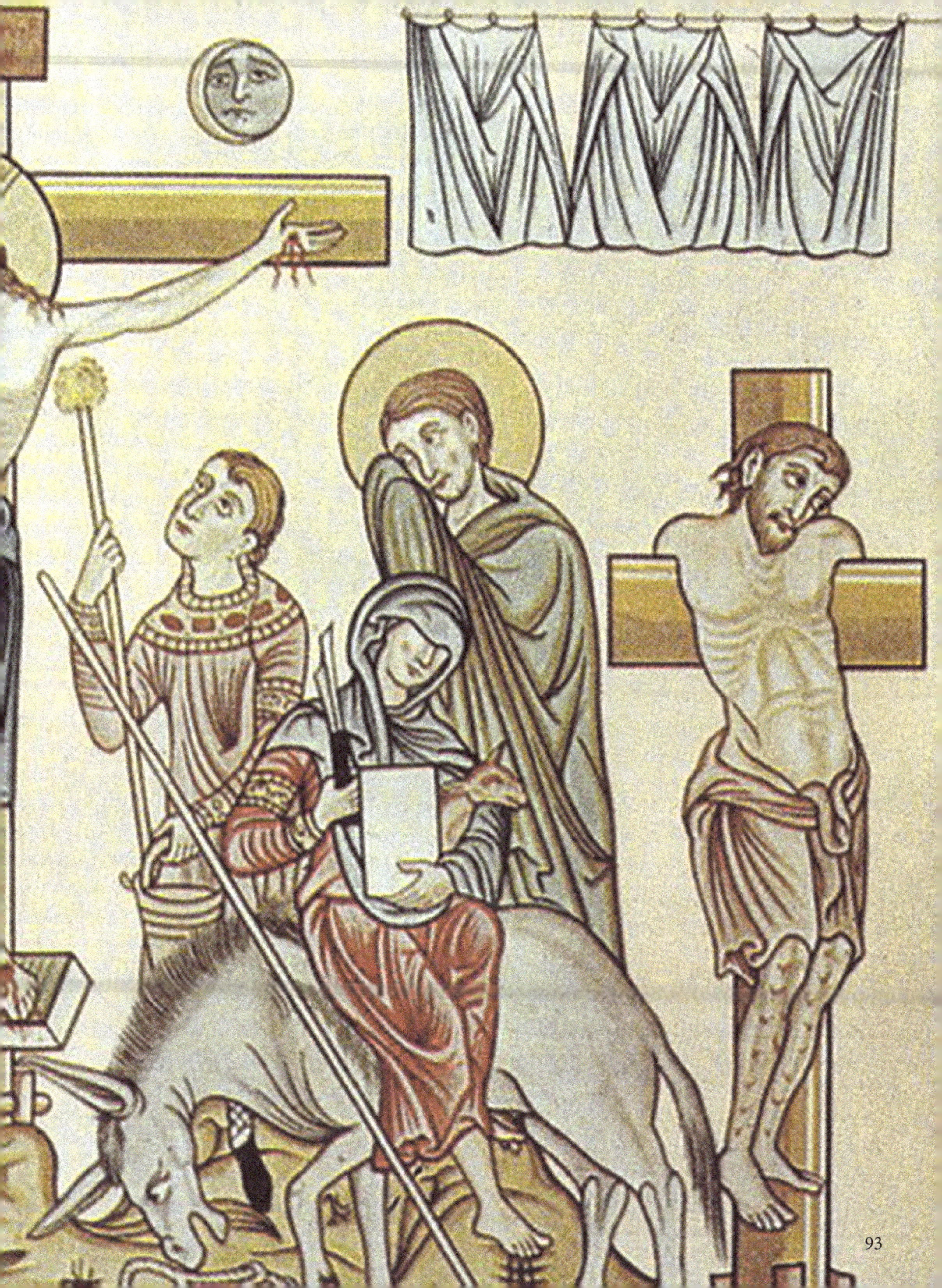

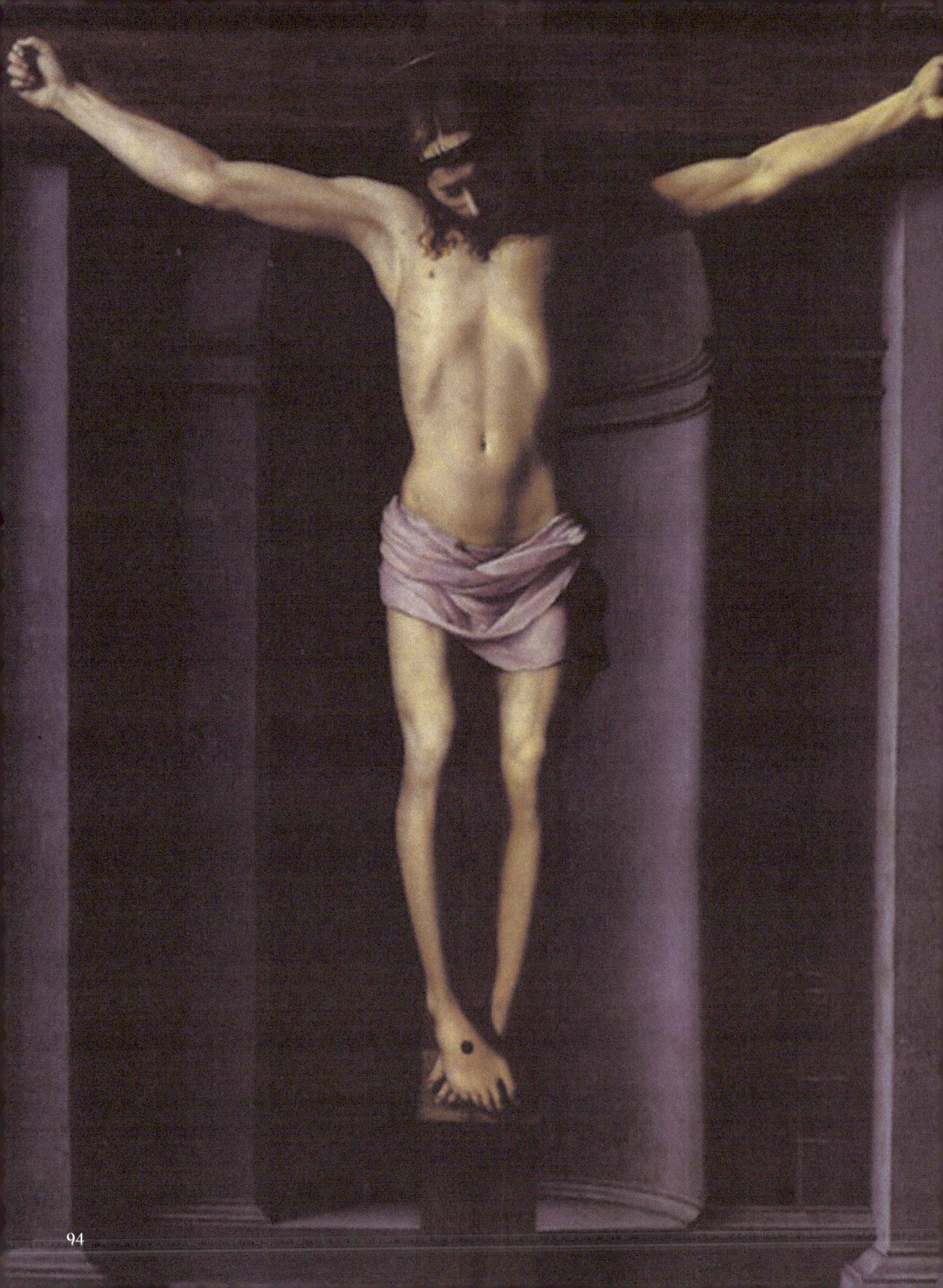

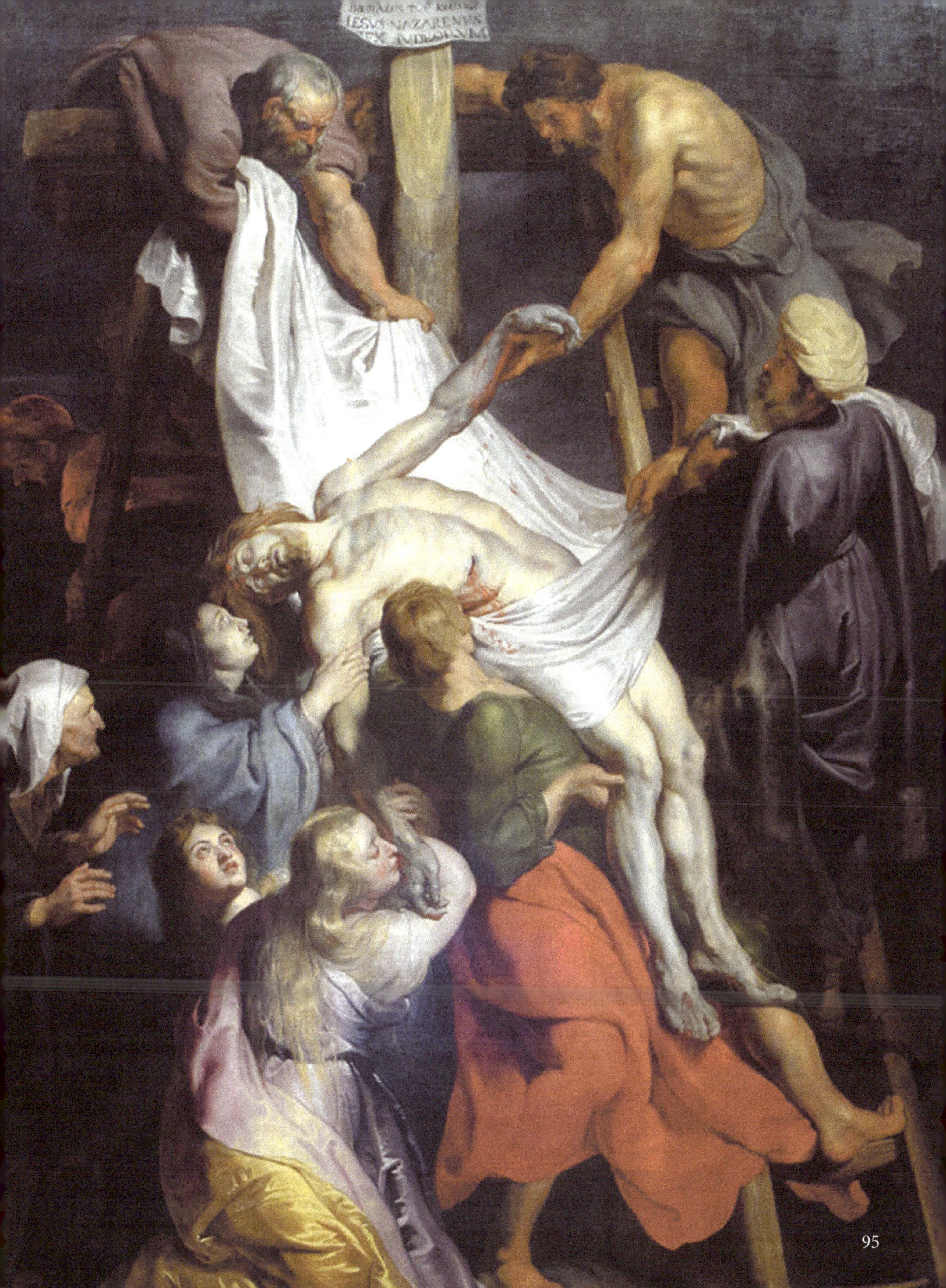

IESVS NAZARENVS
REX IVDÆORVM

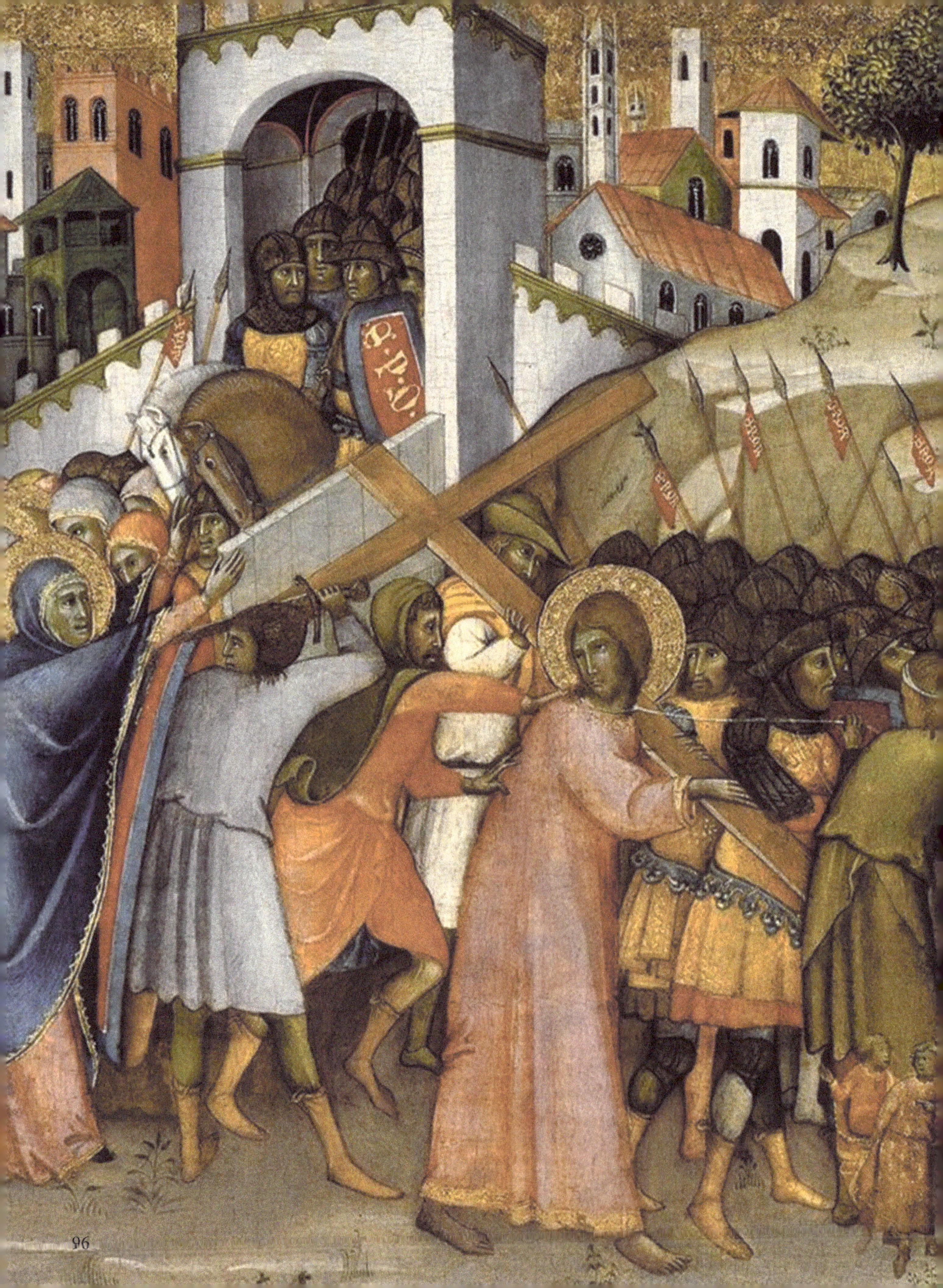
S.P.Q.

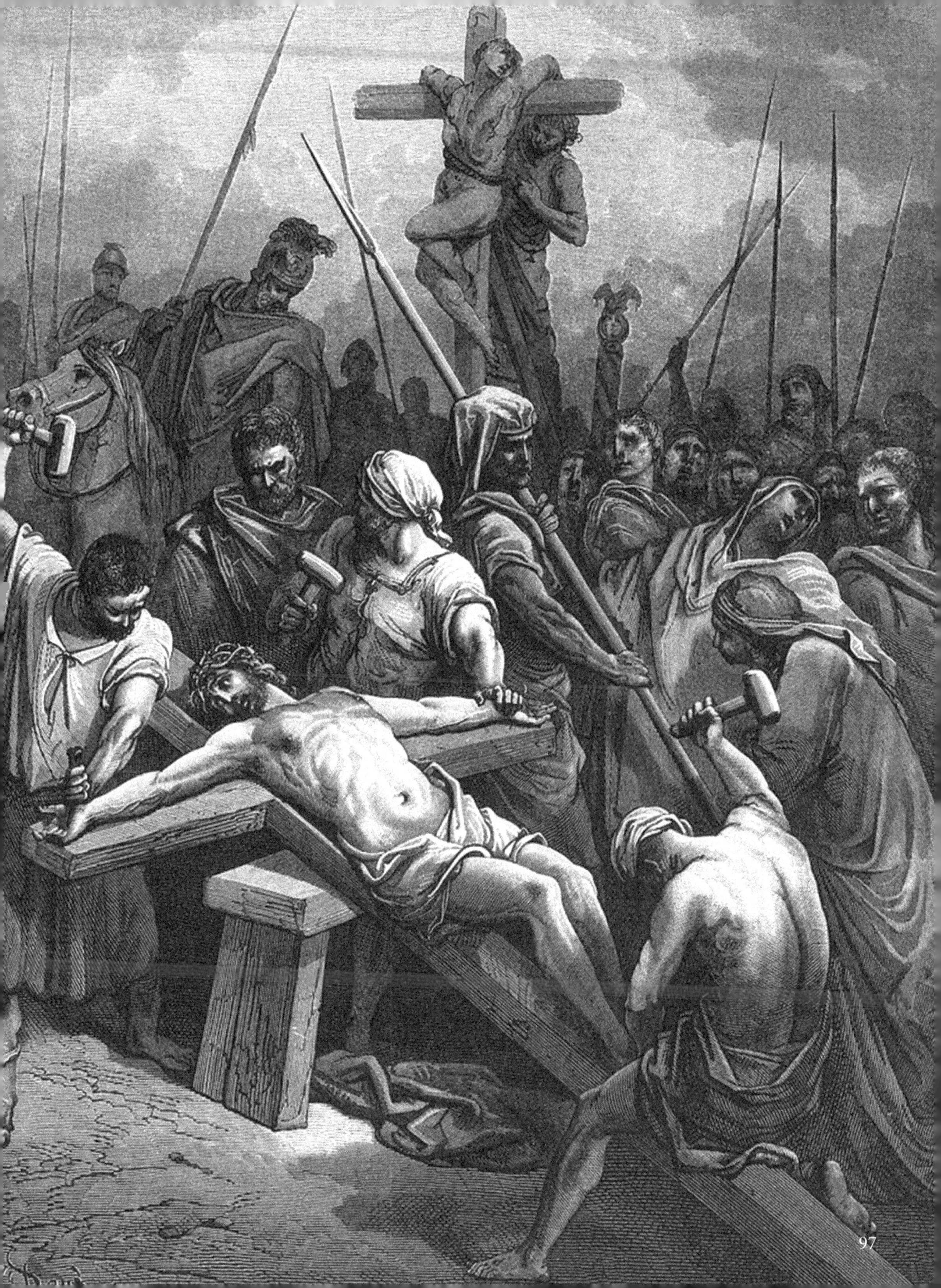

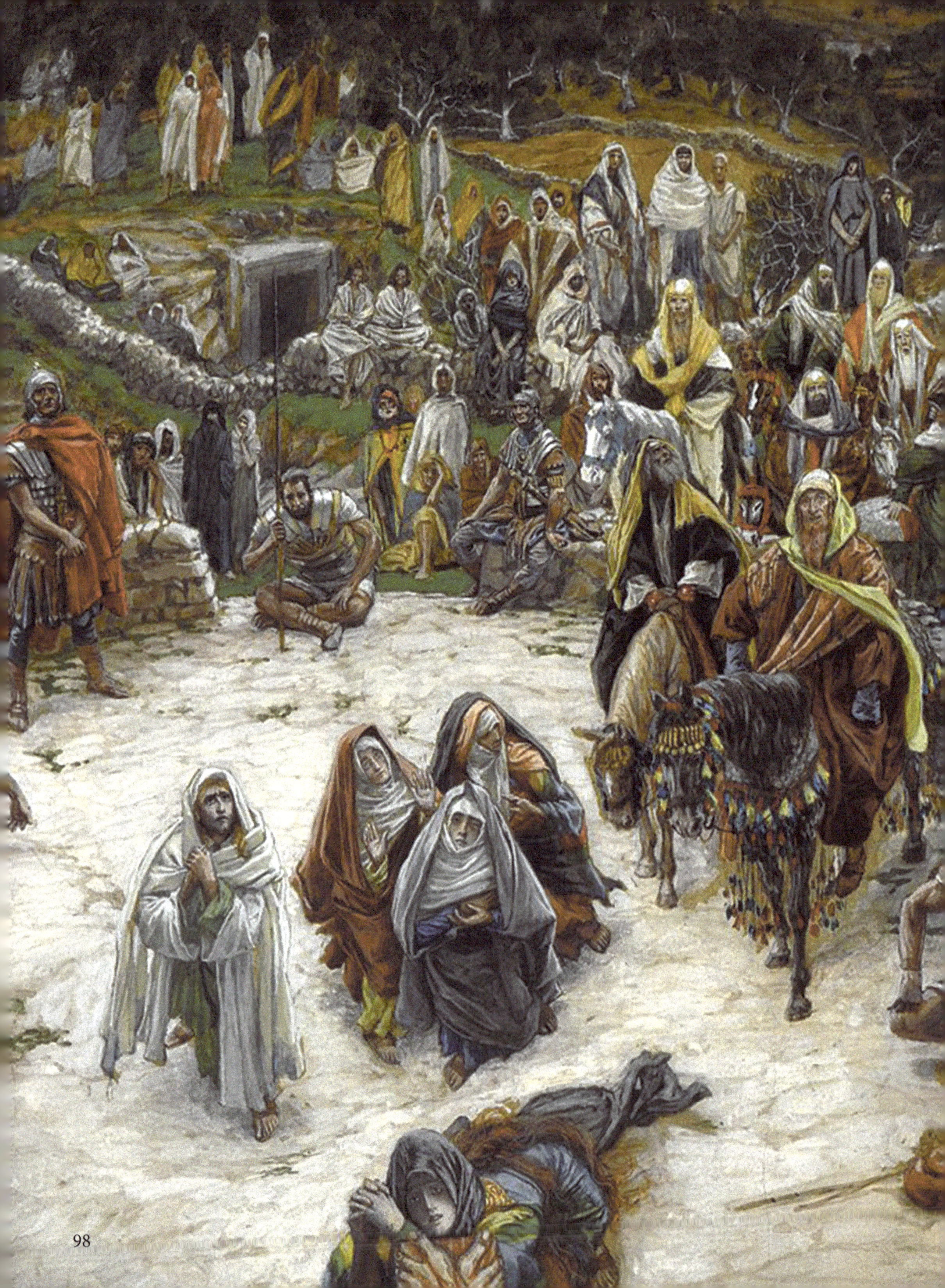

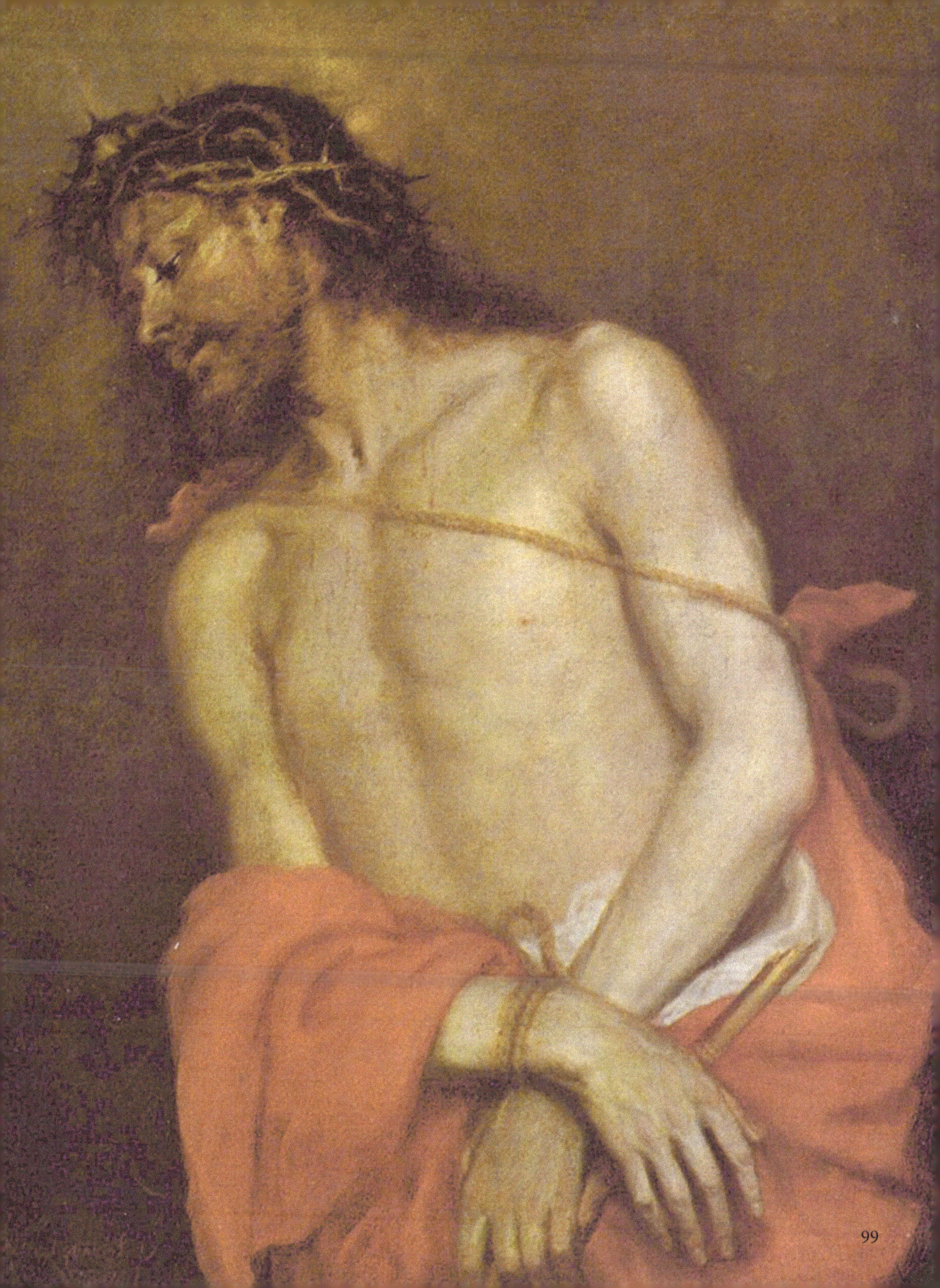

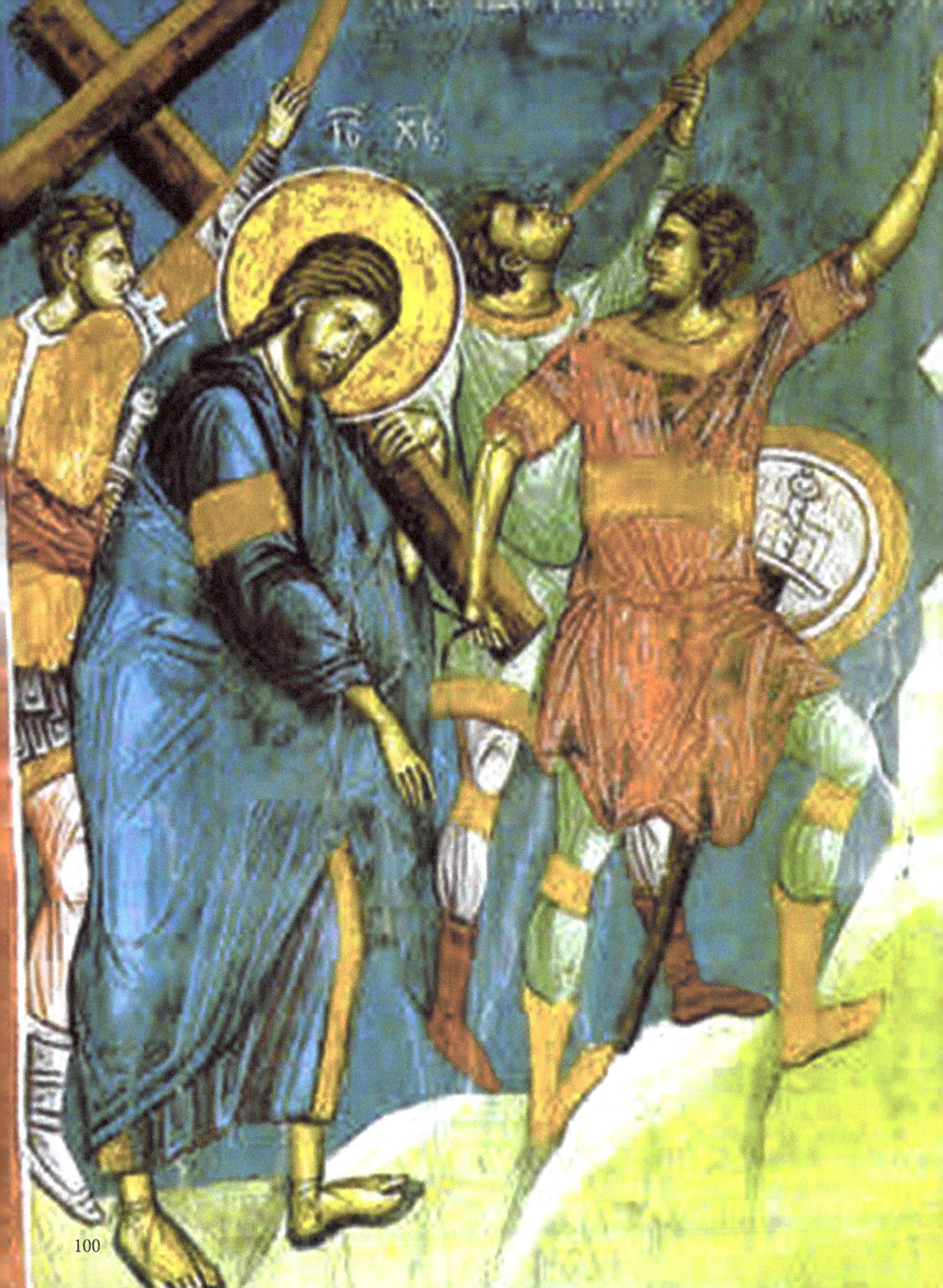

ĪС ХС

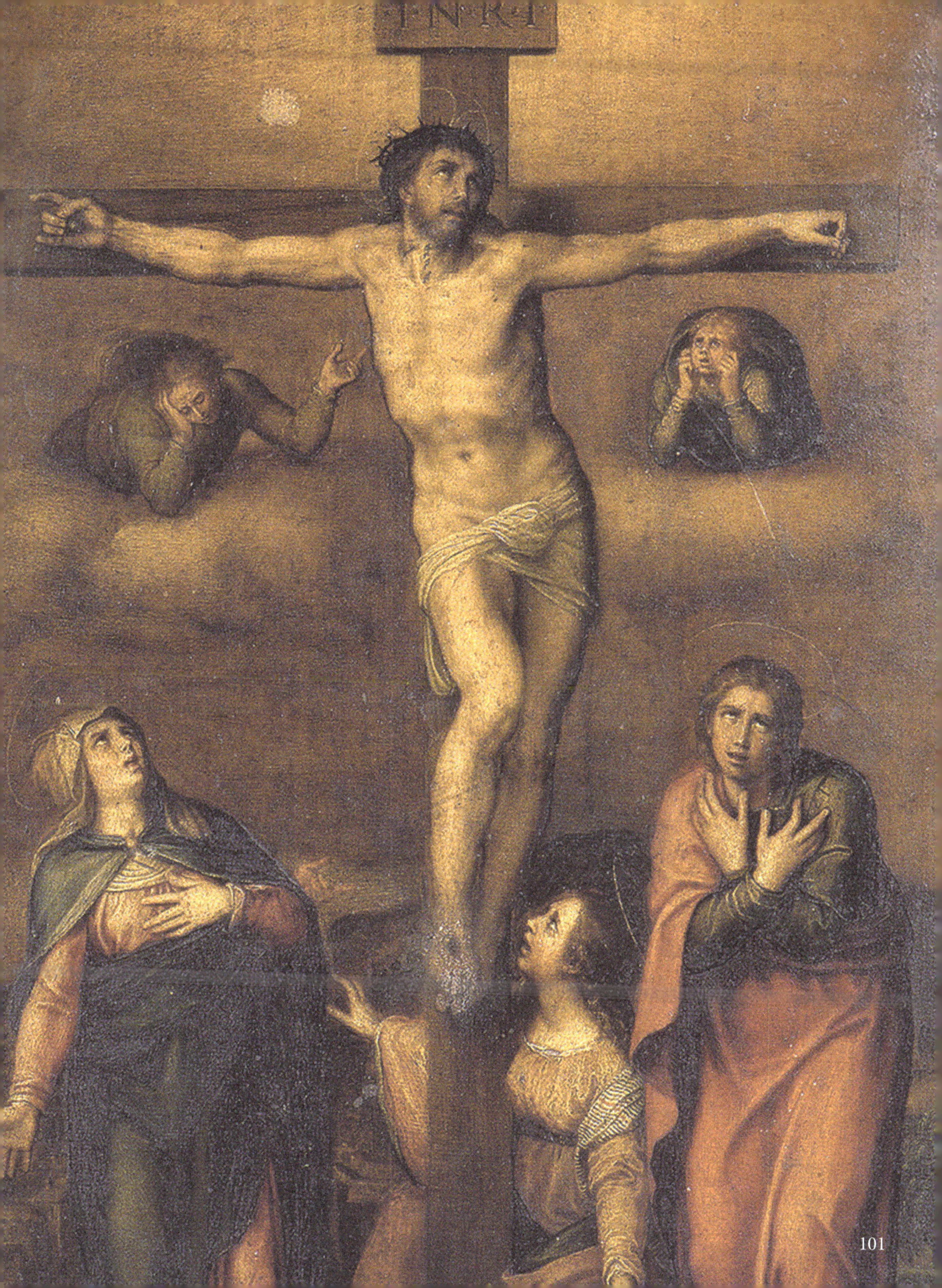
I·N·R·I

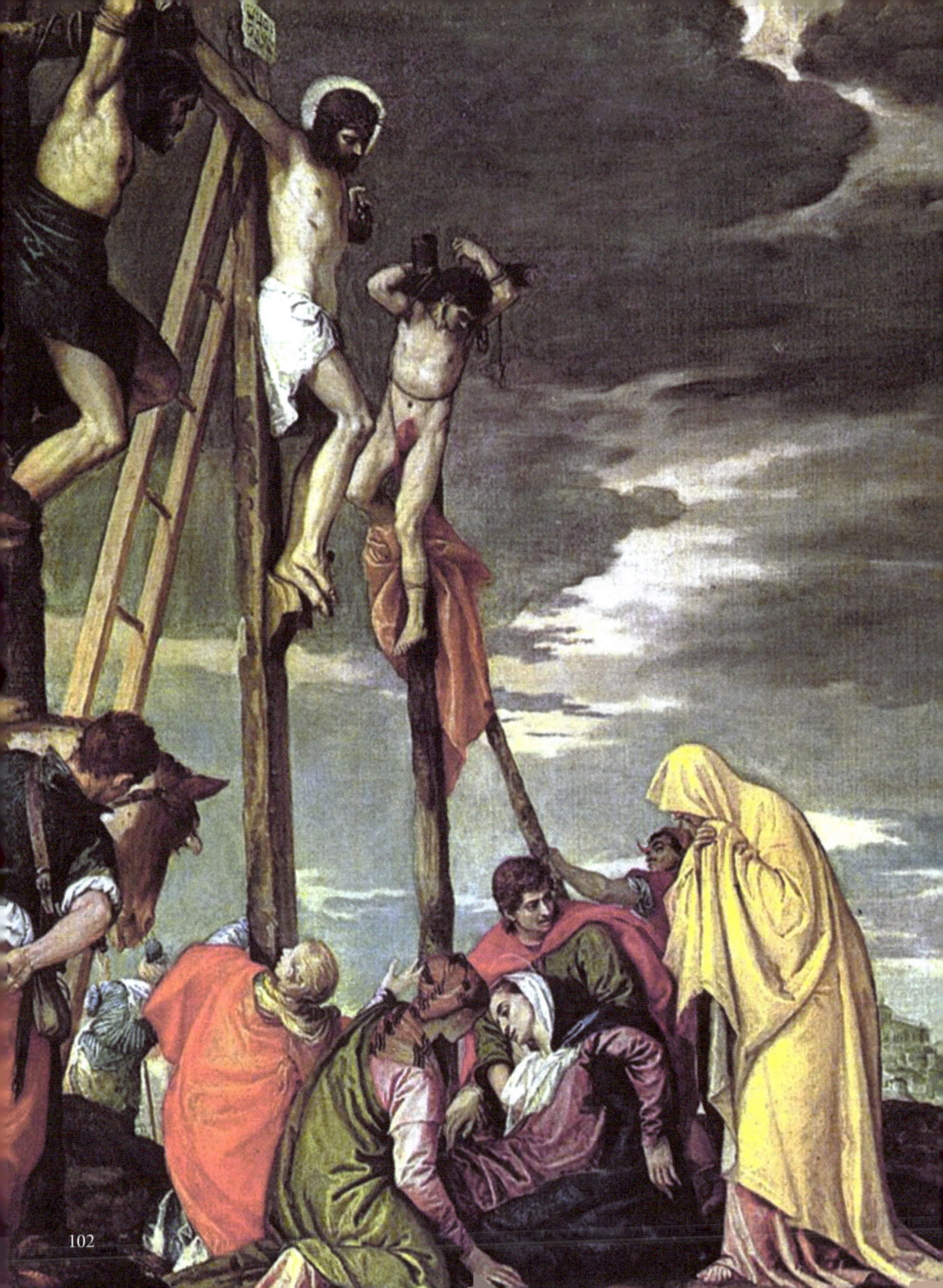

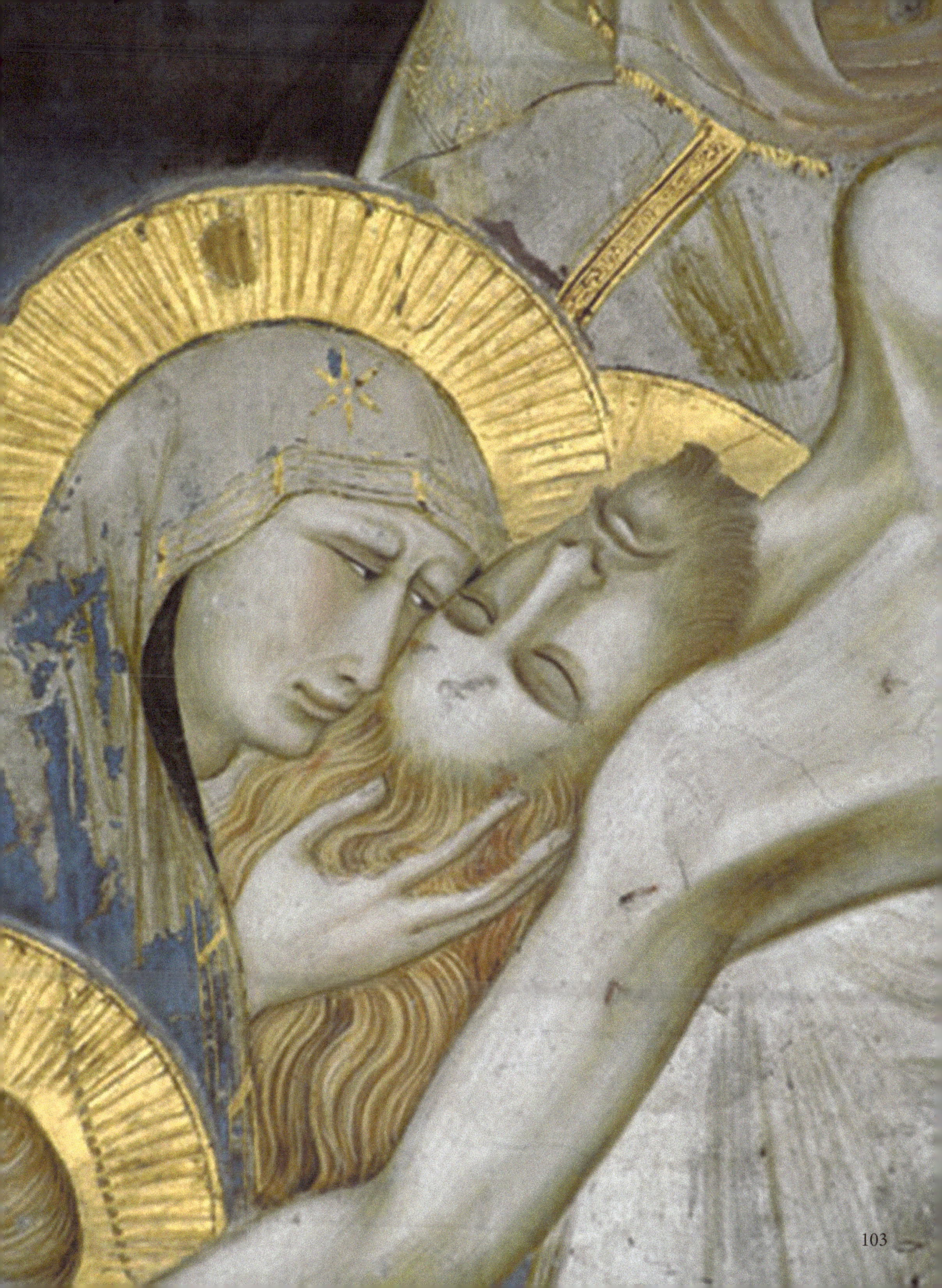

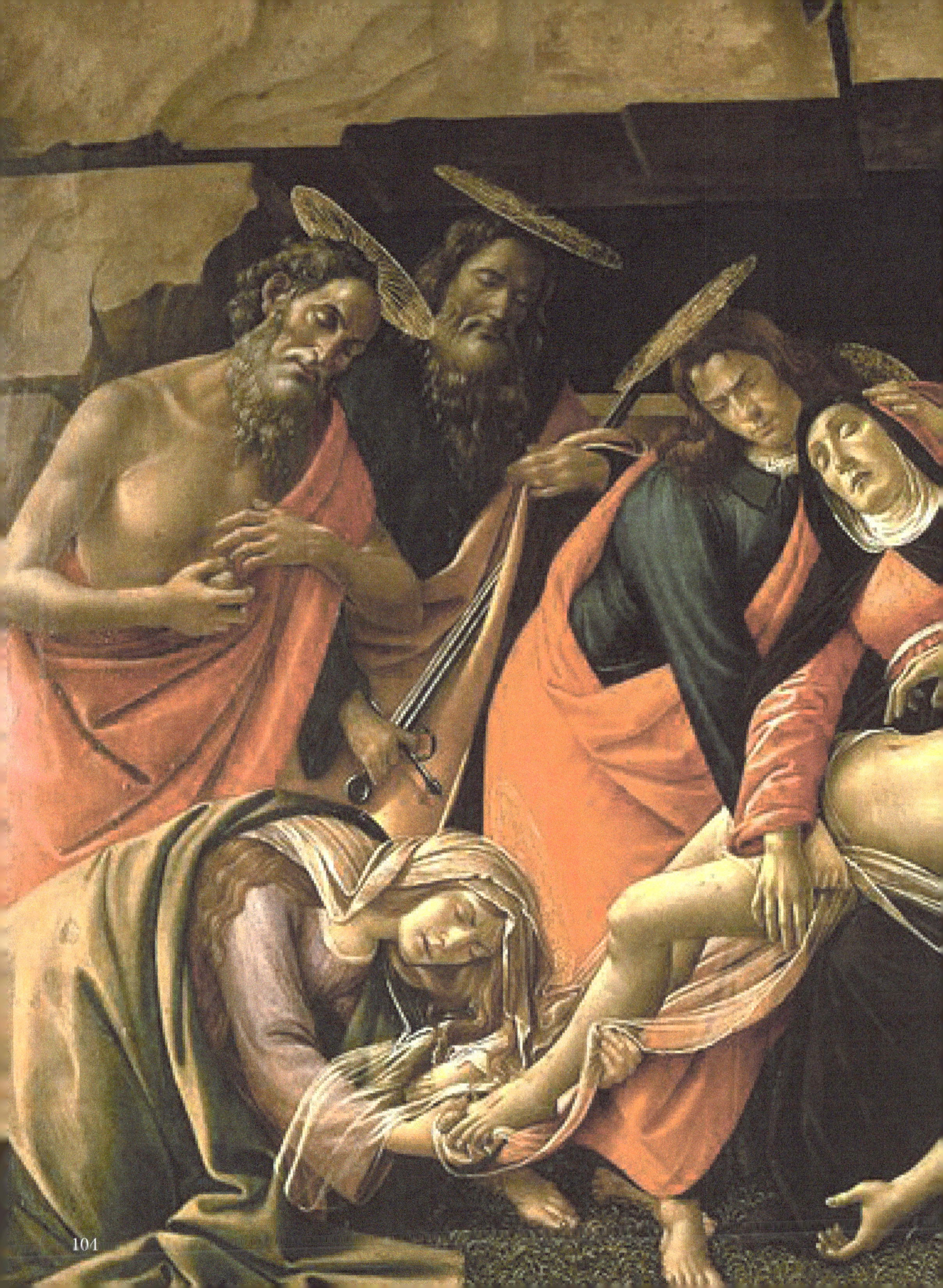

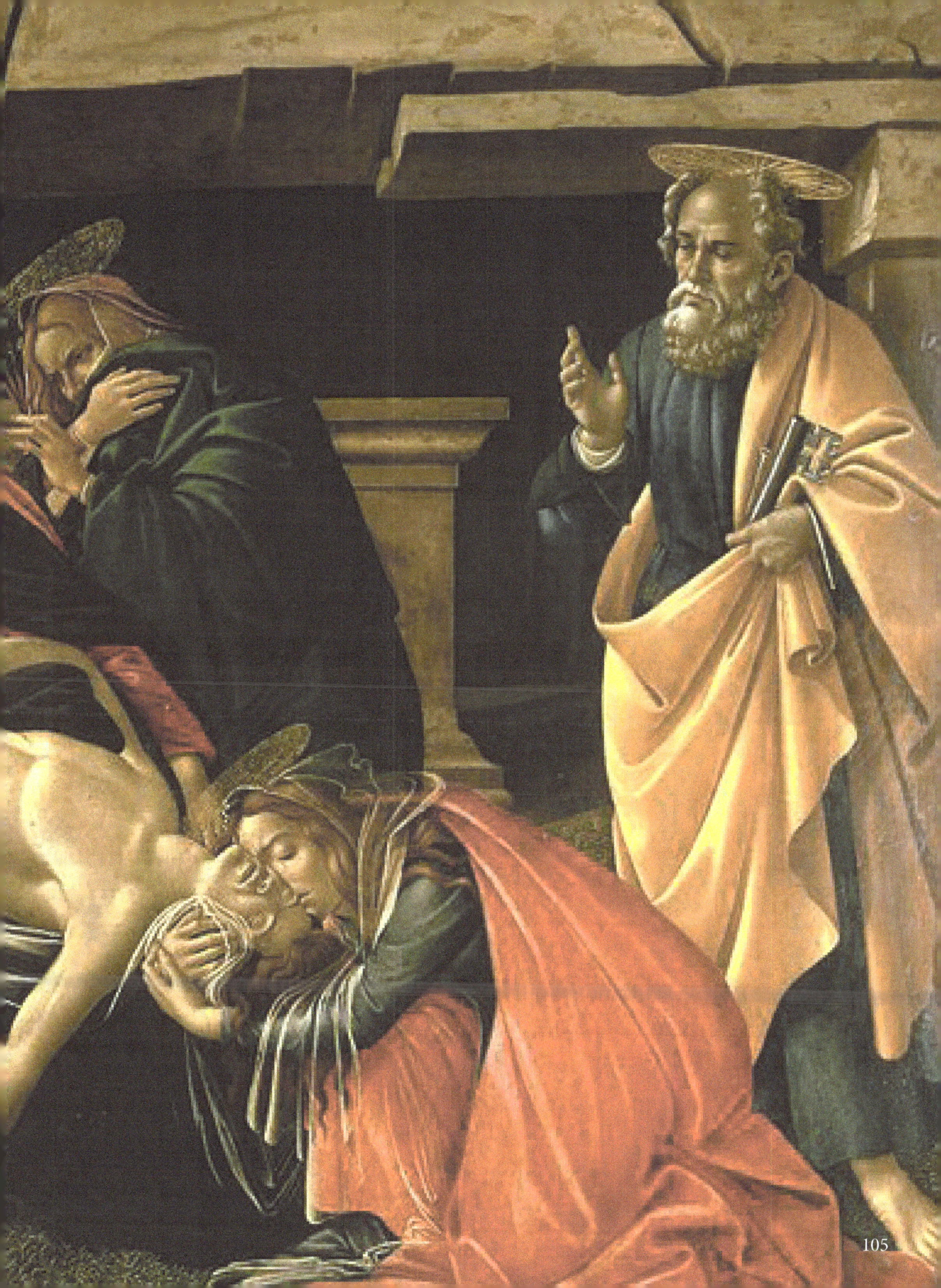

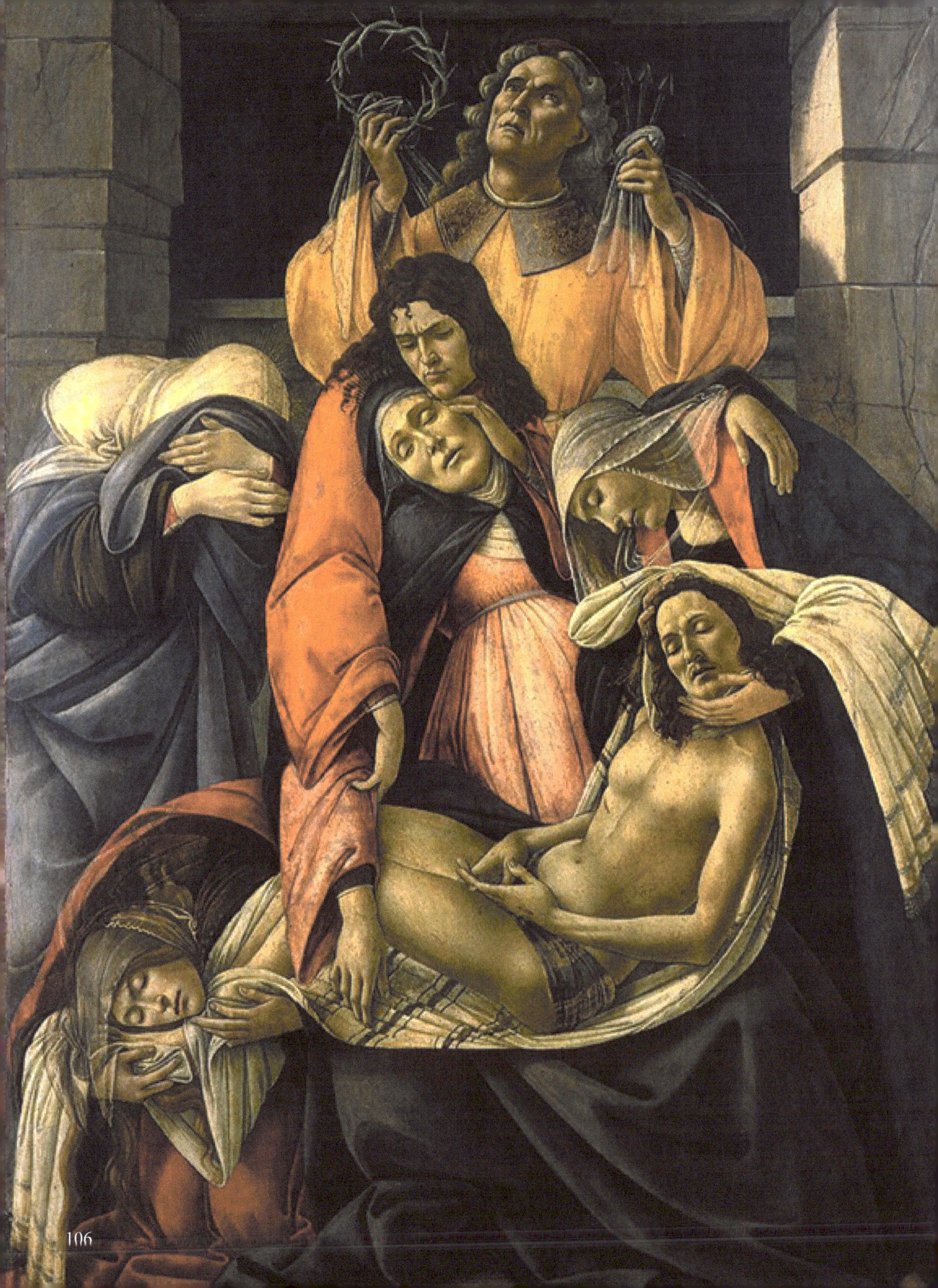

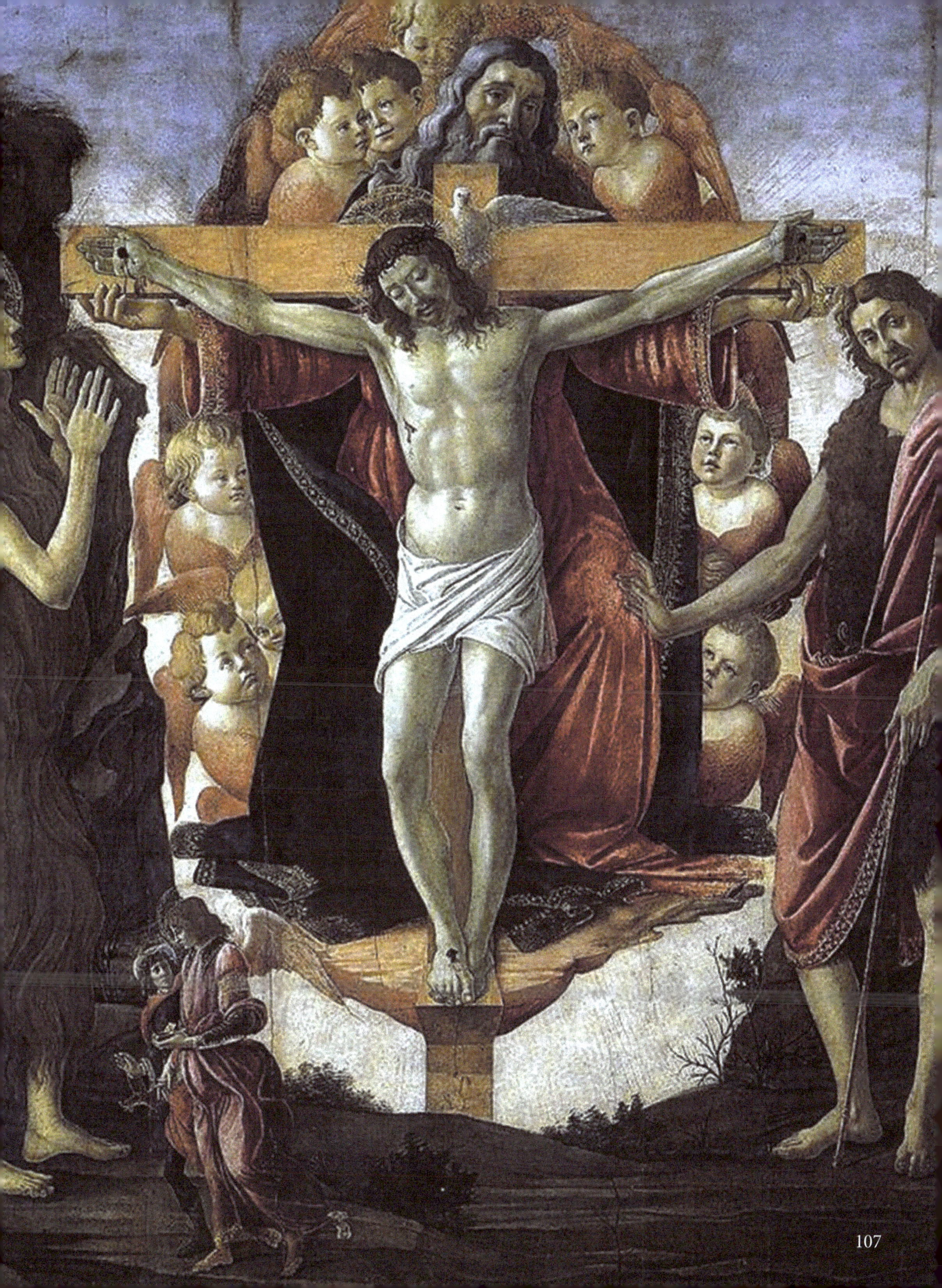

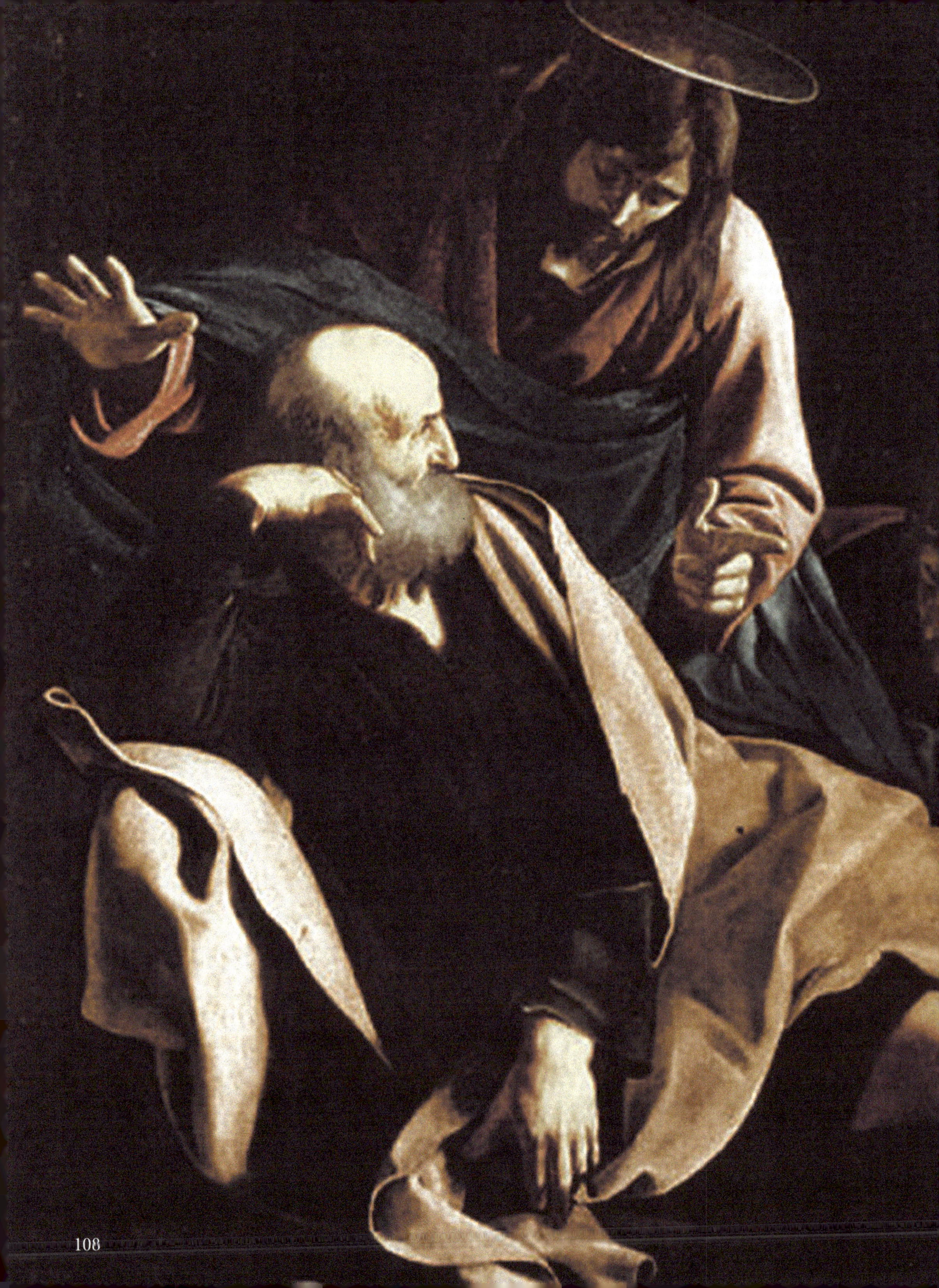

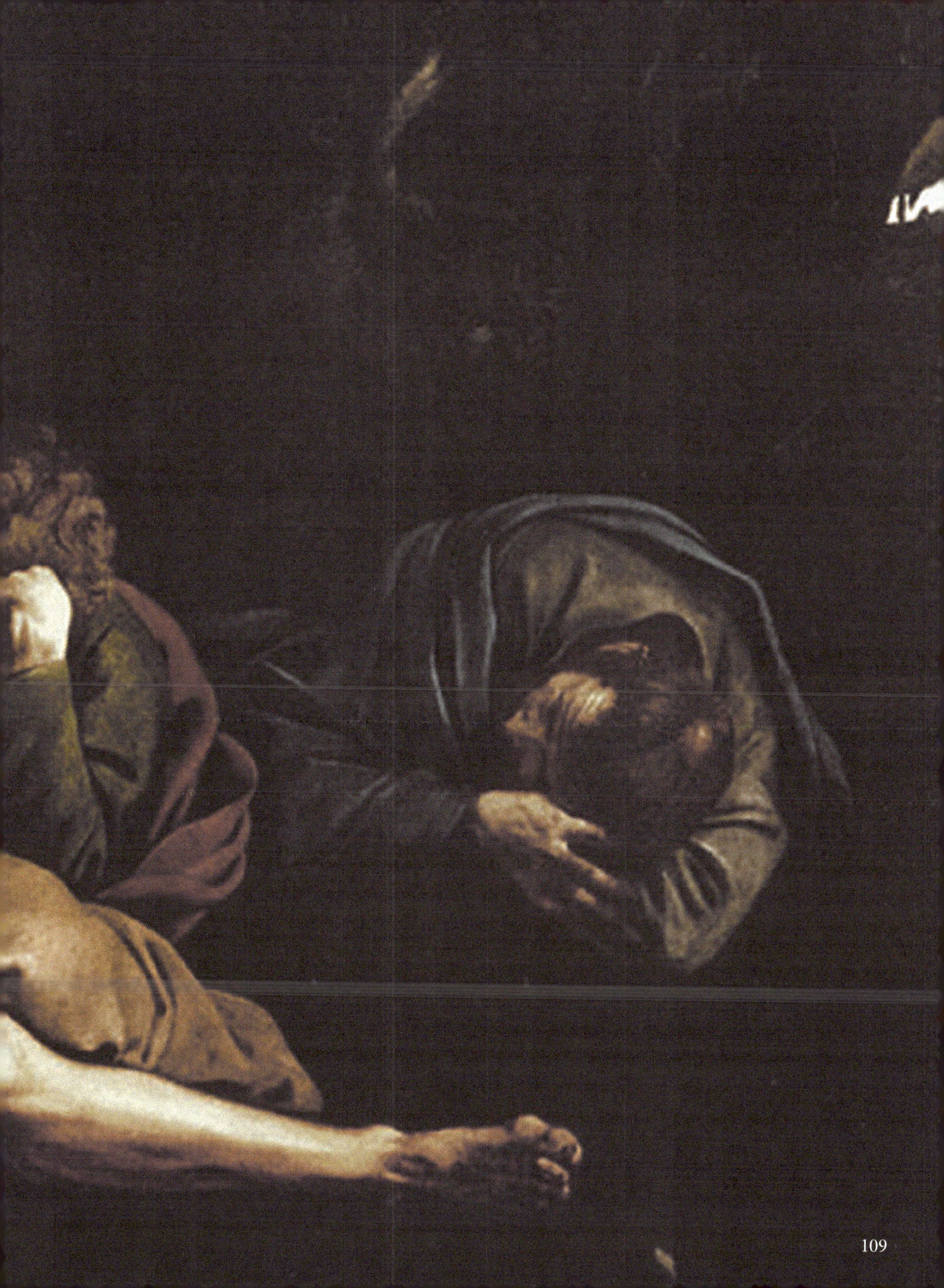

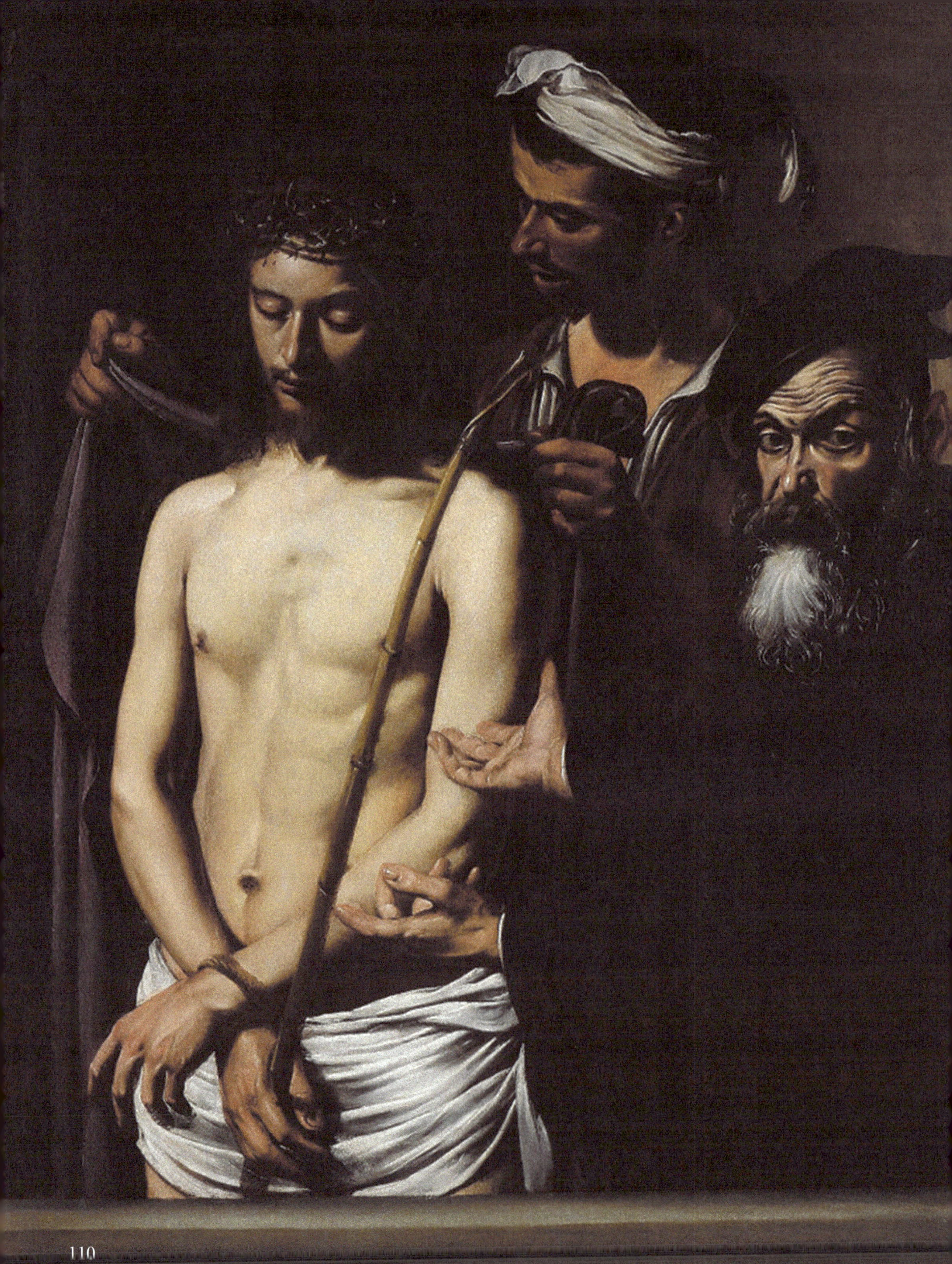

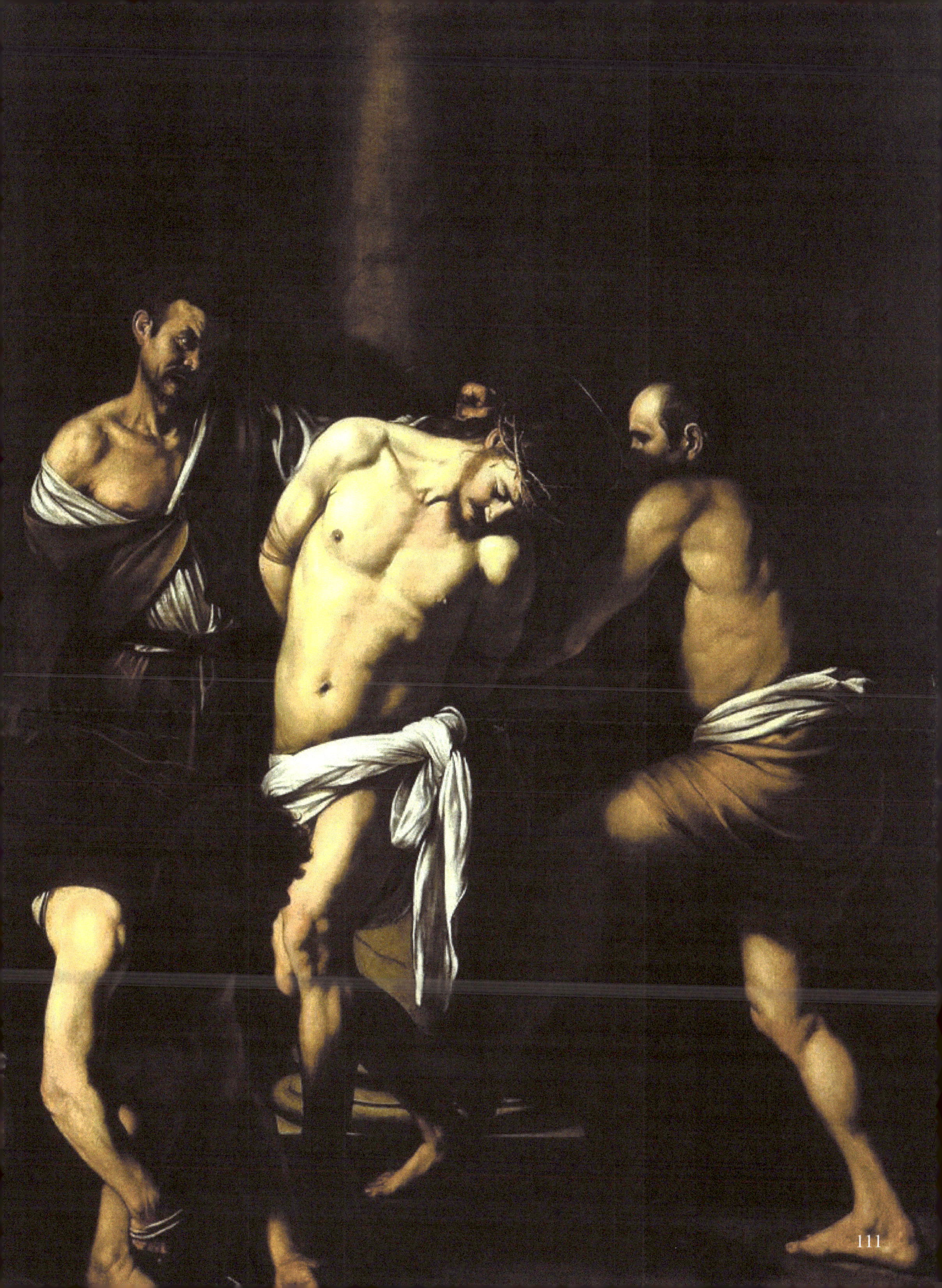

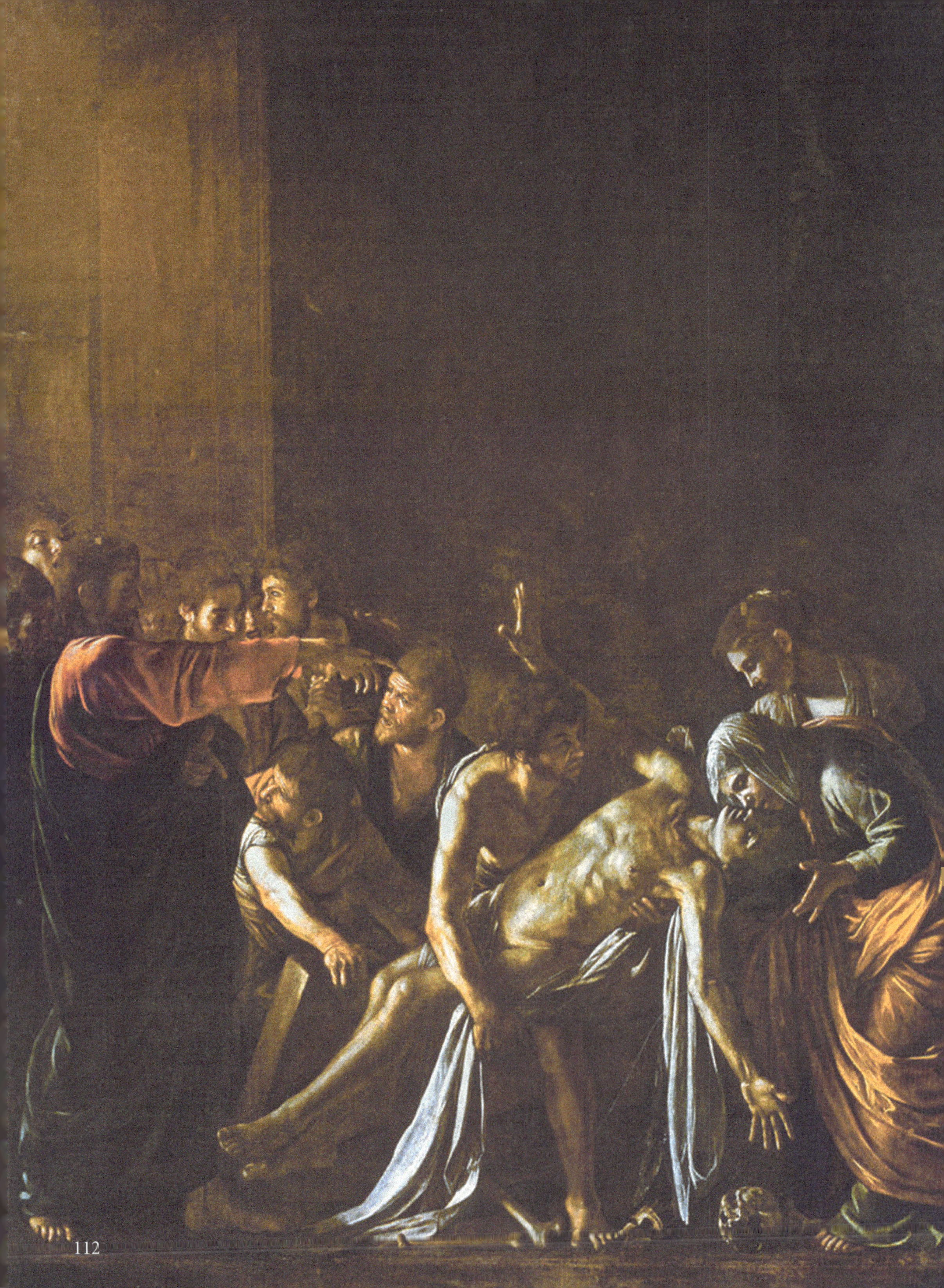

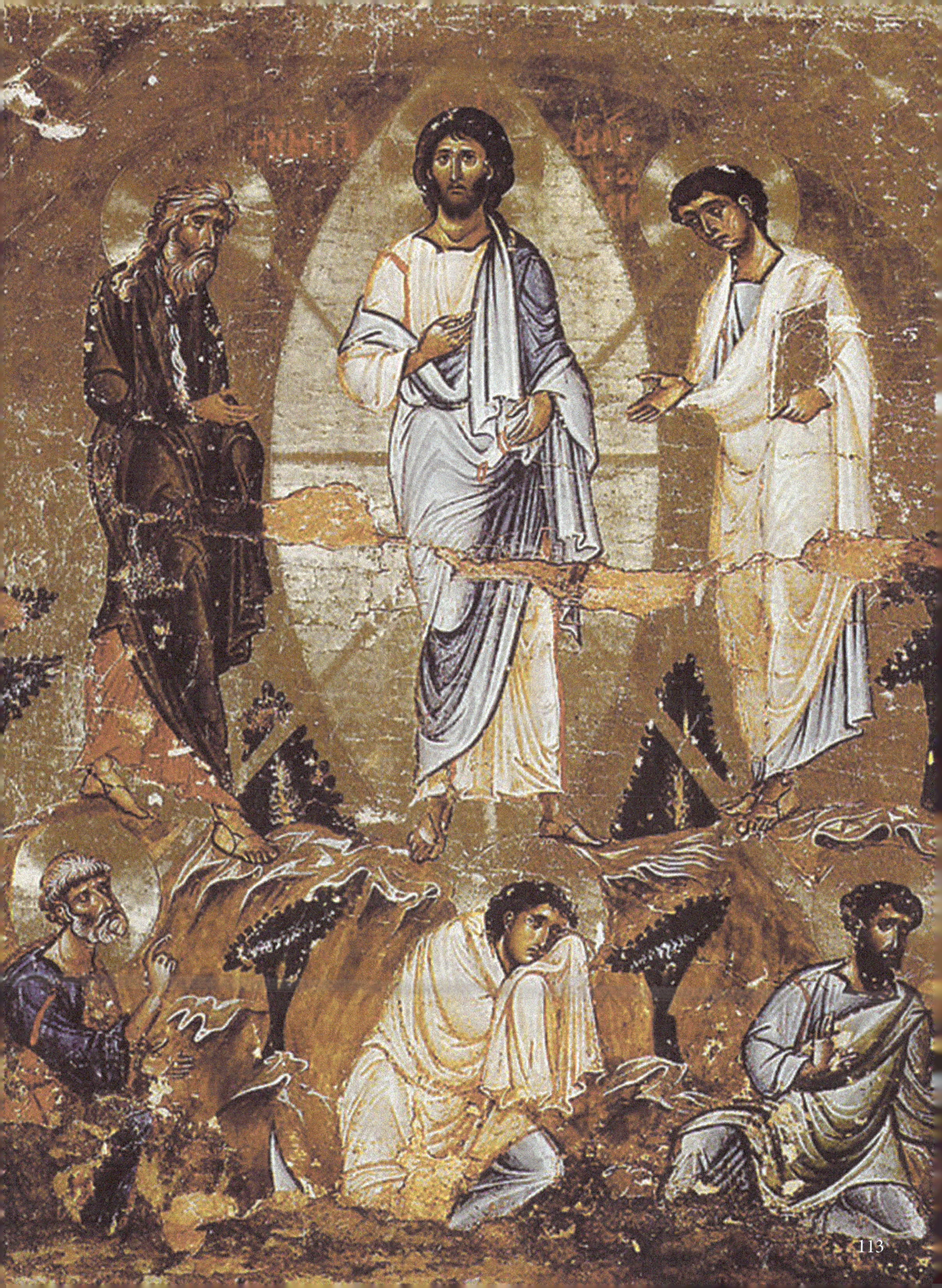

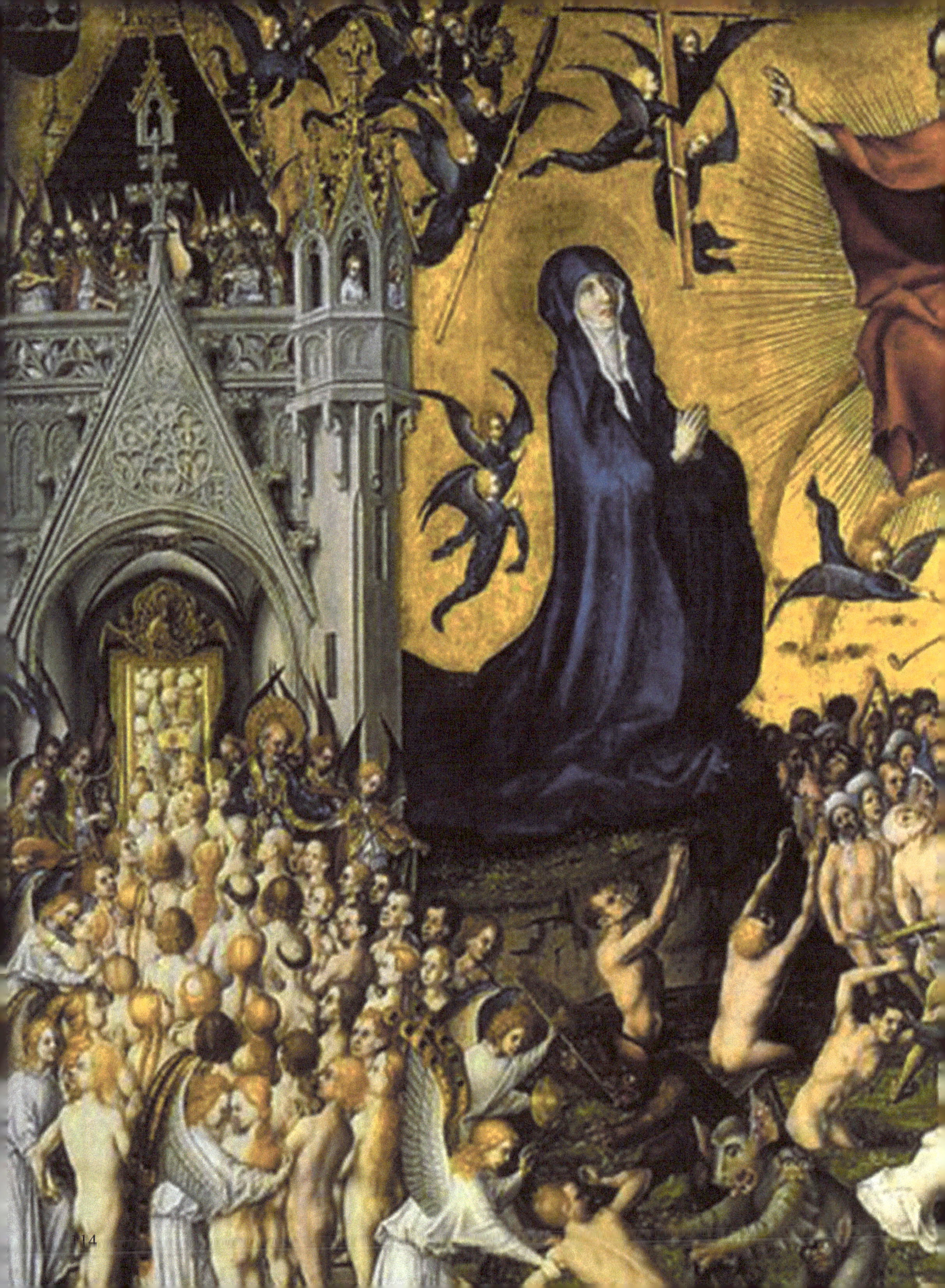

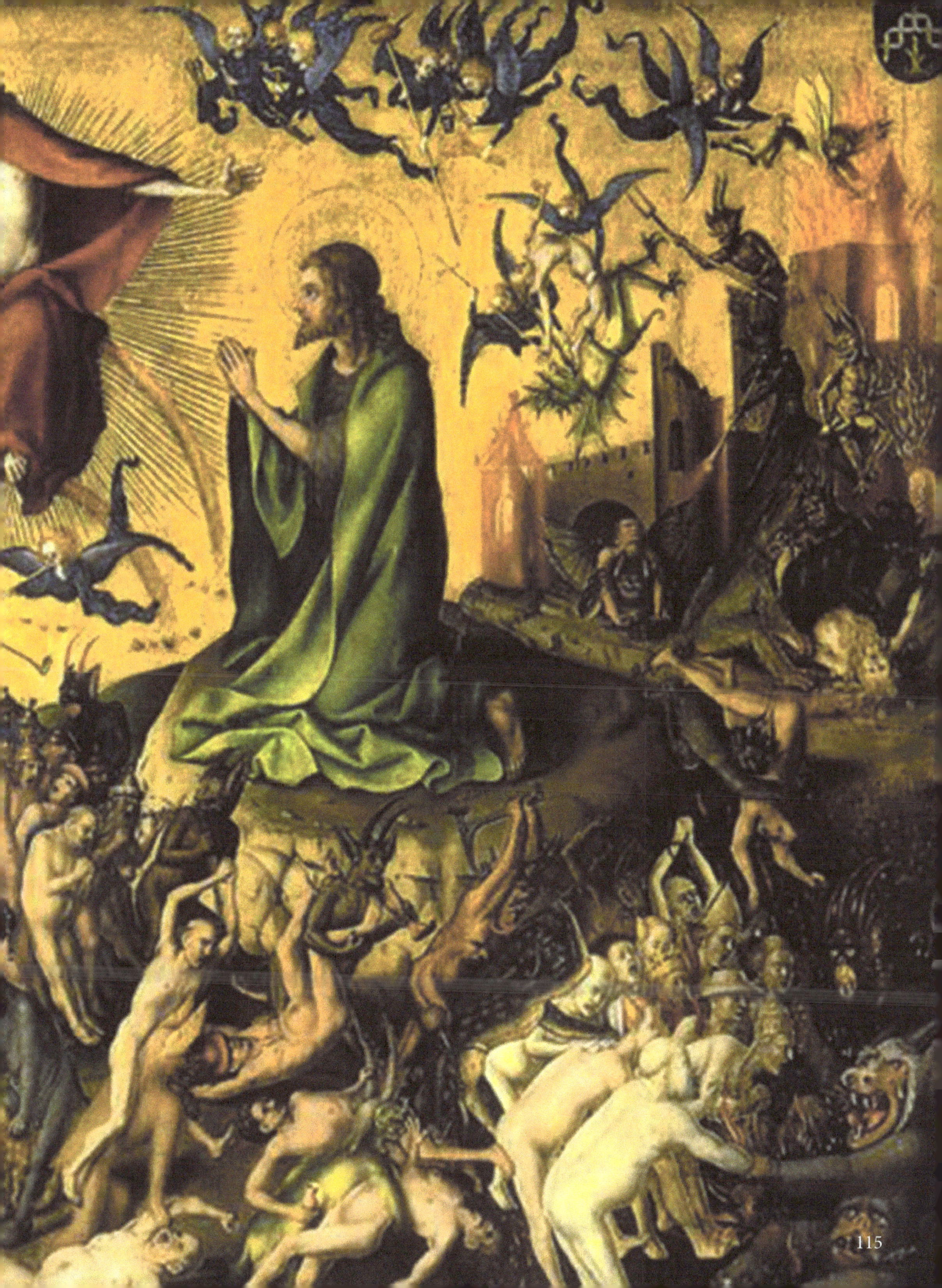

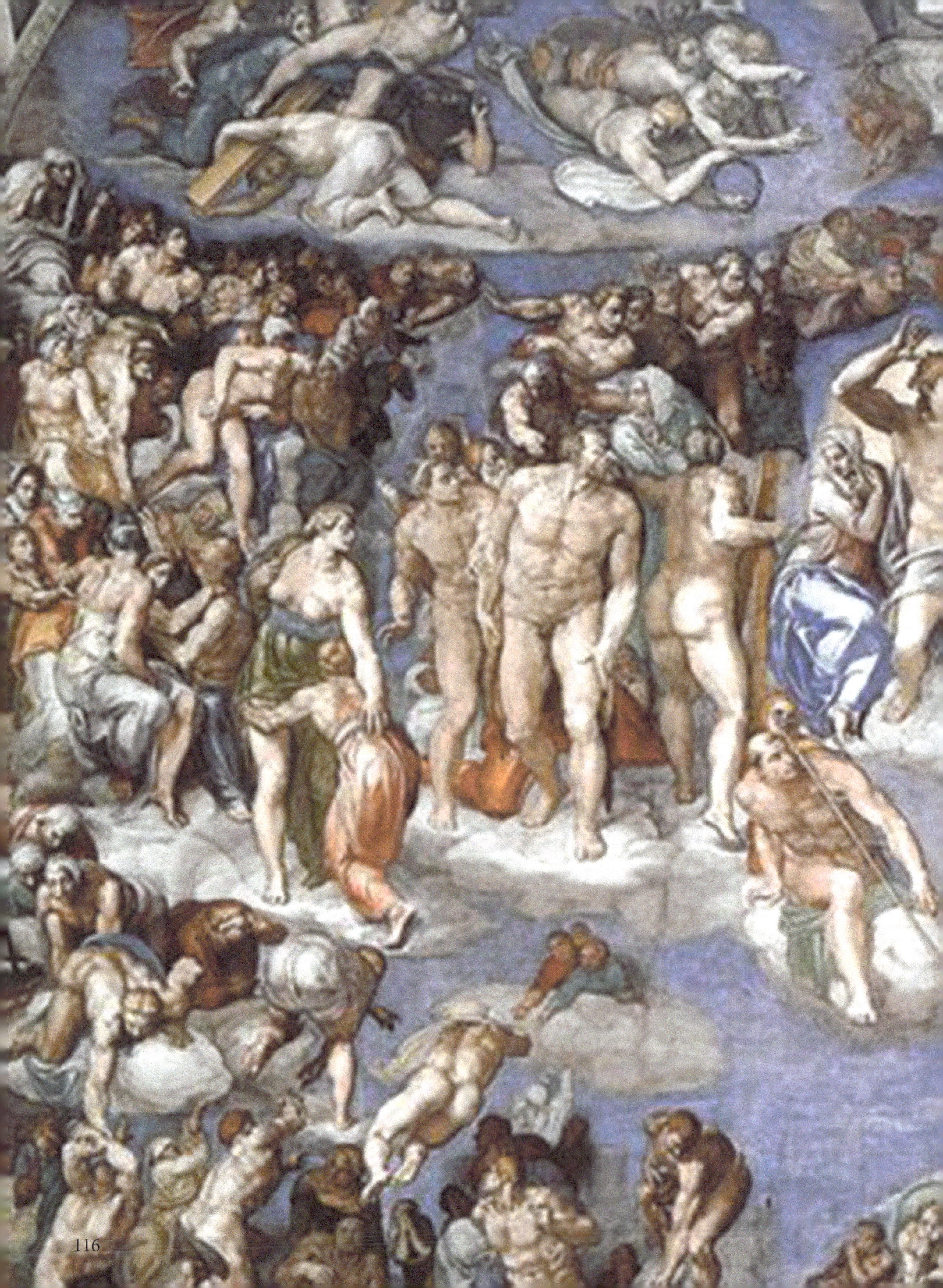

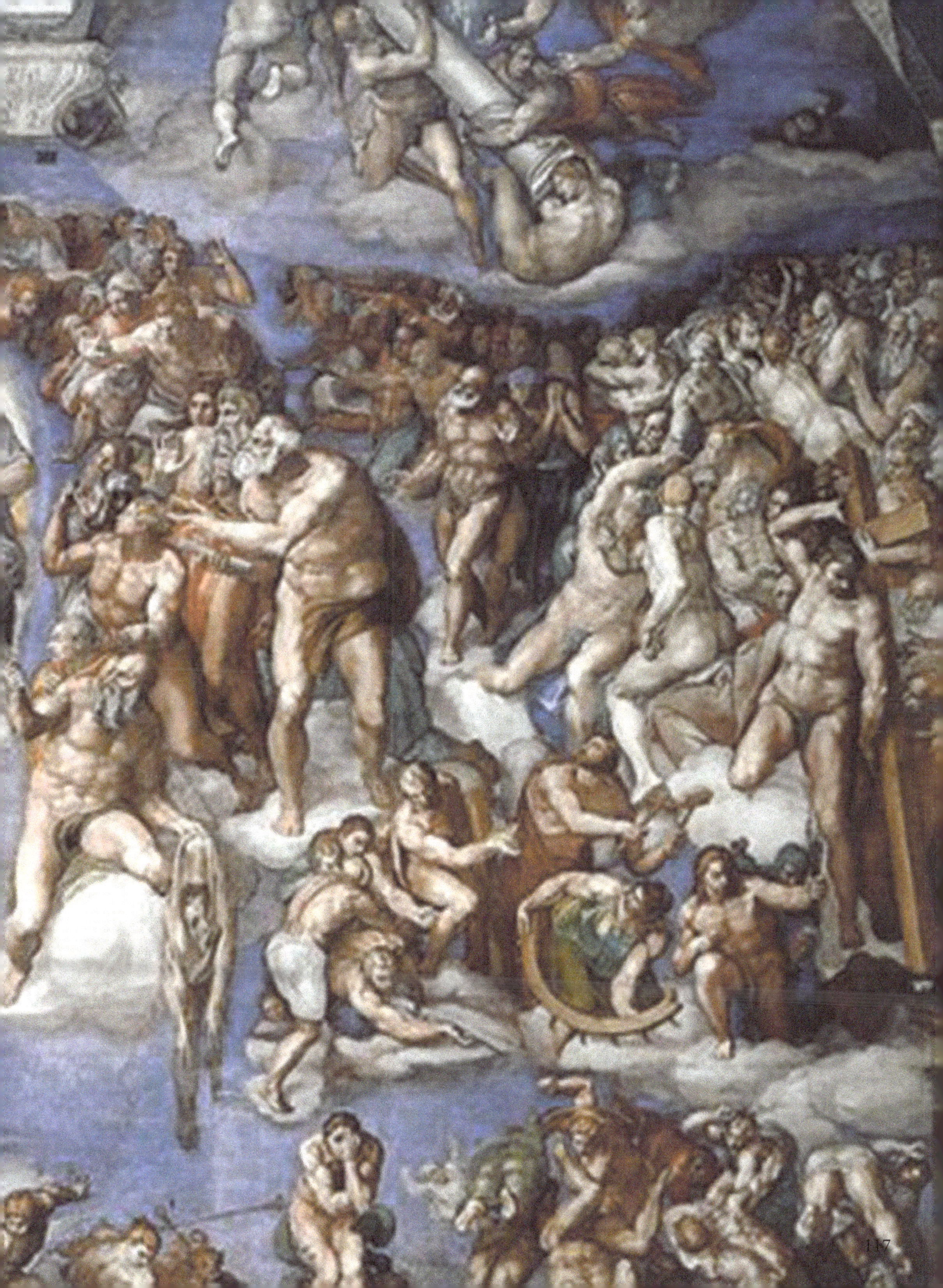

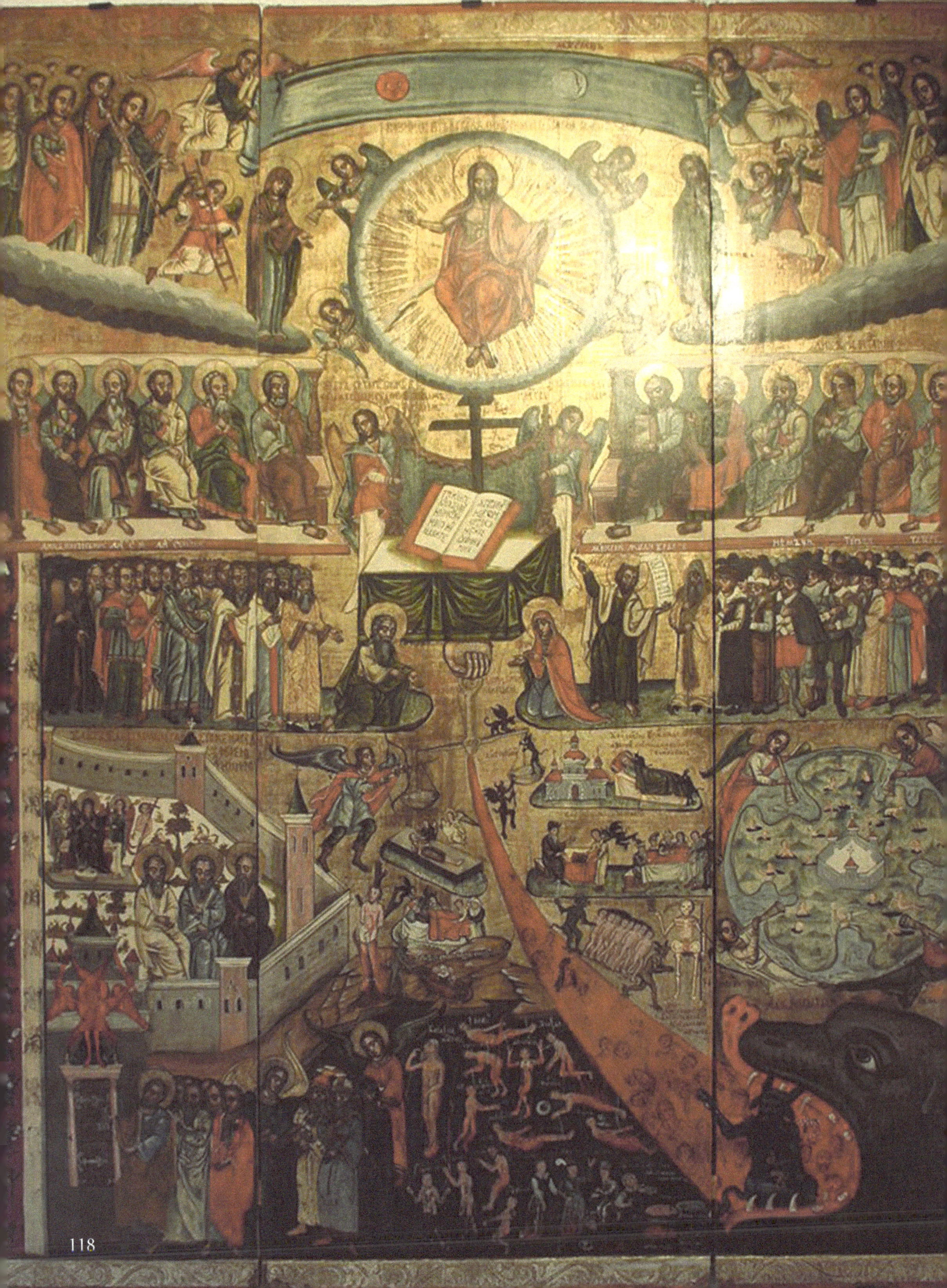

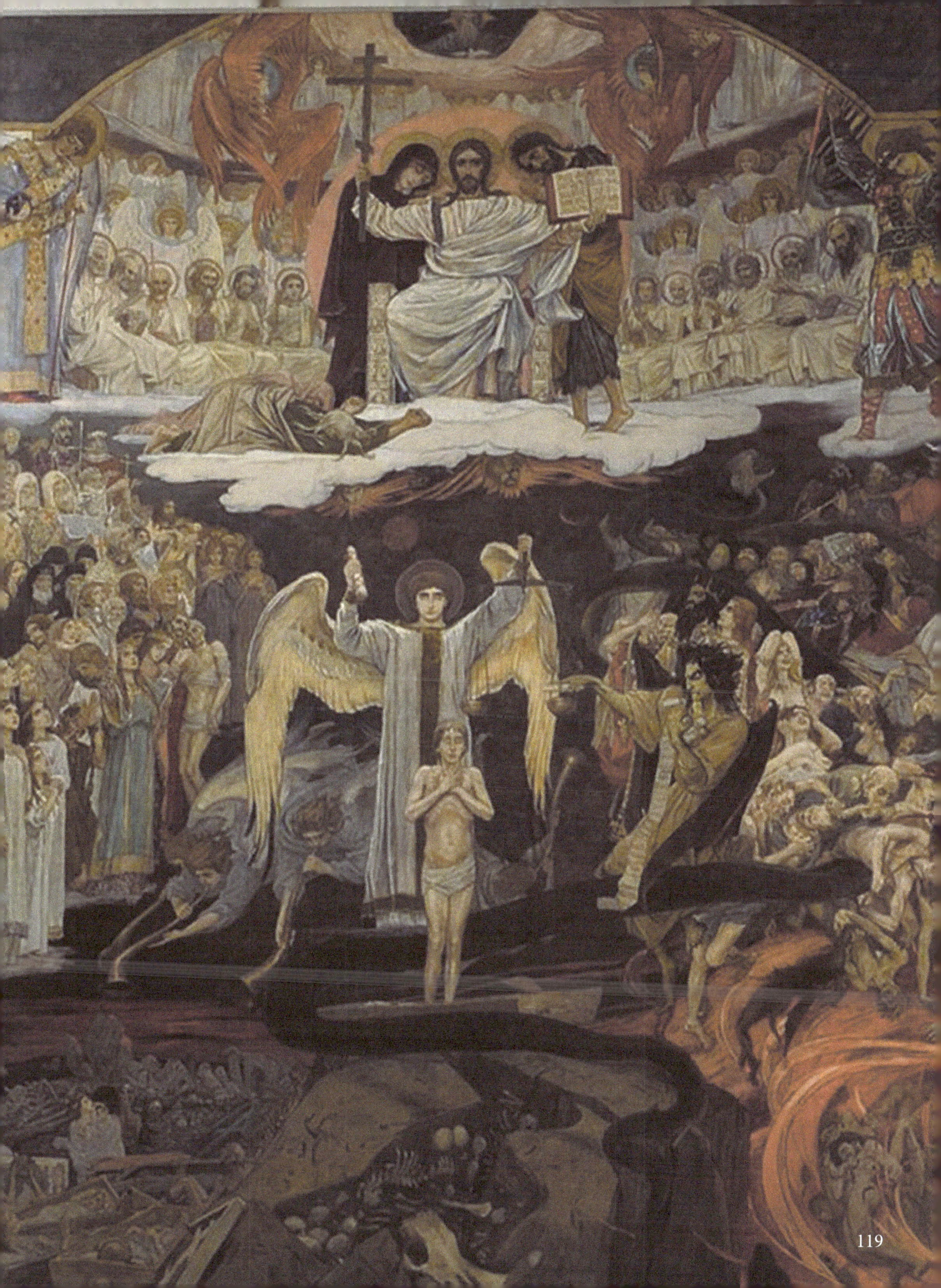

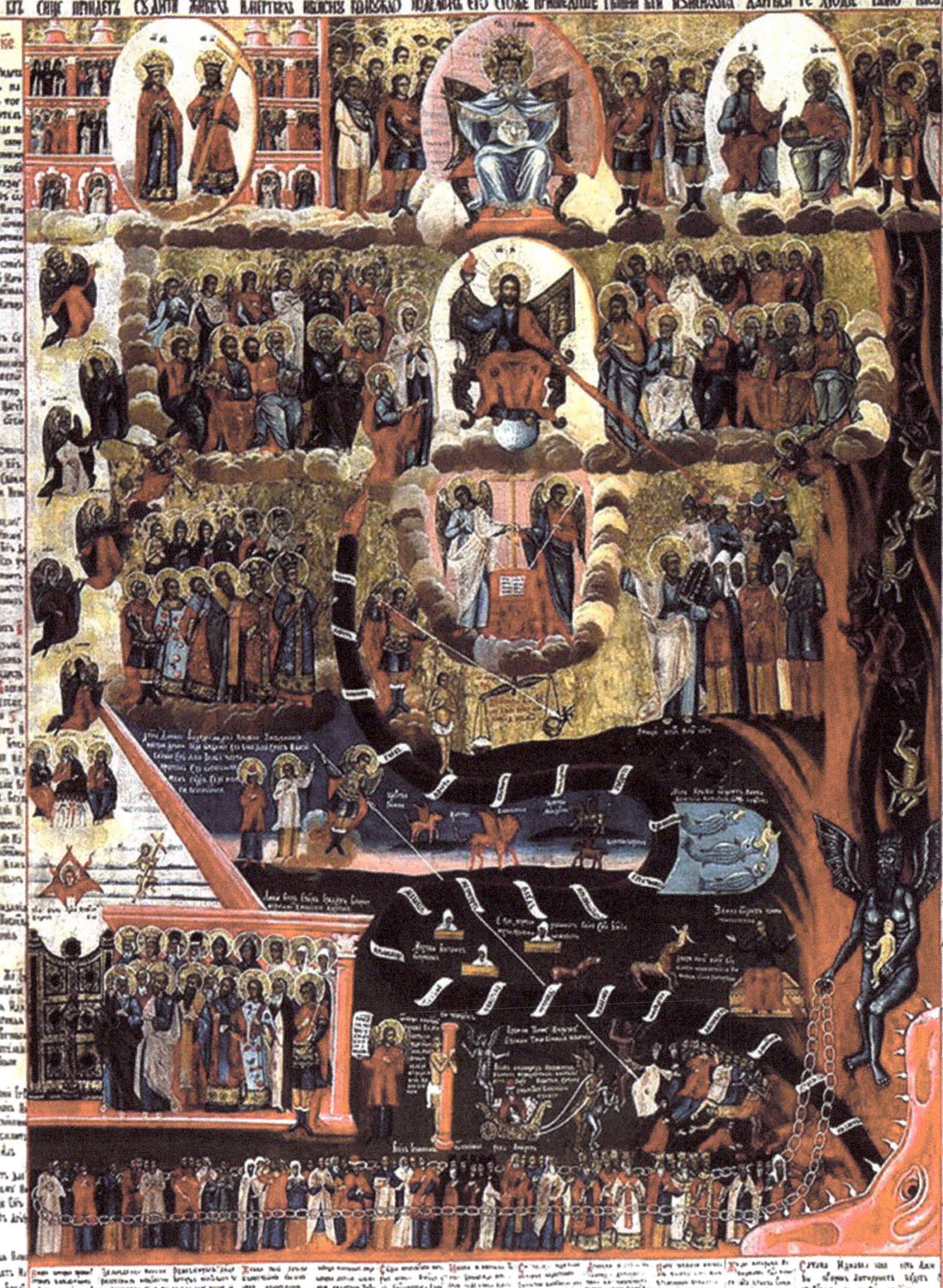

www.ingramcontent.com/pod-product-compliance
Lightning Source LLC
Chambersburg PA
CBHW041031050726
47599CB00018B/1926